Joaquim Antonio de Macedo

A Guide to Lisbon and its Environs

Including Cintra and Mafra

Joaquim Antonio de Macedo

A Guide to Lisbon and its Environs
Including Cintra and Mafra

ISBN/EAN: 9783337180812

Printed in Europe, USA, Canada, Australia, Japan

Cover: Foto ©Andreas Hilbeck / pixelio.de

More available books at **www.hansebooks.com**

A
GUIDE TO LISBON

AND ITS ENVIRONS

INCLUDING

CINTRA AND MAFRA

WITH A LARGE PLAN OF LISBON

BY

JOAQUIM ANTONIO DE MACEDO

PORTUGUESE VICE-CONSUL AT LEEDS.

> Sunt bona, sunt mala quaedam,
> Sunt mediocria plura.

SIMPKIN, MARSHALL & C.º, LONDON.
MATTHEW LEWTAS, LISBON.
1874.

LISBON.
NATIONAL PRINTING OFFICE.
1874.

CONTENTS.

PART I.

PRELIMINARY.

1. Directions to travelers arriving at Lisbon	1
2. British Legation and Foreign consulates	1
3. Banks and bankers	2
4. Hotels	3
5. Eating-houses and cafés	4
6. Public baths	5
7. Clubs and newsrooms	7
8. The Press	8
9. Chronological résumé of the history of Portugal	10
10. Portuguese language and literature, with chronographic map	20
11. Historical sketch of Lisbon	28

PART II.

DESCRIPTIVE.

1. Table by which to ascertain the names of the principal buildings	73
2. Geographical position, population and general view	80
3. The streets of Lisbon	83
4. Climate	92
5. Squares	96
Praça do Commercio	96
Praça de D. Pedro	104
Praça de Luiz de Camões	105
Largo de S. Roque	109
Largo do Pelourinho	110
Largo de Belem	110
Praça do Principe Real	111
Praça da Figueira	111
Praça dos Romulares	111
Largo de S. Paulo	111
Largo do Rato	111
Largo das Amoreiras	111
Campo de Sant'Anna	112
Largo do Carmo	112
Largo do Barão de Quintella	112
Praça das Flores	112
Praça d'Alegria	112

6. Churches and Convents............................ 112
    Basilica de Santa Maria Maior, or Sé de Lisboa .. 113
    Igreja e mosteiro de Santa Maria de Belem....... 117
    S. Roque.. 125
    Collegio Inglez, vulgo os Inglezinhos............ 129
    Igreja do Corpo Santo........................... 130
    Convento de Santa Brigida... 131
    Igreja e mosteiro de S. Vicente................. 134
    Convento de S. Bento........................... 136
    Basilica do Coração de Jesus.................... 139
    Nossa Senhora da Graça.......................... 140
    Igreja e convento de Jesus...................... 143
    Igreja e convento do Carmo...................... 144
    Igreja da Real Casa de Santo Antonio........... 146
    Nossa Senhora da Penha de França.............. 148
    Nossa Senhora dos Martyres..................... 150
    Nossa Senhora da Encarnação................... 150
    Nossa Senhora do Loreto......................... 152
    Igreja de S. Domingos........................... 153
    Igreja de S. José............................... 154
    Convento de Odivellas........................... 155
    Convento de Santos, o Novo..................... 156
    Nossa Senhora do Monte......................... 156
    Igreja de Santos, o Velho....................... 157
    Igreja da Conceição Velha 159
    Igreja de Nossa Senhora do Livramento.......... 159
    Santa Engracia.................................. 161
    Igreja de S. Julião............................. 162
    Igreja de S. Nicolau............................ 163
    Igreja de S. Paulo.............................. 163
    Igreja de Santa Maria Magdalena................ 163
    Igreja de S. Francisco de Paula................ 164
    Igreja das Chagas............................... 164
    Convento de S. Domingos........................ 164
    Convento de Nossa Senhora do Bom Successo..... 164
    Collegio de S. Patricio......................... 165
    Convento da Madre de Deus..................... 165
    Conventinho do Desaggravo...................... 165
    Igreja de Nossa Senhora do Soccorro............ 165
    Igreja de S. Sebastião.......................... 166
    Igreja de S. Pedro de Alcantara................ 166
    Igreja do SS. Sacramento 166
    Igreja de S. Miguel............................. 166
    Igreja de Santo Estevão 166
    Igreja de Santa Izabel.......................... 166
    Igreja de S. João da Praça..................... 166
    Igreja de S. Jorge.............................. 166
    Igreja de Santa Cruz............................ 166
    Igreja de Nossa Senhora da Ajuda.............. 166
    Igreja de Santa Luzia........................... 166
    Igreja de S. Lourenço 166
    Igreja de S. Thiago 166

CONTENTS.

Igreja de S. Thomé	166
Nossa Senhora dos Anjos	166
Igreja do SS. Coração de Jesus	166
Nossa Senhora da Pena	166
Igreja de S. Christovão	166
Nossa Senhora da Conceição, Nova	166
Nossa Senhora da Lapa	166
Igreja de S. Luiz	166
Convento de Sant'Anna	166
Convento de Santa Martha	166
Convento de Santa Monica	166
Convento do SS. Sacramento	166
Convento da Encarnação	166
Convento da Invocação da Santa Cruz	166
Convento das Salessias	167
Convento da Esperança	167
Convento de S. Pedro de Alcantara	167
Convento das Trinas	167
Convento das Albertas	167
Convento de Chellas	167
7. Palaces	167
Ajuda	167
Necessidades	185
Belem	186
Bemposta	187
Queluz	188
Caxias	189
Alfeite	189
8. Public amusements	189
Bull-fight	189
Portuguese Theater	194
Theatro de S. Carlos	196
Theatro de Dona Maria II	198
Theatro de Trindade	198
Theatro do Gymnasio	199
Theatro do Principe Real	199
Theatro da Rua dos Condes	199
Theatro das Variedades	200
9. Libraries	200
Bibliotheca Nacional	200
Bibliotheca da Ajuda	204
Bibliotheca do Convento de Jesus	204
Bibliotheca da Academia das Sciencias	204
10. Picture Galleries	204
Galeria Nacional de Pintura	204
Galeria de quadros no Palacio da Ajuda	210
11. Museums	210
Museu Nacional de Lisboa	210
Museu Colonial	212
Museu do Instituto Industrial	212
Museu Archeologico	212
12. Roman antiquities	212

13. Aqueduct and Fountains.................... 215
14. Observatories............................. 220
    Observatorio Astronomico.................. 220
    Observatorio Meteorologico................ 221
    Observatorio da Marinha................... 221
15. Hospitals................................. 222
    Hospital Real de S. José.................. 222
    British naval hospital.................... 223
    Hospital da Marinha....................... 223
    Hospital da Estrellinha................... 223
    Hospital do Desterro...................... 223
    Hospital de S. Lazaro..................... 223
16. Law Courts................................ 223
    Boa Hora.................................. 223
    Supremo Tribunal de Justiça............... 224
    Supremo Tribunal de Justiça Militar....... 224
    Relação de Segunda Instancia.............. 224
    Tribunaes de Primeira Instancia........... 224
    Tribunal do Commercio..................... 224
    Relação Ecclesiastica..................... 224
17. Arsenals.................................. 224
    Arsenal da Marinha........................ 224
    Arsenal do Exercito....................... 225
18. Prisons................................... 226
    Limoeiro.................................. 226
    Aljube.................................... 227
    Castello de S. Jorge...................... 227
    Torre de Belem............................ 227
    S. Julião da Barra........................ 227
19. Markets................................... 227
    Praça da Figueira......................... 227
    Ribeira Nova (fish)....................... 228
    Ribeira Velha............................. 229
    Feira da Ladra............................ 229
20. Public walks and gardens.................. 229
    Passeio publico........................... 229
    Passeio da Estrella....................... 230
    Passeio de S. Pedro de Alcantara.......... 230
    Jardim botanico........................... 230
21. Public Educational Establishments......... 231
    Escola polytechnica....................... 231
    Escola medico-cirurgica................... 231
    Escola de pharmacia....................... 231
    Instituto agricola........................ 231
    Escola naval.............................. 232
    Escola do exercito........................ 232
    Aula do commercio......................... 232
    Conservatorio real........................ 232
    Curso superior de letras.................. 232
    Instituto industrial...................... 232
    Collegio dos aprendizes do arsenal........ 233
    Lyceu de Lisboa........................... 233

22. Barracks	233
23. Cemeteries	233
Cemiterio dos Inglezes, or Cyprestes	234
Cemiterio dos Prazeres	234
Cemiterio do Alto de S. João	235
Cemiterio da Ajuda	236
Cemiterio de S. Luiz	236
Cemiterio dos Judeus	236
Cemiterio dos Allemães	236
Valle Escuro	236
24. Other public buildings	236
Cocheira Real	236
Castello de S. Jorge	237
Torre de Belem	239
Lazareto	241
Cordoaria	241
Alfandega Grande (Custom-house)	241
Moeda (Mint)	246
Xabregas	246
Statue of S. João Nepomuceno	247
Terreiro do trigo	247
Matadouro	248
Imprensa nacional	249
Casa dos bicos	249
25. Environs of Lisbon	250
26. CINTRA	256
Ramalhão	258
Quinta do Marquez	258
Palacio real	260
Palacio da Pena	262
Castello dos Mouros	262
Convento da Cortiça	263
Collares	264
Pedra de Alvidrar	264
Monserrate	265
Penha Verde	266
Setiaes	266
Quintas	266
27. MAFRA	266

PART III.

SUPPLEMENTARY.

1. Royal family	273
2. Titles of nobility	275
3. Municipality	278
4. Fire signal	279
5. Communications	280
Telegraphic	280
Postal	281

CONTENTS.

Railway	283
Hackney carriages	288
Lisbon Carriage Company	288
Vapores lisbonenses	290
Boats	291
Omnibuses	291
Tramway	291
Steam tramway	292
Steamers	290
6. Money, weights and measures	301
Currency	301
Portuguese to English money	303
English to Portuguese money	307
Portuguese metrical weights compared with English	309
Old Portuguese weights compared with metrical and with English	309
Table for reducing Portuguese to English weight	310
Table for reducing English to Portuguese weight	311
Portuguese Long measure compared with English	312
Old Portuguese Long measure	312
Reduction of Portuguese Long measure to English	312
Reduction of English to Portuguese Long measure	313
Square measure	314
Portuguese dry and liquid measure	314
Old Portuguese liquid measure	314
Centigrade thermometer compared with Fahrenheit	315

PART I.

PRELIMINARY.

1. DIRECTIONS

TO TRAVELERS ARRIVING AT LISBON.

Travelers arriving at Lisbon by sea are required to give up their passports at the police office in the custom-house. Within the space of three days the visitor should present himself at the *Governo Civil*, in the *Travessa da Parreirinha*, near the theatre of S. Carlos, where he will receive a *bilhete de residencia*, or authorization to reside in the capital: his passport will at the same time be returned to him and should be taken to the respective consulate to be viséd. Persons arriving by land must present themselves at the aforesaid *Governo Civil* to receive the *bilhete de residencia*. Neglect of the above formalities is punishable with a fine not exceeding £20. An Englishman, however, intending to stay but a few days in Lisbon need not take out a *bilhete de residencia*, but should get his passport viséd by the consul, without which he will not be able to quit Lisbon by sea, though he may do so by land.

2. BRITISH LEGATION AND FOREIGN CONSULATES.

BRITISH LEGATION.—rua de S. Francisco de Borja
FOREIGN CONSULATES:
  AUSTRIA—Rua Nova de S. Francisco de Paula.
  BELGIUM—Travessa do Sequeiro das Chagas, 1.
  BRAZIL—Rua da Atalaia, 107.

Chili — Rua das Flores.
Denmark — Travessa do Sequeiro das Chagas, 1.
France — Rua Formosa, 108.
Germany — Rua da Emenda.
Great Britain — Pateo do Pimenta.
Greece — Travessa do Sequeiro das Chagas, 1.
Italy — Beco dos Apostolos, 7.
Netherlands — Rua da Emenda.
Perú — Rua de S. Francisco.
Russia — Rua direita do Calvario.
Siam — Rua do Ferregial de Cima, 21.
Spain — Rua da Trindade.
Swiss Confederation — Chiado, 61.
Sweden and Norway — Alto de Santa Catharina.
Turkey — Rua direita de S. Francisco de Paula.
United States of America — Rua do Ferregial de Baixo, 33.
Uruguay — Rua de S. Francisco, 13.
Venezuela — Rua Nova do Almada, 11.

3. BANKS AND BANKERS.

Banco de Portugal — 148, Rua dos Capellistas.
Banco Lusitano — 85, Rua dos Capellistas.
Banco Ultramarino — 74, Rua dos Capellistas.
New London and Brazilian Bank — 75, Rua dos Capellistas.
Banco Hypothecario — Largo de Santo Antonio da Sé.
Fonseca, Santos & Vianna — 120, Rua dos Capellistas.
José Gonçalves Franco, Filhos — 170, Rua dos Capellistas.
Fortunato Chamiço & Filhos — 10, Calçadinha de S. Francisco.
Ricardo Carvalho & C.ª — 156, Rua dos Fanqueiros.
F. H. Van-Zeller & C.ª — Rua, da Horta Secca.
Krus & C.ª — 1, Rua das Pedras Negras.
J. B. Dotti — 49, Rua dos Capellistas.
J. R. Blanco — 19, Largo de Santo Antonio da Sé.

4. HOTELS.

(HOTEIS OR HOSPEDARIAS.)

Lisbon is well supplied with hotels and the prices are moderate, ranging from 4$500 réis to 500 réis (20^s. to 2^s. 3^d.) per day for bed, breakfast and table d'hôte. In the cheaper hotels Portuguese only is spoken, but the traveler may get on pretty well with Spanish. The following are the chief hotels: in the four first English is spoken, in the others French.

BRAGANZA — 41, Rua do Thesouro Velho, considered the first hotel in Lisbon, well situated with a charming view of the Tagus. Prices 1$700 réis (7^s. 6^d.) a day, and upwards according to the quality of bedroom.

CENTRAL — 25, Praça dos Romulares, *vulgo*, Caes do Sodré. A large hotel with excellent table d'hôte. Its situation is very low and is for this reason considered by some to be unhealthy. The stench from the river at low water in summer is a nuisance. Prices from 7^s. 6^d.

DURAND — Largo do Barão de Quintella, much frequented by the English. A comfortable well conducted house. Prices from 7^s.

STREET'S ENGLISH HOTEL — 102, Rua do Alecrim, a good hotel with moderate prices.

HOTEL DOS EMBAIXADORES — 102, Rua Nova do Almada, being a wing of baron Barcellinho's palace. Well furnished lofty apartments. Prices from 7^s.

EUROPA — 16, Rua Nova do Carmo, another wing of the above palace. An old established hotel. Prices from 6^s. 8^d.

HOTEL BORGES — at the top of the Chiado, the most fashionable street in Lisbon. A newly fitted up house, centrally situated and with moderate charges, a good family hotel. Mr. Borges, who was for many years manager of the Allianca, is most solicitous for the comfort of his guests.

GRAND HOTEL DU MATTA, in the building lately occupied as the ministry of the Interior, at the top of the Chiado. A recently established hotel, under the direction of the famed Matta, who may be considered the Soyer of Portugal.

ALLIANÇA — 10, Rua Nova da Trindade, with windows looking into the Chiado, prices from 5ˢ.

UNIVERSAL — 23, Travessa de Estevão Galhardo, also looks into the Chiado. Fair table d'hôte, at which persons not living in the hotel may dine for 3ˢ, or paying by the month for 2ˢ, 3ᵈ, including half a bottle of wine. Prices from 5ˢ.

The prices above stated are for bed, breakfast *à la fourchette*, table d'hôte and service, of course if the visitor take his meals in private, an additional charge is made. In almost all the hotels, half a bottle of ordinary wine *(vinho de pasto)* is allowed per head at dinner. Other wines, which with the exception of Port are as a rule very bad, according to list.

5. EATING-HOUSES AND CAFÉS.

(CASAS DE PASTO E CAFÉS.)

EATING-HOUSES.

MATTA'S — 72, Chiado. All the delicacies of the season served in first rate style, *à la carte*. Dinners, suppers, etc. supplied for balls and parties.

JANSEN'S — Rua do Thesouro Velho, near the hotel Braganza.

RESTAURANT CENTRAL — Rua Aurea, entrance 99, travessa da Assumpção.

UNIÃO — 149, Rua da Conceição, *vulgo*, rua dos Retrozeiros.

ESTRELLA DE OURO — 289, Rua Bella da Rainha (rua da Prata).

PEIXE ASSADO — 72, Rua Larga de S. Roque.

GALLO — 91, Rua de S. Julião (rua dos Algibebes).

MANUEL LOURENÇO — 100, Rua Bella da Rainha (rua da Prata).

In all these eating-houses a number of dishes are always ready cooked, a list of which with prices is placed on the table.

CAFÉS.

CENTRAL — in the Chiado, under the Hotel Universal. Tho' poorly furnished is the best café in the city. Beefsteaks, ham, fried fish and other simple dishes are also supplied contrary to the custom of the Lisbon cafés. It is the only one open after midnight and is much used after the opera. There are several private rooms.

AUREA PENINSULAR — in the rua Aurea.

MARTINHO — Largo de Camões, near the W. end of the theatre of D. Maria II. Much frequented by politicians and men of letters.

MARTINHO DA NEVE — at the N E. corner of the Praça do Commercio or Black horse square. The best ices in Lisbon are to be had here on summer evenings.

MONTANHA — Travessa da Assumpção: a modernly furnished café with six billiard tables.

PRICE OR TABERNA INGLEZA — 76, Caes do Sodré, celebrated for its beefsteaks *à ingleza*, Bass on draught.

JANSEN'S — Rua do Thesouro Velho, near Hotel Bragança. A cool place in summer. A drinkable glass of beer brewed on the spot, may be had here for 40 réis (2^d).

FABRICA DE GELO — Rua da Boa Vista, near the Mint, with an entrance from the *Aterro*. This establishment, attached to an ice and chocolate manufactury, supplies refrigerated beverages of every description including beer and soda-water.

The waiters in all the cafés understand only Portuguese or Spanish, but to compensate for their want of linguistic attainments they are well versed in pantomimicry.

6. PUBLIC BATHS.

(BANHOS PUBLICOS.)

SEA BATHING *(Banhos do mar).* — From the 1.st of July to the 1.st of November, half a dozen barques or floating baths *(barcas de banhos)* are moored in the Tagus, at a short distance from the shore, opposite the Praça do Commercio and Caes do Sodré, where boats are in waiting to convey bathers to the baths. Each barque contains some 20 separate compartments immersed in the water to the depth of 4 or 5 feet. The charge is 100 réis including boat. Each barque has a distinctive name such as *Flor do Tejo, Deusa do Mar, Flor da Praia.*

The water however in this part of the river is not as clear as might be desired, and floating objects unpleasant to contemplate, deposited by the crews of the ships anchored in the vicinity, often make their appearance to the disgust of the poor bathers.

The sandy beach near the tower of Belem is a far more agreeable place and much frequented by sea bathers. There are several bathing establishments which supply rooms or tents, towels, etc., and charge a mere trifle. A visitor staying at Lisbon can take one of the early steamers to Belem, which sail every half hour from the Caes do Sodré, fare there and back 100 réis. On reaching the jetty at Belem, boats meet the steamers and convey the passengers gratis to the bathing establishments.

Many bathers who know how to swim, prefer going to the middle of the river in boats fitted up with canvas for the purpose of undressing, and plunge into the water secured by a cord tied round the wrist.

BATHS OF ALCAÇARIAS *(Banhos das Alcaçarias)* — 80, Rua do Terreiro do Trigo, near the corn market, about half a mile E. of Black horse square. The most ancient in Lisbon having been established from time immemorial. The Romans made use of them and afterwards the Moors. The water, slightly sulphurated, rises in a natural spring and when fresh its temperature is about 85° Fahr., approaching blood heat. The baths are of white marble and kept in good order. Price 200 réis.

BATHS OF THE DUKE *(Banhos do Duque)* — Of the same character as the foregoing and situated a little farther to the E. in the same street.

BATHS OF THE ARSENAL *(Banhos do Arsenal)* — At the S. side of St. Paul's church, in the largo de S. Paulo, under the direction of the proprietor D.r Agostinho Vicente Lourenço. The water springs in the Arsenal (whence the name) and is conveyed hither in pipes. It is considered very efficacious in cases of rheumatism, neuralgia, gout, etc. There is also another water which has its rise near St. Paul's. It is salino-muriatic and said to be good for cutaneous diseases. The prices are as follows: plain sulphur 400 réis, sulphur shower 500 réis, salino-muriatic 240 réis, ditto shower 300 réis, plain cold bath 160 réis.

BATHS OF RILHAFOLLES (*Banhos de Rilhafolles*)— Near the Campo de Sant'Anna. This establishment supplies baths of all descriptions such as Turkish, Russian, douche, emollient, aromatic, gelatinous, etc. Prices from 200 réis to 800 réis.

DR. JOSÉ NILO'S BATHS, 22, Rua nova de S. Domingos, near the Praça de D. Pedro.—All kinds of plain and medicated baths from 300 réis to 1$000 réis.

DR. BRILHANTE'S BATHS, 4, Poço do Borratem near the praça da Figueira.—Cold, tepid, douche, Russian, shower, aromatic, turpentine vapour and local baths. Prices from 200 réis to 700 réis.

7. CLUBS AND NEWSROOMS.

The CLUB LISBONENSE, in the Largo do Carmo, near the ruined church of the same name.

This club is frequented by the best society in the capital. It consists of a fine suit of rooms devoted to reading, billiards, cards, chess, etc. Also a grand ball room with reception rooms adjoining. During the winter, four or five balls and assemblies are given here and are attended by the *élite* of Lisbon. Portuguese, French and English daily papers are in the reading-room.

The GREMIO LITTERARIO, occupies the palace of the late Count Farrobo, in the Largo do Barão de Quintella. The lofty and richly decorated rooms are appropriated to reading, conversation, library, billiards and cards. All the Portuguese newspapers together with many French, English, Spanish, Italian and German daily papers are taken here, as well as a number of reviews and periodicals including the Quarterly, Edinburg and Saturday Reviews, the Lancet, Economist, Illustrated London News, Graphic, Punch and the Scientific American.

The library contains a good collection of Portuguese and French standard works, but only a sprinkling of English literature. Light refreshments and drinkables may be had here up to 3 A. M.

This club is much frequented by statesmen, diplomatists, men of letters and members of the houses of parliament. New members are elected by the committee on proposal by two members.

There are other clubs such as the CLUB PORTUGUEZ, ASSEMBLÉA LUSITANA, ASSEMBLÉA FAMILIAR, which are frequented almost exclusively by the Portuguese.

ASSOCIAÇÃO COMMERCIAL or Commercial Association and Newsroom, situated at the SE. corner of Black horse square adjoining the *Bolsa*. The principal merchants of Lisbon are members, and the reading-room is well supplied with foreign newspapers.

8. THE PRESS.

The greatest possible freedom is allowed, and every kind of opinion political or religious may be openly expressed and advocated; indeed this liberty too often degenerates into licence. The following are the chief daily papers published in the capital:

Diario do governo, the official gazette of the government, is confined exclusively to the publication of official documents, notices and advertisements.

Jornal do Commercio, price 40 réis. Represents commercial interests and advocates advanced liberal opinions.

Revolução de Setembro, 40 réis. A political paper, the organ of the *progressista* party.

Diario de Noticias, 10 réis. Eschews politics and confines itself to giving the latest news, home and foreign, with a circumstancial account of passing events. It has the largest circulation of any paper in Portugal, and is for this reason preferred for advertisements.

Diario Popular, 10 réis, also a widely circulated paper, giving general news, but admitting political articles.

A Nação, 20 réis. An old paper devoted to Miguelite and clerical interests, and circulated principally in the provinces.

Diario Illustrado, 10 réis, with an illustration on the first sheet, a new and progressing paper.

Jornal da Noite, 10 réis. An evening paper.

Besides the above, other papers are constantly appearing and disappearing, having but a mushroom like existence.

The *Correspondencia de Portugal,* price 5$000 réis per annum, is published expressly to go by the mail to the Brasils and other countries. It gives a résumé of home and foreign intelligence up to the latest moment.

The following periodicals are also published in Lisbon:

Annaes do club militar naval, monthly.
Archivo rural, fortnightly.
O Direito, weekly.
Gazeta medica, fortnightly.
Jornal de agricultura pratica, monthly.
Jornal de pharmacia, monthly.
Jornal das sciencias medicas, monthly.
Repertorio das camaras,
Revista agricola, monthly.
Revista de legislação, weekly.
Revista de obras publicas, monthly.
Revista dos tabelliães,
Revista militar, fortnightly.
Revista de Portugal e Brasil, fortnightly.
Artes e Letras, monthly.

9. CHRONOLOGICAL RÉSUMÉ

OF THE HISTORY OF PORTUGAL.

The history of Portugal being little read in England, the following chronological table of the principal events may prove useful to English tourists:—

B. C. 300	—	Subjugation of Lusitania, along with the rest of the Peninsula, by the Carthaginians.
220	—	Roman conquest.
149	—	Viriatus raises the standard of revolt against the Romans.
142	—	Assassination of Viriatus.
A. D. 409	—	Incursion of the Vandals, Alani and Suevi.
711	—	Moorish invasion.
1095	—	Count Henrique receives from Alfonso VI. of Leon and Castile the investiture of Portugal, along with the hand of his daughter Theresa.
1112	—	Death of Count Henrique, is succeeded by his infant son Affonso Henriques under the regency of his mother.
1139	Affonso Henriques.	Battle of Campo d'Ourique. Affonso proclaimed king of Portugal.
	1147	Siege and capture of Lisbon from the Moors by Affonso, assisted by a party of English and Flemish Crusaders.
	1158	Alcacer-do-Sal taken after 60 days siege: the whole Moorish garrison slaughtered.
	1185	Death of Affonso Henriques ‹the Conqueror› aged 74. Lies in a magnificent tomb in the Church of Santa Cruz, Coimbra; is succeeded by his son,
1185	Sancho I.	‹Father of his Country.›
	1189	Silves taken: the sovereign adds to his title that of *King of Algarve*.
	1211	Death of Sancho aged 57: lies in the Church of Santa Cruz, Coimbra; is succeeded by his son,
1211	Affonso II.	‹The Fat›.

		1211	Assembly of the first Parliament at Coimbra.
		1217	Battle of Alcacer-do-Sal which had been retaken by the Moors in 1190.
		1223	Death of Affonso II. aged 37: lies in the Convent at Alcobaça; is succeeded by his son,
1223	Sancho II.		«Capello».
		1245	Rebellion of the aristocracy and clergy, deposition and flight of the king to Toledo, where he died in 1248, and is buried in the cathedral of that city: succeeded by his brother,
1245	Affonso III.		«Of Boulogne.»
		1249	Taking of Faro and complete conquest of the Algarve.
		1254	Cortes assembled at Leiria, at which delegates from the municipalities for the first time appear.
		1279	Death of Affonso III. aged 69: buried at Alcobaça; succeeded by his son,
1279	Diniz.		«The Husbandman» who marries St. Isabel in 1281.
		1285	Civil war, the king's younger brother claiming the throne.
		1318	Rebellion of the king's son Affonso.
		1289	University of Lisbon founded.
		1320	Military order of Christ founded.
		1325	Death of Diniz aged 64: buried at Odivellas; succeeded by his son,
1325	Affonso IV.		«The Brave».
		1340	Battle of Salado: the Moorish power in the Peninsula finally crushed.
		1354	Clandestine marriage of the Infante D. Pedro with the beautiful Ignez de Castro.
		1355	Civil war between the king and his son D. Pedro: murder of Ignez de Castro.
		1357	Death of Affonso IV. aged 67: buried in the Cathedral at Lisbon; succeeded by his son,
1357	Pedro I.		«The Severe».
		1361	Exhumation and Coronation of the murdered Ignez de Castro.
		1367	Death of Pedro I. aged 47: buried at Alcobaça; succeeded by his son,
1367	Fernando.		«The Handsome».
		1370	War with Castile.

	1373	Alliance with the Duke of Lancaster, son of Edward III.
	1383	Death of Fernando aged 38: buried in the Convent of S. Francisco at Santarem; succeeded by an,
	INTER-REGNUM.	D. Juan I. of Castile claims the kingdom in right of his wife Dona Beatrice, daughter of Fernando, but D. João, Master of Aviz, his natural son is elected king by the Cortes at Coimbra. Nuno Alvares Pereira distinguishes himself on the national side.
1385	João I.	«Of Good memory».
	1386	14.th August. Famous Battle of Aljubarrota, 6:000 Portuguese completely routing in half an hour 25,000 Spaniards. D. João thrown from his horse, is rescued by Gonçalo de Macedo. Artillery for the first time used in Portugal.
	1387	D. João I. marries Philippa of Lancaster and founds the royal Convent of Batalha.
	1415	Conquest of Ceuta in Africa.
	1420	Discovery of Madeira by João Gonçalves Zarco and Tristão Vaz.
	1418	Discovery of Porto Santo by Bartholomeu Perestrello.
	1422	Adoption of the Christian era in place of that of Cæsar. The Infante D. Henrique lays the foundation of the maritime greatness of Portugal.
	1433	Death of João I. aged 76: buried in the convent of Batalha, which he had founded to commemorate the battle of Aljubarrota; succeeded by his third son.
1433	DUARTE.	«The Eloquent».
	1437	Battle of Tanger: defeat of the Portuguese; captivity and martyrdom of the Infante D. Fernando.
	1438	Death of Duarte aged 47: buried at Batalha; succeeded by his son,
1438	AFFONSO V.	«The African» with his uncle D. Pedro as Regent.
	1438	Civil war between the king and the regent.
	1449	Battle of Alfarrobeira; defeat and death of D. Pedro.

	1476	Battle of Toro in Spain: the Portuguese defeated in their attempt to take the crown of Castile.
	1449	Discovery of the Açores. African conquests. Affonso resigns and re-assumes the crown.
	1481	Death of Affonso V. aged 49: buried at Batalha; succeeded by his son,
1481	João II.	«The Perfect». Conspiracy of nobles against the king.
	1482	Discovery of Guiné by Diogo d'Azambuja.
	1483	Duke of Bragança beheaded.
	1484	Duke of Viseu stabbed by the king at Setubal.
	1486	Discovery of Angola and Benguella by Diogo Cão.
	1487	Cape of Good Hope doubled by Bartholomeu Dias. Affonso de Paiva and João da Covilhã set out by land to discover India, but never return.
	1495	Death of João II. aged 40: buried at Batalha; succeeded by his cousin, son of the Infante D. Pedro and grandson of Duarte.

HOUSE OF VIZEU.

1495	Manuel.	«The Fortunate».
	1496	Expulsion of the Jews.
	1498	Discovery of India by Vasco da Gama.
	1500	Brazil discovered by Pedro Alvares Cabral.
	1506	Discovery of Madagascar by Ruy Pereira Coutinho.
	1507	Discovery of the Maldiva islands by Lourenço d'Almeida.
	1508–10	Conquest of Ormuz, Malaca and Goa, the three chief emporiums of Asia.
	1517	Discovery of China by Fernão Peres de Andrade.
	1521	Death of Manuel aged 52: rests in the convent of St. Jerome at Belem, Lisbon; succeeded by his son,

1521	João III.	«The Pious».
	1530-49	Colonization of Brazil. Portugal attains the height of its glory.
	1536	Establisment of the Inquisition in Portugal.
	1540	Entrance of the Jesuits, with St. Francis Xavier.
	1546	Taking of Diu by D. João de Mascarenhas.
	1557	Death of João III: buried in St. Jerome's Belem; succeeded by his grandson,
1557	Sebastião.	«The Regretted» with his grandmother as regent.
	1562	Cardinal Henrique regent.
	1574	D. Sebastian's first visit to Africa.
	1578	Fatal expedition composed of 16,000 men, including the flower of the Portuguese aristocracy, headed by D. Sebastião, and accompanied by Muley Hamet who disputes the crown of Morocco with Muley Maluco.
	1578	4.th of August. Battle of Alcacer-Quibir, defeat and disappearance of Sebastião, whose fate remains a mystery. The Portuguese army is utterly destroyed. Sebastião at the time of his disappearance was aged 24: his supposed remains, brought to Portugal by Philip II, are deposited in St. Jerome's, Belem: succeeded by his great-uncle, 7.th son of king Manuel,
1578	Cardinal Henrique.	«The chaste».
	1580	Death of the Cardinal King aged 68: buried in St. Jerome's Belem. The throne is claimed by Philip II. of Spain; Antonio, Prior do Crato; João, Duke of Bragança; Emanuel Philibert, Duke of Savoy; the Prince of Parma; Elizabeth of England, and the Pope. The claimants resolve themselves into Philip II. of Spain and the Prior do Crato. The duke of Alva invades Portugal, and Philip prevails.

CASTILIAN USURPATION.

The 60 years captivity.

1581	Philippe I.		(II. of Spain) «The Prudent».
		1589	Siege of Lisbon by the Prior do Crato.
		1588	The invincible fleet of 150 ships sails from Lisbon to conquer England, but is driven back by contrary winds and many of the ships wrecked. Various impostors give themselves out as D. Sebastian, the most notable being a man who appeared at Venice having marks on his body corresponding exactly with D. Sebastião. Many Portuguese believe in his identity, but Philip casts him into prison where he perishes. Rapid decline of the Portuguese empire.
		1598	Death of Philip I. aged 71: buried in the Escurial, near Madrid. Succeeded by his son,
1598	Philippe II.		(III. of Spain) «The Idle». The Dutch ruin the Portuguese empire in Asia and conquer nearly the whole of Brazil.
		1610	Expulsion of the Moors from Portugal and from the rest of the Peninsula.
		1621	Death of Philip II. aged 43: buried in the Escurial; succeeded by his son.
1621	Philippe III.		(IV. of Spain) «The Unfortunate».
		1625	Bahia retaken from the Dutch.
		1640	1.st December. The Portuguese tired of the tyranny of Spain resolve to expel the foreigner. A vast conspiracy is formed headed by D. João, 8.th Duke of Bragança, and by a preconcerted plan, in a single day, all the Spaniards are either assassinated or driven from the country.

HOUSE OF BRAGANÇA.

1640	João IV.	«The Restorer» proclaimed in Lisbon. Portuguese India and Brazil also expel the Spaniards. War of Independence with Spain; lasts 28 years.
	1644	Battle of Montijo; the Spaniards defeated.
	1643–54	War with the Dutch; the islands in the Atlantic, Angola, Maranham, and Pernambuco recovered. The Portuguese influence gradually re-established.
	1646	The king chooses Nossa Senhora da Conceição patroness of the kingdom.
	1656	Death of João IV. aged 52: buried in St. Vincent's Lisbon; succeeded by his son,
1656	Affonso VI.	«The Victorious». The Dutch expelled from Brazil.
	1658	Successful battle with the Spaniards at the Linhas de Elvas.
	1663	Ameixial.
	1665	Montes Claros.
	1668	The king deposed and falsely declared insane, is banished to the Island of Terceira, where he remains 6 years: his brother D. Pedro named regent.
	1683	Death of Affonso VI. aged 40, at the palace of Cintra, where he had been confined nine years in a small room: buried in St. Vincent's; succeeded by his brother the regent,
1683	Pedro II.	«The Pacific». Spain renounces all claim to Portugal.
	1703	Treaty with England.
	1706	Death of Pedro II. aged 58: buried at St. Vincent's; succeeded by his son,
1706	João V.	«The Magnanimous».
	1716	Lisbon made a Patriarchate.
	1717–30	Erection of the Basilica at Mafra.
	1717–38	Construction of the great aqueduct to supply Lisbon.
	1748	Pope Benedict XIV. concedes the

			title of «Most Faithful» to king John and to his descendants.
		1750	Death of João V. aged 61: buried in St. Vincent's; succeeded by his son,
1750	José I.		«The Most Faithful» who placed such faith in his minister Sebastião José Carvalho, afterwards created Marquis of Pombal, that this statesman was the real ruler of the kingdom during José's reign.
		1755	Great earthquake which destroys the greater part of Lisbon, 30,000 of its citizens falling victims.
		1758	Pseudo-conspiracy of members of the aristocracy against the king's life.
		1759	Expulsion of the Jesuits.
		1762	War with France and Spain.
		1777	Death of José I. aged 62: buried in St. Vincent's, Lisbon; succeeded by his daughter,
1777	Maria I.		«The Merciful» who had married her uncle Pedro III, son of John V. Disgrace and banishment of the Marquis of Pombal.
		1789	Insanity of the Queen.
		1807	Napoleon proclaims that the house of Bragança has ceased to reign.
		1807	First French invasion under Junot. The Royal family sail to Brazil.
		1808	English army under Sir Arthur Wellesley enters Portugal, and having gained the battles of *Roliça* and *Vimeiro*, oblige the French to evacuate the country. Convention of Cintra.
		1809	Second French invasion under Soult: they enter Oporto, but are soon vanquished by the Anglo-Portuguese army.
		1810–11	Third French invasion under Massena: they are defeated at the battle of *Bussaco*, march on Lisbon pursued by the allied army, and are driven out of Portugal.
		1811	Death of Maria I. at Rio de Janeiro aged 30: translated to Portugal and buried in the church of Estrella, which she had founded at Lisbon; succeeded by her son,

1816	João VI.	«The Mild» who had acted as regent since 1789, when his mother became insane. The court resides in Brazil.
	1820	The Constitution proclaimed. The king returns to Portugal and accepts it, surrendering Brazil to his son D. Pedro as regent.
	1821	D. Miguel, the king's 2.nd son, revolts against the constitution.
	1824	D. Miguel again revolts, and is banished to Vienna.
	1825	Independence of the Brazils acknowledged.
	1826	Death of João VI. aged 59: buried at St. Vincent's, Lisbon; succeeded by his son,
1826	Pedro IV.	«The Soldier King» first Emperor of Brazil.
	1826	29.th April. The king signs the Constitutional Charter and abdicates in favor of his daughter D. Maria, on condition that she observe the constitution and marry her uncle D. Miguel.
	1828	D. Miguel returns from banishment and is acclaimed king.
	1832	D. Pedro IV. lands in Portugal, with an army of 7,500, to vindicate the cause of his daughter. Battle of Ponte Ferreira, near Oporto: the Miguelites defeated, the Duke of Terceira's expedition from the Açores.
	1833	Sir Charles Napier annihilates the Miguelite fleet.
	1834	Battle of Asseisseira. Miguelites finally defeated. Convention of Evora Monte. D. Miguel resigns the kingdom. Extinction of the monastic orders in Portugal. Death of D. Pedro IV. aged 36: buried at St. Vincent's, Lisbon.
1834	Maria II.	«The Virtuous» proclaimed.
	1836	Outbreak for a modification of the Constitution.
	1846	Revolution against the government of Cabral. Spanish forces under general Concha, and English fleet called in to establish order.
	1853	Death of D. Maria II. aged 34: buried in St. Vincent's, Lisbon; succeeded by her son,

1853	Pedro V.	'The Hopeful' under the regency of his father the king consort D. Fernando.
	1855	D. Pedro V. assumes the reins of government.
	1861	Death of D. Pedro, regretted by all, aged 24: buried in St. Vincent's, Lisbon; succeeded by his brother,
1861	Luiz I.	

10. PORTUGUESE LANGUAGE AND LITERATURE.

The Portuguese language is well worth being studied, not only for the sake of its literature, but also on account of its usefulness in travel and commerce, being spoken in a wide extent of territory, especially in the Brazils and in many parts of Africa.

A great number of people labor under the idea that Portuguese is a dialect of Spanish, so accustomed are they, from infancy, to see the two nations united in one map in the atlases, and although physically they are close neighbors, and there is at the same time a great similarity between their languages, yet as regards their customs, character, and literature they are very wide apart. It is only recently that a Portuguese-Castilian dictionary has been published, though a Chinese-Portuguese dictionary was printed many years ago. Indeed ever since the Spanish domination, which ended in 1640, the Portuguese have kept themselves aloof from every thing that savored of Spain, so that Spanish books are scarcely to be met with in Portugal. The Spaniards, on the other hand, think it quite beneath them to read Portuguese.

The origin of the Portuguese language is the same as that of the Spanish, both being transformed dialects of Latin. Strictly speaking there is no such language as *Spanish;* what is generally called by this name is *Castilian. Spain* is a political and geographical expression like *Great Britain;* but nobody ever calls the latter's official language *Britannic!* Yet Spain includes within its area languages quite as distinct from each other as English, Welsh and Gaelic.

When the Romans entered the Peninsula B. C. 225, they found many different languages established in different regions, but having colonized it and kept it in their possession for more than six centuries, they left it speaking almost entirely Latin (except in the mountains), but with different pronunciations and dialects in different parts of the country, according to the various languages previously spoken by the aborigines.

Indeed, as early as the time of Julius Caesar, the inhabitants of southern Spain understood and therefore spoke Latin, as may be inferred from the following passage:

« Caesar, concione habita Cordubae, omnibus generatim gratias agit: civibus Romanis, quod oppidum in sua potestate studuissent habere, *Hispanis, quod praesidia expulissent; Gaditanis, quod conatus adversariorum infregissent,* seseque in libertatem vindicassent. »
Caes., *De bello civili.* lib. II, XXI.

Strabo, who lived in the time of Augustus, says that the inhabitants of southern Spain had adopted Roman manners and even forgotten their vernacular language:

«Turdetani autem, maxime qui ad Boerim sunt, plane Romanos mores assumpserunt, *ne sermonis quidem vernaculi memores,* ac plerique facti sunt latini. »
Strabo, *De rerum geographarum,* lib. III, page 224.

Now if there were many people in the time of Augustus who spoke Latin, is it not safe to assume that after a further sway of the Romans of upward of four centuries, the Latin language would have become the general language of the people?

Some proud Spaniards go so far as to say that Castilian is not derived from Latin, but Latin from Castilian!

« Algunos han querido que no el romance del latin sino el latin del romance nuestro, habia tomado su origen. »
Sarmiento.

It is a remarkable fact that many of the Latin writers in the silver age were born in Spain, as for instance, the two Senecas, Columella, Lucanus, Quintillianus, Martialis, Mela, etc. Latin then, having become the general language of the Peninsula, but with various dialects, one of these was the foundation of the Galician language, and another of the Castilian. The former has been developed into Portuguese. So that Castilian and Portuguese have grown up side by side independent of each other, but as their foundations were dialects of one and the same language, there is a very close resemblance between the two, but they stand in the same relation to each other as Spanish and French.

Portuguese is as near Latin as may be, after abolishing the case-endings and introducing prepositions in their stead.

To shew the very close connection between Portuguese and Latin let us take one of Cicero's letters and compare all the verbs, adverbs, nouns, pronouns and adjectives, viz:

«Tullia nostra venit ad me pridie Idus Junias, cujus summa virtute et singulari humanitate graviore etiam sum dolore affectus nostra factum esse negligentia ut longe alia in fortuna esset atque ejus pietas ac dignitas postulabat. Nobis erat in animo Ciceronem ad Caesarem mittere, et cum eo Cn. Sallustium. Si profectus erit, faciam te certiorem. Valetudinem tuam cura diligenter. Vale.»

Omitting proper names and putting the nouns and adjectives in the abl. and the verbs in the first per. singular, present indicative, we have.

Latin.	Portuguese.
nostra	nossa
venio	venho
me	me
pridie	No equivalent adv.
Junio	Junho
cujus	cujo
summa	summa
virtute	virtude
singulari	singular
humanitate	humanidade
grave	grave
sum	sou
dolore	dor
affecto	affecto
facto	facto
negligentia	negligencia

Latin.	Portuguese.
longe	longe
alia	outra
fortuna	fortuna
pietate	piedade
dignitate	dignidade
postulo	postulo
animo	animo
mitto	remetto
eo	elle
proficiscor	parto
facio	faço
te	te
valetudine	saude
certo	certo
curo	curo
valeo	valho

Indeed so much alike are the two languages that Antonio de Sousa de Macedo has published a collection of orations both in prose and verse, which may be read as Portuguese or Latin. The following is a sample:

«O quam gloriosas memorias publico considerando quanto vales, nobilissima lingua lusitana cum tua fecundia excessivamente nos provocas, excitas, inflammas, quam altas victorias procuras, quam celebres triumphos speras, quam excellentes fabricas fundas, quam perversas furias castigas, quam feroces insolencias rigorosamente domas, manifestando de prosa e de verso tantas elegancias latinas».

«Alta resurge pio felix de principe terra
Et renova palmas lysia clara tuas
Vive triumphando charissima patria vive
Que fama, imperio gloria maior eras
Et tra de mundo certo celeberrima lingua
(Extinguas voces lingua latina tuas)
Prospera continuos dando fortuna favores
Conserva gentes forte benigna suas.»

After the overthrow of the Roman empire, Portugal successively fell a prey to the Vandals, Suevi, Alanos,

Visigoths, Arabs and Moors, the latter occupying the country for more than three centuries and introducing into its language many Arabic words which are still retained and generally begin with *al*, like *alfandega*, custom-house; *alfinete*, pin; *almoço*, breakfast.

After the expulsion of the Moors, the language may be said to have undergone no radical change; the difference between Portuguese of the XVI century, and that of the present day, is principally a change of orthography and latterly the introduction of French words and gallicisms.

Portuguese literature may be said to begin with Gil Vicente, who flourished in the first half of the XVI. century: the following are the chief classic authors since that period:

    Bernardim Ribeiro.
    Sá de Miranda, 1495–1558.
    João de Barros, 1496–1570.
    Damião de Goes, 1501–1573.
    Jeronymo Osorio, 1506–1580.
    Fernão Mendes Pinto, 1509–1583.
    Camões, 1524–1580.
    Antonio Ferreira, 1528–1569.
    Diogo Bernardes, 1530 (?)–1605.
    João de Lucena, 1549–1600.
    Frei Luiz de Sousa, 1555–1632.
    Freire de Andrade, 1597–1657.
    Antonio de Sousa de Macedo, 1606–1682.
    Padre Vieyra, 1608–1697.
    Manuel de Mello, 1611–1666.
    José Agostinho de Macedo, 1761–1834.
    Bocage, 1765–1805.
    Garret, 1798–1854.

Of men of letters of the present day the number is great, and journalism being the shortest cut to place and power, many ambitious men take to the pen, not from a love of literature, but as a means to an end. However there are many distinguished writers in all branches of literature, and at the head of the list stand the names of Visconde de Castilho, Herculano, Mendes Leal, Castello Branco, Latino Coelho.

To an Englishman, Portuguese is by no means an easy language to learn. It contains many niceties of expression and pronounciation. There are 21 distinct vowel sounds represented by the five vowels *a, e, i, o, u,* and 20 consonant sounds represented by 18 letters, by which are formed the 1,800 syllables and 40,000 words composing the Portuguese language. The vowels *e* and *o* are each pronounced in six different ways without any accents to guide foreigners, indeed the only way to acquire a tolerably correct pronunciation is by constant practice and residence in the country; all rules given in grammars are of little use, it being impossible to apply them in practice. It is as necessary to educate the ear for language as for music, and it is only after a year or two that an Englishman begins to distinguish the pronunciation of a Portuguese from that of a Brazilian, tho' to the natives there is as great a difference as between cheese and chalk.

The principal difficulty to be got over by an Englishman is the *s chiante* and the double *r*, which must be very distinctly articulated to distinguish it from the single *r*. The easiest way to learn Portuguese is to master thoroughly the paradigms of the verbs and the rules of concordance. There is nothing more profitable than learning phrases by heart, so as to be able to write them down from memory. Before committing any thing to memory care must be taken to give each word its proper pronunciation. By this means the learner will not only acquire a knowledge of the genders, irregular verbs, signification of words, orthography and pronunciation, but he will also learn to put the right word into the right place; for there are many synonyms in Portuguese, the use of which practice alone will teach, and which if wrongly employed sound very odd to Portuguese ears, just as to an Englishman it would sound strange to hear any one say *Mendelssohn's moonshine sonata* tho' the signification of moonshine and of moonlight is exactly the same.

The Portuguese are very vivacious in familiar conversation, and often make use of onomatopeias to enliven their discourse. Thus in recounting the exploits of a warrior who cut off the head of his enemy, they would imitate the action by a wave of the hand and the noise of the percussion by *zaz*.

In Portuguese like in Latin the personal pronouns are not used with the verbs, except for the sake of emphasis or to prevent ambiguity, and this feature of the language makes it especially adapted for epic poetry. The same may be said with regard to the relative positions of the nominative, verb and object which can be varied infinitely more than in English.

The best English-Portuguese grammar is Vieyra's, but it does not contain any exercises. There is also a method of teaching Portuguese by Cabano, on the Ahn system; it is not a bad book, but the Portuguese part is full of errors. A small book of exercises by the Rev. A. J. D. D'Orsey tho' printed in London is more correct, as well as his «Colloquial Portuguese».

The best Portuguese-English dictionary is that by Lacerda. Vieyra's though less copious is much cheaper, and quite sufficient for beginners. It is correct as far as it goes.

The distinction between *ser* and *estar*, both represented by *to be* in English, offers considerable difficulty at first, which practice alone will overcome. *Ser* is derived from the Latin *esse*, and *estar* from *stare*; but their use and signification are very different in the two languages. The former corresponds with archbishop Whately's *inseparable accident*, and the latter with his *separable accident*. Many nice shades of meaning arrise from the combination of the three auxiliaries *haver*, *estar* and *ter*, with the verb «to be» *ser*, by which existence is predicated as commencing, continuing or ending. In conversation, however, there is no time for metaphysical subtilties, and the student will find it by far more profitable to learn the practice first and the theory afterwards.

Portuguese differs from all the other European languages in possessing a *personal* infinitive in addition to the impersonal one, and this circumstance does away with ambiguity in those propositions, where the subject of the infinite is different, from that of the finite verb.

Chronographic Map of the principal Portuguese Classic writers compared with those of Italy, Spain, France and England

There are three modes of address called *tratamentos,* like in French. The second person singular *tu* is used in addressing near relations, intimate friends, and lower servants; the second person plural *vos* in place of the singular, is now almost obsolete; and the third person *o Senhor, Vossa Senhoria, Vossa Excellencia,* is used with equals and superiors, and may be safely used by a foreigner in addressing all classes of society: *O Senhor quer jantar?* Like *Monsieur, veut-il dîner?* In addressing ladies *Vossa Excellencia* is always used.

An Englishman speaking French can get on very well in Lisbon or Oporto, but if he intend to travel in the interior of the country, a knowledge of Portuguese is indispensable.

There may be said to be no patois in Portugal if we except the province of the Minho, whose inhabitants are in the habit of changing the *v* into *b* and vice-versa. Along the Spanish frontier also, slight modifications of pronunciation may be observed, but they can scarcely be said to amount to dialects.

The following chronographic map presents at one view, the relative position in point of time, of the principal Portuguese classics compared with those of Italy, Spain, France and England down to the end of the last century. The map is divided by the thicker horizontal lines, into five centuries, which are again subdivided into decades. The numbers at the top and bottom of each figure denote the years of birth and death. The perpendicular space covered by each figure represents the duration of the writer's life.

11. HISTORICAL SKETCH OF LISBON.

The origin of Lisbon is lost among the nebulae of remote antiquity. Like most cities of the Peninsula, its historians claim for its foundation a remoteness which carries us back to the regions of fable; and much learned time has been spent in attempting to prove that the Elysian fields were situated in Portugal; that the Lima was the river of oblivion, and that *Lisus* or *Lusus,* who accompanied Bacchus in his travels, was the founder of Lisbon and progenitor of the Lusitanians:

> Lusus the loved companion of the God,
> In Spain's fair bosom fixed his last abode,
> Our kingdom founded, and illustrious reign'd,
> In whose fair lawns, the blest Elysium feign'd,
> Where winding oft the Guadiana roves,
> And Douro murmurs through the flowering groves.
> Here with his bones he left his deathless fame,
> And Lusitania's clime shall ever bear his name.
>
> (CAMOËS, cant. VIII.)

Others again with no less zeal contend that Lisbon owes its origin to *Elisa*, great-grandson of Noah, and with marvelous precision determine the exact date to be 2150 B. C. or 278 years after the deluge. The popular belief, however, is that it was founded by Ulysses after the destruction of Troy, and though there is no definite authority in favor of Homer's astute hero, yet he has been generally adopted by the poets in their lucubrations, and the story has thus gained currency with the people. It is related that Ulysses after long contending with the tempestuous ocean, entered the Tagus for the double purpose of repairing the damage his ships had sustained in a storm, and of giving an interval of repose to his weary followers; that after a considerable delay, when he proposed to resume his voyage, he found few or none willing to exchange the security of a delightful harbor for the stormy perils of an unknown ocean, that in this emergency he adapted himself to circumstances, and in accordance with the wishes of his men, traced out the foundations of a new city which he called Olyssippo, and built in it a temple to Minerva; that the predatory habits of these conquerors of Troy soon drew upon them the hostility of the natives, and that the prudent chief representing to his followers this opposition as an insurmountable obstacle to their plans of permanent colonization, induced them to abandon the place and to sail with him once more in search of Ithaca:

> That other chief th'embroidered silk displays,
> Tossed on the deep whole years of weary days,
> On Tagus' banks at last his vows he paid.
> To Wisdom's God-like power, the Jove born maid.
> Who fired his lips with eloquence divine,
> On Tagus' banks he reared the hallowed shrine,
> Ulysses he, though fated to destroy
> On Asia's ground the heaven built towers of Troy,
> On Europe's strand, more grateful to the skies,
> He bade th'eternal walls of Lisbon rise [1].
>
> (LUSIAD., cant. VIII — IV, V.)

But leaving the regions of fiction we find that the first certain event recorded of Lisbon is its reduction with the rest of Spain under the dominion of Carthage. In the wars which the African republic waged against Rome, its citizens joined the standard of the victorious Hannibal.

The lasting hatred against the Romans infused by that general into his followers, displayed itself in the pertinacious struggle which the Lusitani maintained under the immortal Viriatus; and long after Carthage had fallen beneath the power of her rival, they still fought for independence under the conduct of Apimanus and Sertorius.

The unequal contest at last terminated in the destruction of Lusitanian liberty, and the whole of further Spain was reduced into the form of a Roman province. Under the Emperors, good military roads were constructed, connecting Lisbon with the other principal

---

1. This tradition is the subject of Antonio de Sousa de Macedo's epic poem «Olyssippo» written in the middle of the 17.th century, and considered one of the classic works in the Portuguese language.

towns of Lusitania: its ancient name Ulysippo[1] was changed into the more classical one of *Felicitas Julia,* as that of Beja was into *Pax Julia.* Both appellations were bestowed by Julius Caesar, and the same Emperor gave to Lisbon the privileges of a Roman *Municipium.*

From the time of Julius Caesar nothing worthy of notice occurs till the reign of Honorius, when the Gothic invaders of the Roman empire, after desolating the fairest provinces of Italy and Gaul, scaled the Pyrenees, and scattered their countless legions over the Peninsula. Lisbon soon attracted the attention of the barbarians. The terrified inhabitants, following the temporizing policy of Rome, met with a calamity similar to that which befel the Latin capital. A prodigious sum procured the departure of the foe: the same year witnessed his return. The interval had been employed in providing additional means of defence, and the garrison had been raised to twice the number of men. For three months all the efforts of the barbarians to force an entrance had proved unavailing. At length a termination was put to the struggle by the treachery of Lucidius, the commander of the garrison. The besiegers were admitted, and the city was given up to plunder. Yet whatever Lisbon may have suffered from the rapacity of the invaders, she could not complain of preëminence in disaster: every city of Spain bore its share in the general calamity. The Gothic invasion, however, was not without its advantages. Impoverished by the successive exactions of Roman governors, the country had little to lose, perhaps much to gain, by a change of masters. The Goths by incorporating themselves with the natives, gradually spread among them ideas of independence, all tendency to which the suspicious policy of Rome had been careful to suppress; and thus, if the people under the Gothic sway retrograded in civilization, the evil was partly compensated by the onward move they made in liberty. Among the nations which had followed

1. Pliny and Gruter assert that the ancient name of Lisbon was *Olisipo* or *Olisippo*, a word of Phœnician etymology meaning a pleasant bay. In the inscriptions still extant of the time of Domitianus and of the middle of the 3.rd century, it is styled *Olisipo.*

the standard of Alaric, the principal were the Goths or Visigoths, the Vandals, Suevi, Alani and Siligni. Each tribe had its own chief and professed independence. These divisions soon proved a fertile source of discord, and the conquered country, after being exposed to the miseries of invasion, was doomed to experience the horrors of civil war. Lisbon was a second time besieged and taken.

The Visigoths, under Theodoric finally gained the ascendant, and during the space of two hundred years thirty Visigothic kings successively wielded the scepters of Spain and Portugal. Roderic closed the series; a man remarkable only for his shameful irregularities, which after having earned for him the detestation of his subjects, finally occasioned the loss of his crown and life after the fatal battle with the Moors, on the banks of the Guadelete in 713.

The followers of Mahomet had at this period extended their power from the eastern border of Arabia to the shores of the Atlantic. One only fortress bade defiance to their arms. This was Ceuta. Before this important place, Musa, the general of Caliph, appeared with an army of 140,000 men. For a considerable time the efforts of the infidel were without success, and his army would probably have wasted away before this impregnable rock had not the governor himself treacherously given him admission, to revenge an insult which Roderic had offered him in the person of his daughter. Count Julian not only became an apostate and a traitor, but offered to head the expedition which had for its object the subjugation of the Peninsula to the Mahometan yoke. The appearance of the forces after landing on the coast of Spain, under Yarrick, the lieutenant of Musa, is thus described by Southey: —

> There on the beach the unbelievers spread
> Their banners flaunting to the sun and breeze;
> Fair shone the sun upon their proud array,
> While turbans, glittering armor, shield engrailed
> With gold, and scymitars of Syrian steel,
> And gently did the breezes, as in sport,
> Curl their long flags outrolling, and display
> The blazoned scrolls of blasphemy.

The landing of the Moors was an event the more appalling as it was unexpected. No adequate means of checking the progress of the invaders had been provided; town after town was either forced or terrified into submission, and within the space of two years from the appearance of the Moslem fleet, the standard of Mahomet waved from every principal city in the Peninsula.

The dominion of the Moors forms a long and dreary night in the history of Lisbon. In the year 793, after a christian army had rallied round the king of Asturias, a successful effort was made by Don Alonzo, surnamed «the Chaste», to wrest the city from the hands of the infidels. But though he gained, he was unable to retain possession of it. During a period of 300 years the Christians and Moors were alternately its masters. The importance of its position was equally felt by both parties, and many and bloody were the contests carried on, either within the city itself, or in its immediate neighborhood. In the meantime its population decreased; the appearance of the temples changed according to the religion of the victors; and its public buildings and ancient monuments were remorselessly pulled down to aid in constructing works of defense. Even its name was destined to undergo a change. The ancient appellation of Lispo, the abbreviation of Olisipo, was transformed into Lisbo, an alteration easily accounted for by the fact that the letter *p* does not exist in the Moorish alphabet.

Such was the situation of Lisbon, when in the year 1095 Don Affonso VI, king of Castile, gave with the hand of his daughter, the investiture of the whole of Portugal to the valiant Prince Henry, duke of Burgundy. This prince, by a series of victories over the Moors, had well nigh succeeded in realizing, before the end of his long reign, a title which when bestowed was only nominal. At his death he left a son, whose achievements were to form the first and brightest page in the history of the Portuguese monarchy. This was Affonso Henriques. Assuming the reins of government when only eighteen years old, he first combated and quelled an unnatural cabal in the regency, which had for its object to deprive him of the rights which he inherited from his father. His next efforts were directed against the Moors. They were his avowed and natural enemies. Putting himself at the head of an army he advanced into Estremadura, crossed the Tagus, and carried devastation into the country south of that river. To arrest his progress the infidels united their forces. Five Moorish kings assembled their respective armies on the plains of Ourique. Victory declared for Affonso, who with 13,000 men defeated a host of 200,000, and returned laden with spoil and with glory[1]. His chief object in this expedition had been to strike terror into the enemy by ravaging the open country as he passed. An unsuccessful attempt on Lisbon closed the campaign. The great battle of Ourique was fought in 1139.

After a short repose he again took the field. From Lamego, where he had been proclaimed by the three estates, he marched once more in the direction of Lisbon. Leiria and Santarem were taken by assault; the smaller towns surrendered at discretion, and no further opposition was attempted till he came in sight of the Moorish

[1]. Tradition says that on the eve of the battle, while the count was meditating on the vast superiority of his enemy's forces, a hermit suddenly entered his tent and told him in God's name, to go forth next morning on hearing the bell ring for mass, and turn his face towards the east. He obeyed and beheld the image of our crucified Saviour surrounded by a bright halo, who promised him not only victory, but a regal crown:

> A matutina luz serena e fria,
> As estrellas do polo já apartava
> Quando na Cruz o Filho de Maria,
> Mostrando-se a Affonso, o animava.
> Elle adorando quem lhe apparecia,
> Na Fé todo inflammado, assi gritava:
> Aos infieis, Senhor, aos infieis,
> E não a mim, que creio o que podeis!
>
> Com tal milagre os animos da gente
> Portugueza inflammados, levantavam
> Por seu rei natural este excellente
> Principe, que do peito tanto amavam:
> E diante do exercito potente
> Dos imigos, gritando o céu tocavam.
> Dizendo em alta voz: Real, Real,
> Por Affonso, alto rei de Portugal.
>
> Camões.

capital. Here the infidels had determined to make a final stand. Having concentrated within the walls the best and bravest of their forces, they bade defiance to all the efforts of the besiegers. A strong wall defended by seventy seven towers, surrounded the place. Stores of every kind had been abundantly provided, and the energies of the Christian army would probably have wasted away in as vain attempts as those that had been made the preceding year, had not a fortunate and unexpected occurrence taken place, which ultimately decided the contest in favor of Affonso. This was the arrival of a fleet of some two hundred galleys on its way to Palestine with an army of Crusaders, composed principally of English, French, Germans and Flemings.

Having been driven to Oporto through stress of weather, Affonso did not lose the golden opportunity. He represented to the commanders of the expedition that the infidels whom he was besieging were in effect the same as those whom they had bound themselves to conquer, and that to aid him in expelling from his dominions these enemies of the Christian name, was as meritorious and honorable an entreprise as if they had landed on the shores of Palestine. His arguments and entreaties prevailed. The forces amounting to 20,000 men were landed at Lisbon, and the siege was continued with the combined strenght of both armies.

Who the leaders of these Crusaders were has long been a *vexata quæstio* among historians. Several distinguish-

Thus translated by Mickle:

> "T was morn's still hour, before the dawning grey,
> The stars' bright twinkling died away;
> When lo, resplendent in the heaven serene,
> High o'er the prince the sacred cross was seen.
> The godlike prince with faith's warm glow inflamed,
> Oh, not to me, my bounteous God, exclaim'd,
> Oh, not to me, who well thy grandeur know,
> But to the Pagan herd thy wonders shew.
>
> The Lusian host, enraptured, mark'd the sign,
> That witnessed to their chief the aid divine:
> Right on the foe they shake the beamy lance,
> And with firm strides, and heaving breasts, advance,
> Then burst the silence, Hail, O King, they cry;
> Our King, our King, the echoing dales reply.

ed names are mentioned, such as Eric, king of Denmark, the duke of Burgundy and the court of Flanders. Some authors are of opinion that the expedition was under no particular chief, but that it was an heterogeneous multitude, who had taken the cross in different countries and trusted more to the guidance of Heaven, than to that of their leaders.

The following account of the siege of Lisbon by Affonso Henriques is taken from a letter written in 1147 by one of the Crusaders, a nobleman named Arnulfo, to the bishop of Jerona, in France, and published at Paris 1724 in a work entitled *Veterum Monumentorum* by two Benedictine monks of St. Maurus[1].

«On Monday, entering the bar of the river called Douro, we arrived at Oporto where we found the bishop of that city joyfully awaiting our arrival by order of the king, and there we stayed eleven days for count Arnoldo de Ardescot and the Constable, who had been separated from us by a tempest, and we were liberally supplied with wine and other delicacies by the generosity of the king.

«Count Arnoldo and the Constable having arrived, we set sail and on the second day, the vigil of the apostles SS. Peter and Paul (28.th June) we reached Lisbon, which city according to the Moorish historians, was founded by Ulysses after the destruction of Troy. It is admirably constructed both as to its walls and towers and is situated at the top of a hill almost impregnable to

---

1. For the benefit of those who take an interest in antiquities we give the Latin text of this curious document:

«Secunda feria a Portucallim per alveum fluminis, qui Dorius dicitur, applicuimus, ubi Episcopum civitatis ejusdem adventum nostrum cum magno gaudio juxta praeceptum Regis praestolantem reperimus. Ubi per dies xi adventum comitis Arnoldi de Ardescot nec non Christiani Constabularii, qui a nobis praedicta tempestate divisi erant expectantes, nequam redditionem tam vini, quam caeterarum deliciarum ex benevolentia regis habuimus.

«Eandem comite Arnoldo simulque Stabulario receptis, navigantes secunda die apud Ulixibonam in vigilia apostolorum Petri et Pauli appulimus. Quae civitas, sicut tradunt historiae Saracenorum, ab Ulixe post excidium Troiae condita, mirabili structura tam murorum quam turrium, super montem humanis viribus insuperabilis fundata est.

human forces. Pitching our tents around it we captured the suburbs, by divine assistance, on the 1.st of July. After this, assaulting the walls in various places, with great loss to ourselves and to the enemy, we spent the time till the 1.st of August in making military machines. We constructed two towers near the shore, one on the east side where the Flemings were located, and the other on the west side where the English had pitched their camp. We constructed also four bridges in the ships, to gain admission to the city by scaling the walls.

On St. Stephen's day (3.rd August) we advanced with the ships, but being driven back by contrary winds and damaged by the engines of war, we had to withdraw them. Then, while we were fighting with the Moors, the English having been remiss in the defense of their tower, it was suddenly set on fire and the flames could not be extinguished. In the meantime we began to undermine the wall by means of a machine, but the Moors observing this, poured burning oil on to it, and the machine was set on fire. After which they killed a large number of our men by their darts and engines and were themselves severely punished by us. Our men, somewhat downcast by the destruction of their machines and the damage they had received, rely-

---

«Circa quam, figentis tentoria Kalendis Julii suburbana ejus Divina virtute adjuti, cepimus. Post hace assaltus, varios circa muros non sine magno nostrorum et illorum detrimento facientes, usque ad kalendas Augusti in machinis faciendis tempus protraximus. Siquidem duas turres juxta litus unam in orientali parte, ubi Flandrigenae consederant, alteram in occidentali, ubi Angli castra locaverant, magno sumptu construximus.

«Pontes etiam quatuor in navibus, per quos nobis aditus super urbis muros paterent, construximus.

«Hace in inventione B. Stephani Protomartyris admoventes, vento contrario repulsi, nec non magnellis quodammodo laesi, naves retraximus. Deinde nobis ex nostra parte pugnantibus cum Saracenis, Anglici minus caute suam turrim custodientes hanc ex improviso igne succensam extinguere non potuerunt. Interim nos quadam machina murum citodere coepimus. Quod videntes Saraceni igne oleo admixto, eandem machinam in favillam redegerunt, praeterea mortes innumeras, tam magnellis quam sagittis, nostris inferentes, ipsi quoque a nostris puniti sunt. Nostri de fractura machinarum et suorum contritione aliquantis perfracti, in misericordia Dei sperantes, ingenia et machinas reparare coeperunt.

ing on the mercy of God, set to work to repair their losses.

Meanwhile the Moors, who had abundant provisions, refused to share them with their needy brethren, many of whom died from hunger. Some of them, however, did not hesitate to eat cats and dogs, but the greater number went over to the Christians and received the sacrament of baptism. Some of them, sinking on the walls with their hands cut off, were stoned to death by their fellow citizens.

Many other events which happened, some in our favor and others against us, according to the varying chances of war, we pass over in silence to avoid prolixity.

About the Nativity of St. Mary (8.th September) an engineer, a native of Pisa, a man of great ability, devised a wooden tower of immense height, in the same place where that of the English had been destroyed, and this praiseworthy undertaking was completed at the expense of the king, and with the assistance of the whole army, about the middle of October. In like manner, a certain individual, by his genius and the help of many others, made huge excavations under the walls of the city. The Moors, annoyed at this, made a sally on the feast of St. Michael (29.th September), about ten o'clock in the morning, and fought over the fosse

«Interea Saraceni civitatis qui alimentis abundabant, suis concivibus egentibus alimenta adeo subtrahebant ut quamplurimi eorum fame morerentur; quidam autem eorum canes et cattos non abhorrebant devorare. Horum pars plurima Christianis se obtulit et Baptismi Sacramenta suscepit. Quidam autem illorum truncatis manibus ad murum remissi, a suis concivibus lapidati sunt.

«Multa nobis adversa seu prospera secundum quod varius eventus est belli acciderunt, quae propter prolixitatem vitandam silentio transivimus.

«Tandem quidam Pisanus natione vir magnae industriae circa Nativitatem Sanctae Mariae turrim ligneam mirae altitudinis in ea parte qua prius Anglorum turris destructa fuerat, coaptavit, et opus laudabile tam ex regio sumptu quam ex totius exercitus labore circa medium Octobris consummavit. Similiter quidam sub muro civitatis ingentes cavationes suo ingenio et multorum auxilio fecit, quod Saraceni moleste ferentes in festo Sancti Michaelis circa horam tertiam latenter exeuntes, nobiscum usque ad vesperum super fossam pugnam continuabant.

with our men till evening. Attacking the enemy with
our archers, we so obstructed the road by which they
hoped to return, that scarcely a single one of them escaped without a wound. After this, our men, working
day and night, completed the mine and filled it with
sticks, on the same day that the king together with
the English, applied their tower to the walls. On the
night of St. Gallus (16.th October) having set fire to the
wood in the mine, a part of the wall, about 200 feet in
length, fell down. Our soldiers awakened by the crash,
seizing their arms, with a loud shout rushed to the assault, expecting that the defenders would flee from the
walls, but when they came to the breach they found
before them a hill of difficult ascent and a crowd of
Moors prepared for the defense. Nevertheless our men
made the attack, nor did they retire from the battle,
which began at midnight, till the ninth hour of the
next day, and having suffered various repulses, they
quitted the fight just as the tower was being brought
up, and by this the Moors were very much disheartened.

At length the tower, filled with brave warriors, was
placed against the wall, and at the same time the army
on our side and the Lorenese at the breach in the wall,
made a vigorous attack on the Moors.

«Nos autem, sagittariis eis oppositis, vias per quas redire
sperabant adeo vallavimus, ut vel nullus, vel vix aliquis eorum
sine plaga evaderet. Hinc nostri die noctuque laborantes opus
subterraneum lignis levigatis impletum eadem die consummaverunt qua rex cum anglicis muris turrim suam applicabat. Siquidem in ipsa nocte Sancti Galli Abbatis, igne fossae imposito, lignisque ardentibus, corruit murus spatio ducentorum pedum.

«Nostri de tanta ruina somno expergifacti, sumptis armis cum
magno clamore assiliebant, spectantes vigiles custodes murorum
fugisse. Ad ruinam autem cum venissent mons aditu difficilis
supereminebat, et turba Saracenorum parata stabat in defensione. Nihilominus autem nostri assiliebant nec a pugna media
nocte inchoata usque ad diei horam nonam cessabant. Tandem
variis percussionibus attriti, pugnae se subtrahebant quosque
communicatio turris admoveretur et sic Saracenorum populus
hinc inde vexaretur. Et ecce turris viris bellicosis impleta, muro
supereminebat. Eadem hora exercitus nostrae partis, Lotharinges,
ad fracturam murorum indicio pugnantibus, Saracenos mirabili
assaltu impetebant. Interim milites regis qui in arce turris pugnabant, magnellis Saracenorum territi, minus viriliter pugna-

Meanwhile the king's soldiers, who were fighting at the top of the tower, being terrified by the engines of the enemy, were resisting with little spirit, so that the Moors would have burnt the tower, had not some of our men who had gone thither by chance, prevented it. When the news of this danger reached our ears, we sent the best part of our forces to defend the tower, lest our hopes in it should be destroyed. When the Moors saw the Lorenese and Flemings ascending to the top of the tower with so much alacrity, they were seized with such terror that they threw down their arms and held out their hands in sign of peace.

Whence it resulted that their chief, the alcaide, concluded the following treaty with us, viz that our army should receive all their moveable goods, gold and silver, and that the king should have the city with its inhabitants and all their lands.

This divine rather han human victory over 200,500 Moors was consummated on the feast of the eleven thousand Virgins (21.st October) 1147.

The first care of Dom Affonso after his victory was to bury the dead. The remains of his own followers he caused to be interred in the spot where he had fixed his encampment on the eastern side of the city and he erected a church over the place. By a similar disposition he consecrated to God the resting place of his allies who had fallen in the siege, on the western declivity, when they had advanced to the assault. The former spot is now covered by the church of St. Vincent, the latter by that of our Lady of the Martyrs.

bant usque adeo, quod Saraceni exeuntes turrim concremassent siquidem de nostris qui casu ad eos venerant non obstitissent. Haec periculi fama cum ad nostras venisset aures, meliores exercitus nostrae partis ad defendendam turrim, ne nostra spe in ea adnullaretur transmisimus. Videntes autem Saraceni Lotharingos et Flamengos tanto fervore in arcem turris ascendentes, tanta formidine territi sunt ut arma submitterent et dextras sibi in signum pacis dari peterent.

«Unde factum est ut alchaida princeps eorum hoc pacto nobiscum conveniret; ut noster exercitus omnem supellectilem eorum cum auro et argento acciperet, rex autem civitatem cum nudis Saracenis et tota terra obtineret. Consummata est autem haec divina non humana victoria in ducentis millibus et quingentis viris Saracenorum in festa undecim millium Virginum.»

In return for the effectual services rendered to him by the crusaders, Affonso bestowed on all who chose to remain, lands, which extended along the north bank of the Tagus as far as Villa Franca, and another tract at Almada, on the south side. Numbers, principally English, accepted the reward; the rest embarked for Palestine. It is perhaps owing to the above circumstance that the first person nominated to the bishopric of Lisbon after the expulsion of the Moors was an Englishman. His name was Gilbert. He had quitted his native country with the crusaders and having remained with the English who accepted lands, was selected by Affonso to head the list of Lisbon's prelates. The final conquest of Lisbon from the Moors forms a grand epoch in the history of the city and was an event of the utmost importance to the infant monarchy. The Moors, in their brave but unsuccessful efforts to defend it, did not over-rate its value:

> E tu, nobre Lisboa, que no mundo
> Facilmente das outras és princesa,
> Que edificada foste do facundo,
> Por cujo engano foi Dardania accesa:
> Tu, a quem obedece o mar profundo,
> Obedeceste á força Portugueza,
> Ajudada tambem da forte armada,
> Que das Boreaes partes foi mandada.
>
> Lá do Germanico Albis e do Rheno,
> E da fria Bretanha conduzidos,
> A destruir o povo Sarraceno,
> Muitos com tenção santa eram partidos:
> Entrando a bôca já do Tejo ameno,
> Co'o arraial do grande Affonso unidos,
> Cuja alta fama então subia aos céos,
> Foi posto cerco aos muros Ulysseos.
>
> Cinco vezes a lua se escondera,
> E outras tantas mostrara cheio o rosto,
> Quando a cidade entrada se rendera
> Ao duro cerco, que lhe estava posto.
> Foi a batalha tão sanguina e fera,
> Quanto obrigava o firme presupposto
> De vencedores asperos e ousados,
> E de vencidos já desesperados.
>
> (CAMÕES, cant. III.)

From this time, the history of Lisbon presents scarcely any event of importance till the reign of Fernando, towards the close of the fourteenth century, when the greater part of the city was burned by Don Henrique, king of Castile. On the death of Peter the Cruel, king of Castile, Fernando of Portugal laid claim to the vacant throne as great-grandson of Don Sancho. It was however seized by Don Henrique, the bastard brother of Peter and his supposed murderer. A bloody and protracted war ensued between the claimants. At last Fernando was prevailed upon to accept the mediation of Pope Gregory IX, and a treaty of peace was solemnly entered into at Evora on the last day of March 1371. Fernando, however, broke through his engagements, repudiating his queen Dona Leonor, the daughter of Don Henrique, and in open defiance of law and common decency, and in spite of the clamors and remonstrances of his subjects married Dona Leonor Telles de Menezes, wife of João Lourenço da Cunha. Hereupon Don Henrique enraged to the highest degree at the insult offered to his daughter, and still farther inflamed by the pressing instances of the wretched husband, who had fled from Portugal and taken refuge in his court, entered Beira with a powerful army, declaring that he would not sheath his sword till he had taken a terrible vengeance. After reducing that province almost to a desert he advanced into Estremadura, and meeting with but a feeble resistance, took possession of the unfortified part of Lisbon, and inflicted on its innocent inhabitants all the cruelties which a capricious and insatiable revenge could invent. Finding himself unable to reduce the castle of St. George, the only part of Lisbon not in his hands, he resolved to draw off his forces to some distance; but before he retired he destroyed all the outworks that had fallen into his power and burnt the city to the ground [1]. The desolation he caused is thus hinted at by Camões:—

---

[1] Some historians assert that Lisbon was set on fire by its inhabitants in order to rid themselves of the hated invaders, and force Fernando to come to terms with Don Henrique.

The stern Castilian drew the vengeful brand,
And strode proud victor o'er the trembling land.
How dread the hour, when injured Heaven in rage
Thunders its vengeance on a guilty age!
Unmanly sloth the king, the nation stained.
And lewdness fostered by the monarch reigned.
Such was his rage for beauteous Leonore,
Her from her husband's widowed arms he tore,
Then with unblest unhallowed nuptials stained
The sacred altar, and its rights profaned.
Alas! the splendor of a crown how vain
From Heaven's dread eye to vail the dimmest stain.

This terrible blow had the effect of humbling the pride of Fernando, who had during this time been safely lodged with a small army in Santarem, and he reluctantly submitted to the conditions of peace dictated by the conqueror. Returning to Lisbon he ordered its walls to be rebuilt. The work was begun on the 13.th September 1373 and terminated in July 1375.

Upon the death of Fernando, his queen or paramor Dona Leonor Telles assumed the reins of government, as regent for her daughter Beatrice, who had been married to the king of Castile. At the same time Dom João, the son of Dom Pedro and the unfortunate Inez de Castro, was proclaimed at Lisbon. Upon this, that ill-fated prince was seized and imprisoned in Spain, and shortly after the king and queen of Castile were proclaimed by Dona Leonor in Lisbon to the great dissatisfaction of the people. This woman whose character is one of the most infamous in history, so exasperated the Portuguese by her iniquitous rule and the decided preference she always showed for foreigners, that a report spreading through the city that Dom João the brother of the late king, and Grand Master of the order of Aviz, had assassinated in the Palace her chief adviser and favorite, a Spaniard of the name of Juan Fernandez Andero, upon whom she had bestowed the title of Conde de Ourem, the populace of Lisbon rushed to arms, and meeting the bishop Don Martiño also a Spaniard and one of her creatures, they pursued him to the cathedral. Here he ascended the tower and began to ring the tocsin, as a signal to the troops to come to his assistance, which so infuriated the populace that bursting open the doors of the church they hurled him headlong from the tower. They then rushed to the palace (now the prison) of Limoeiro, and elected Dom João regent by acclamation. Upon this the king of Castile entered Portugal with a powerful army and besieged Lisbon, while his fleet took hostile possession of the Tagus.

The regent though destitute of a fleet, and almost without troops and money, resolved to make a determined stand for his country's liberties. He was indefatigable in his exertions; and owing to a secret correspondence he maintained with several Portuguese who surrounded the Castilian monarch, he anticipated all his attacks with vigor and success, and made several sorties which spread consternation through the camp of the besiegers.

He commissioned the Prior do Crato to raise an army in the north and invade Castile, and that brave patriot gained several brilliant advantages over the generals opposed to him. In the meantime, a squadron which had been equipped in Oporto, sailed out of the Douro, captured several of the enemy's ships, and entered Lisbon with provisions. The king had now grown weary of the siege, when a pestilential disease appeared in his army and swept away vast numbers of his troops. Notice was also brought that Nuno Alvares Pereira, the Lord High Constable, was approaching with a strong force from Evora: upon which he broke up the siege in great haste, and covered with ignominy, led back the miserable remnant of his army to Spain.

The following account of the siege of Lisbon by Don Juan, king of Castile was, in 1384, given by Lorenzo Fougace, one of the ambassadors from Portugal, to the Duke of Lancaster in England:

"Don Juan of Castile arrived with his whole army before Lisbon, and by his manner of forming the siege, plainly shewed he would not break it up until he had it in his power. He menaced the Master of Aviz (the Regent) who was within the town, that, if he could take him, he would put him and all the rebels to an ignominious death.

«The army of Don Juan was very numerous; and the Castilians and the French, who had come to his assistance, had so closely surrounded Lisbon that no one could come out or go in without danger of being taken. When any Portuguese were made prisoners by the Castilians in a skirmish or otherwise, their eyes were torn out, their legs, arms, or other members were cut off; and in such maimed state, they were sent back to Lisbon, and bid tell their town's folk, that they had been so treated in despite of the Lisboners and their Master of Aviz, whom they were so eager to crown king; and that they would keep the siege until they had won the town by storm or famine, when they would shew mercy to none, but put all to death, and give up the city to fire and flame.

«The Lisboners, however, did not revenge themselves so cruelly, for whenever they made any prisoners, their king afforded them every comfort, and did not send them back with hurt of any sort. This made many of the army say he was a gallant fellow thus to return good for evil.

«During this siege of Lisbon, which lasted upwards of a year, there were every week two or more skirmishes, in which many were killed and wounded on both sides. The town was besieged by sea as well as by land; and the besiegers had plenty of all things, for provisions came to them from different parts of Spain.

«The Spaniards made one course up to the very gates of Lisbon; when Lourenço da Cunha (the governor) sallied forth out of the barriers with his pennon and after a severe skirmish, was slain by a dart which pierced through his armor and body: he was succeed in the government of Lisbon by his cousin da Cunha, who revenged his death in several successful sorties.

«The siege of Lisbon was continued to the great dismay of the inhabitants; for no succor seemed likely to come to them from any quarter. When their hopes began to fail of help from England, the king was advised to embark for that country, as their ambassador had brought intelligence thence, that assistance would be sent: and that your Grace would bring reinforcements:
«In God's name that is very true», replied the Duke of

Lancaster, "for I was on the point of sailing, having every thing prepared, when the war in Flanders broke out. The men of Ghent called on England for aid, and they had given to them all, or at least the greater part, of those troops which I was to have led into Portugal. The bishop of Norwich carried them with him beyond the sea, and thus retarded the expedition to Portugal'. 'I vow to God, my lord,' said the Ambassador, 'we in Lisbon thought that there had something happened in England to prevent your coming to us'.

"We managed, however, as well as we could, and bore up against the power of the king of Castile, which was not small; for he had upwards of sixty thousand men on sea and land, and menaced daily to destroy us without mercy, and burn Lisbon to the ground.

"During this siege of Lisbon, a lord of our country called de Acosta, did us a notable piece of service, and gained by it great renown. He freighted and armed twenty galleys at Oporto, with good men-at-arms and provisions, with which he put to sea, and by the grace of God, having a favorable wind to second their exertions, passed though the Spanish fleet, consisting of one hundred great vessels, that were lying at anchor before Lisbon, so opportunely that, whether they would or not, he arrived in the port with all his galleys unhurt, carrying with him four of the enemy's vessels which he had conquered. The inhabitants were very much rejoiced at the success and arrival of the lord de Acosta. The siege lasted upwards of a year, for the king of Castile had sworn he would never break it up until Lisbon were under his obedience, or until some more powerful prince should force him from it.

"Considering what happened, the king of Castile religiously kept his vow of not breaking up the siege, unless forced to it by a more powerful lord, as I will explain. A most destructive pestilence burst out in his camp so that persons died suddenly whilst in conversation with each other. Upwards of twenty thousand were carried off by this plague; which so much alarmed the king, that he was advised to break up the siege and retire to Santarem, or elsewhere, and disband his army until the disorder should be checked. He consented to this very unwillingly; but he was forced to it by the principal lords in his army, who pressed him to march to Santarem». The Spaniards were closely followed in their retreat, and suffered severely from the active exertions of the Portuguese.

In the beginning of April 1385, the regent was, by a solemn act of the cortes assembled at Coimbra, chosen to fill the throne, which was considered vacant by the imprisonment of Dom João in Castile, and which was declared to have been forfeited by the Castilian monarch, owing to his hostile invasion of the realm. He took the name of Dom João I, and shortly afterwards gained the famous battle of Aljubarrota, in which 6,600 Portuguese completely routed 30,000 Castilians, who lost in the battle and pursuit, one third of their entire army[1].

The year 1496 was remarkable for the departure from Lisbon of Vasco da Gama and his discovery of the passage to the East Indies round the Cape of Good Hope. For some time previous the enterprising spirit of the Portuguese had prompted them to undertake voyages along the coast of Africa. When they commenced their first voyage of discovery, it is probable that they had nothing further in view than to explore those parts of the coast of Africa, which lay nearest to their own shores. But success animated them to fresh exertions and prompted them to advance along the western shore of the African continent far beyond the utmost boundary of ancient navigation. At length they became more adventurous, despised dangers which formerly appalled them, and overcame difficulties which they once deemed insurmountable. When, in the torrid zone which the ancients had declared to be uninhabitable, they found rich and fertile countries occupied by populous nations, and perceived that the continent of Africa, instead of extending in breadth towards the west, according to

---

1. It was not till this reign that Lisbon became fairly the capital of the kingdom and wrested that honor from Coimbra, which hitherto had been the permanent residence of the court. In 1394 it received the further honor of being raised to the rank of an archbishopric.

the opinion of Ptolemy, contracted itself nwards to the east, more extensive prospects opened before them, and inspired them with hopes of reaching India, by continuing to hold the same course. After several unsuccessful attempts to accomplish this object a small squadron sailed from the Tagus on the 3.rd of July 1497 under the command of Vasco da Gama. Though the abilities and courage of this officer fitted him to conduct the most arduous enterprise, yet as he was unacquainted with the proper season and route of navigation over the vast ocean through which he had to steer his course, his voyage was long and dangerous. At length he doubled that cape, which for several years had been an object of terror and of hope to his countrymen. Thence after a prosperous navigation he arrived at the city of Melinda, whose inhabitants he found to be so far advanced in civilization and the various arts of life, as to carry on an active commerce, not only with the nations of their own coast, but with the remote countries of Asia. Conducted by their pilots, he sailed across the Indian Ocean, and landed at Calicut, on the Malabar coast, in 1498, ten months and seventeen days after his departure from Lisbon.

Here he was exposed to numerous dangers from the open attacks or secret machinations of the Indians; but he extricated himself from them all with singular prudence and dexterity, and at last departing with his ships laden not only with the commodities peculiar to that coast, but with many rich productions of the eastern part of India, he arrived in the Tagus, after an absence of two years, and landed amid the enthusiastic greetings of the whole population of Lisbon. The discoveries made in this arduous voyage led the way to all the great results which modern enterprise has effected: whilst to the Portuguese they opened an avenue to wealth and power far beyond their loftiest aspirings. From this time all the treasures of the east were poured out for centuries in one unceasing tide on the banks of the Tagus; and so rapidly did Lisbon rise in splendor and commercial importance that it soon became one of the richest and busiest emporiums of Europe. In grateful acknowledgment to Heaven for the prosperous termination of this memorable voyage, king Emmanuel the Great, built the magnificent monastery and church of Santa Maria de Belem which will be fully noticed hereafter[1].

In the year 1506 Lisbon was the scene of one of the most wanton massacres on record. During the celebration of a festival on the first Sunday in April in the Church of São Domingos, an extraordinary refulgence was said to have been observed by some, to radiate from one of the crucifixes. A *Christão novo* (the title given to converted Jews) was overheard to express his disbelief in the miracle, whereupon the congregation became excited and seizing the unhappy man, dragged him into the square (Rocio) and having beat him to death, cast his body into a fire which they kindled for that purpose. Some dominican friars now appeared, and haranguing the crowd, crucifix in hand, called upon them to wreak vengeance on the enemies of their faith. Thus incited, a number of the populace formed themselves into a gang and paraded the streets, killing every *christão novo* or Jew they could lay hands upon. According to the testimony of Damião de Goes, over 500 jews were massacred during the first day.

With the approach of night the riot increased. The king, court, and civil and military authorities were absent from the capital, which was at this time suffering from a dreadful pestilence. On Monday morning the number of the mob had increased to 2,000 and the carnage con-

---

1. The same spot which saw the departure of Vasco's glorious expedition, witnessed in 1578 the departure of Dom Sebastião the Regretted, with all the chivalry of the kingdom, destined never to return. The king and his army were cut to pieces at the battle of Alcacer-Quibir and their bones were left to whiten in the sandy plains of Africa.

> Dos lusitanos reys com tanta gloria
> Governada será, que em todo o mundo
> Perpetua ficará sua memoria,
> E de Lisboa o nome, sem segundo.
> Porém (ó cruel caso, ó triste historia,
> Que o sentimento excede mais profundo)
> Tanta gloria, adquirida em tantos annos
> Roubam n'uma hora os campos africanos.
> (ULYSSIPPO, cant. 14-13.)

tinued with unabated rage. As no more jews were to be found, the maddened crowd still thirsting for blood, entered many private houses and dragged forth their trembling inmates, man, woman, and child, into the streets, where they were ruthlessly sacrificed, their bodies, some still alive, being afterwards cast into the fire. Some of the victims sought refuge in the churches, but the infuriated mob regarded not the sacredness of the place, but pursued them to the very steps of the altar and dragged them from the foot of the cross to which they clung for protection. A second night of terror followed and on the morning of the third day the wild disorder still prevailed. Many were the private enmities revenged on this occasion. At last the people were glutted with blood and plunder: the city had been abandoned by all who had any thing to lose or were likely to excite the resentment or covetousness of the populace, and in the evening, the governor, Alvaro de Castro, arrived with a body of troops and put a stop to the riot, which had lasted three days and two nights, and cost the lives of thousands.

The next events of importance were the taking of the city by Philip I. in 1580 and the conspiracy against Spanish domination which broke out in Lisbon on the 1.st of December 1640, and ended in the revolution which seated the Bragança family on the Portuguese throne.

After the death of Cardinal Dom Henrique, who had succeeded the unfortunate Sebastian, no fewer than seven candidates laid claim to the vacant throne. These were Philip II. of Castile; Emmanuel Philibert, Duke of Savoy; Antonio, Prior of Crato; the Prince of Parma; João, Duke of Bragança: Elisabeth of England, and the Pope. The people of Lisbon declaring for the Prior, he was proclaimed at Santarem on the 24.th June 1580, and immediately advancing to the capital, he issued laws, coined money, and opened the prisons, as if his claims had been acknowledged throughout the whole realm. He met, however, a powerful and successful antagonist in Philip of Spain. Although the Prior of Crato was proclaimed king with all the formalities usual at such ceremonies, yet he was supported only by the lower orders, the chief nobility retiring from Lisbon. Philip's army under the duke of Alba having obtained possession of Estremoz, Evora and Montemaior, directed their steps upon Setubal. Notwithstanding the enemy's near approach the Prior does not seem to have taken any vigorous measures to resist their entry into Lisbon. He had no other army than a turbulent rabble composed of the lower class of citizens, a few friars and negroes, without any experience or knowledge of the art of war.

Having entered Setubal without resistance, Alba was joined by the Spanish fleet in which he embarked his forces and landed at Cascaes, taking its castle without much difficulty. The Prior, seeing the enemy so near, was almost driven to despair, but resolved on defending himself to the last. He placed himself at the head of his rabble army, and encamped behind the stream of Alcantara, whilst Alba with the Spaniards advanced and captured the fort of São Julião, whose governor capitulated with precipitancy. This was the death blow to the Prior's hopes, yet he awaited the enemy and on the general attack, which took place on the 25.th August 1580, he displayed during the battle great personal courage, and defended the bridge of Alcantara to the last extremity, receiving several wounds. His army, however, being totally routed and dispersed, he galloped off, passing through the city, and took refuge in Santarem.

Alba with his army now entered Lisbon, which they had agreed to spare, but on finding themselves within its walls, the Spaniards, disregarding the terms they had made, pillaged a great part of the city and committed the greatest atrocities. On the 19.th April 1581, Philip was proclaimed at Thomar king of Portugal, and shortly afterwards made his public entry into Lisbon, when he was received with great demonstrations and festivities prepared by his new subjects, in the hope of ingratiating themselves with their new master.

Philip dying in 1598, left the crown to his son Philip III., who in the twentieth year of his reign visited his Portuguese dominions: upon which occasion the inhabitants of Lisbon voluntarily incurred an enormous expense in preparations for his reception, hoping thereby to conciliate his clemency and induce him to relax the odious oppression, under which they were groaning.

He remained among them only four months and dying in 1621, was succeeded by his son Philip IV. This prince never once visited Portugal, and it would seem that he and his creatures, in whose hands were placed all the offices of state and posts of rank in this unhappy kingdom, studied to provoke the wrath of Heaven, and goad the Portuguese into rebellion by their open and shameless violation of almost every one of the privileges, which had been solemnly guaranteed to them by his royal grandsire.

At last so universal did the detestation of the Spanish government become, that a numerous body of Portuguese nobles entered into a conspiracy to throw off the odious yoke. Their measures were taken with the greatest secrecy: they held many conferences before they proceeded to action and it was agreed that, after clearing the palace of the execrated foreigners who had so long tyrannized over them, they should proclaim Dom João, 8.th Duke of Bragança, king, and then unite in one grand effort to expel the Spaniards from the country.

Having selected the 1.st of December 1640 for the daring enterprise, they met as soon as it was dark, in the Terreiro do Paço, and as soon as the clock struck nine, which was the signal agreed upon, each one attacked the position which had been assigned him, with such vigor and success, that in three hours the whole revolution was accomplished. In this short space of time the Spanish minister Miguel de Vasconcellos, was seized and slain, the queen Regent, Margaret of Savoy, Duchess of Mantua, who was entirely in the interests of the foreigners, was imprisoned in the palace and forced to sign an order to the governor of the Castle to surrender it to the conspirators; Philip IV. was deposed: Dom João proclaimed king of Portugal: and the Spanish domination overthrown, after it had for sixty years been a scourge to the country. This great event which placed the present royal family on the throne, is still commemorated by an annual festivity in Lisbon on the first of December.

Under the wise and politic administration of the new monarch, the whole kingdom, and especially the capital, recovered by a slow, but steady progress from the injuries which had been inflicted on them during the galling tyranny of Spain. The commercial spirit of the people received a new impulse from the revival of national independence, new fleets were equipped, and the wealthy resources that had been for sixty years turned from their natural channel into the insatiable coffers of the Spanish monarchs, once more flowed into the exhausted treasury of Lisbon.

But it was not till some years after the death of the «Restorer» and the accession of his grandson Dom João V., that the kingdom regained its pristine power and splendor. During the reign of this fortunate monarch Lisbon was enriched and beautified by many works of art and public utility. Of these the most remarkable is the great aqueduct, which conveys the waters from Bellas, over the deep valley of Alcantara, to the city. This structure had been long in contemplation, but its accomplishment was reserved to Dom João V., surnamed the «Magnificent», who laid the foundation of it in 1713. During this reign Lisbon may be said to have attained to the height of its splendor and prosperity, and was the richest and handsomest capital in Europe. In 1716 it was elevated to the rank of a patriarchate.

From the period of the revolution of 1640, Lisbon enjoyed comparative quiet, being neither attacked from without, nor disturbed by commotions within, till the year 1755, when the greater part of the city was destroyed by one of the most tremendous earthquakes on record.

Five years previously an unusually severe shock had been felt. During the four years that succeeded, there was so excessive a drought that several springs which till then had yielded plentiful supplies, were totally dried up. The predominant winds were north and north east, accompanied with frequent though very slight tremors of the earth. The first part of the year 1755 proved very wet; the summer was cooler than usual and for forty days before the earthquake, the weather was clear. On the 1.st of November, early in the morning, a thick fog arose, but was soon dissipated by the heat of the sun and the whole atmosphere became perfectly serene and clear. At thirty five minutes past nine a. m. a low rumbling noise was heard, resembling that of distant thunder, which gradually increased until it became as loud as the roar of artillery. It was at that moment that the first shock of the earthquake took place. The buildings rocked from side to side like a ship in a heavy sea, and such was the violence of the commotion that the upper stories immediately gave way, and fell crushing their occupants to death, as well as those who were passing in the streets below. The motion of the earth was so great that it was impossible to stand, and the terrors of this awful and sudden calamity were still more fearfully aggravated, by the extreme darkness which succeeded to the light of day. Numbers precipitated themselves from the windows to avoid being buried in the ruins of their falling habitations. All who could, forced their way over the mass of ruins, to the open squares or to the river side in order to escape the stones and pieces of timber that threatened to fall upon them from the houses in the narrow streets. As the first of November is the great festival of All Saints, the churches were crowded, and in them perished great numbers crushed under the falling buildings. Most of the churches in the city were destroyed. A mingled multitude rushing to the quays raised to Heaven the loud cry of supplication «Mercy, mercy, O Lord, have mercy».

In the midst of this desolation, a second shock, almost as violent as the first, completed the work of destruction. Shrieks of agony and despair resounded from every side. The church of St. Catharine already much injuried by the first shock, fell to the ground with a tremendous crash, killing vast numbers who had fled for safety to the height on which the building stood.

But the most dreadful consequences of this second shock were felt by those who had congregated in the neighborhood of the river, which from being in a state of perfect calm was suddenly elevated at its bar, and thence came rolling onward in one mountain wave, overwhelming in its course the streets and quays along its banks. In vain the crowds attempted to flee; the irruption was too rapid to allow of any escape and they were all buried beneath the waves. At the same time a magnificent marble quay at the Terreiro do Paço, which had been recently finished, sunk by the opening of the earth and totally disappeared, with all who were on it. A number of boats and small craft that were anchored near and attached to the quay and which were filled with persons who imagined that the river would afford a place of safety, were at the same moment swallowed up.

Several of the vessels at anchor were dashed from their moorings and driven ashore or against each other, while others were ingulfed in whirlpools, or capsized by the violent heaving of the water. A captain of a ship that survived these perils and who witnessed the phenomena, stated that the city appeared to him as if waving to and fro like the waves of the sea, when agitated by a rising wind, and that such was the commotion under water that the anchor of his own vessel became visible at the surface.

The river rose three fathoms and as suddenly fell again. The calamity now appeared to be at its height, when a third shock succeeded. Though this was less violent than the preceding ones, it had the effect of making the river rise and retire with the same rapidity and impetuosity as before, so that vessels anchored in seven fathom water were suddenly stranded. This alternate rise and fall of the river, continued at intervals for a considerable time, and each fluctuation caused a fresh damage and loss of live. The terrified inhabitants believed that the final day of doom had arrived, or at least that their city was being swept away from the face of the earth. At length, however, the shocks ceased, but only to be succeeded by a calamity no less awful and destructive. A fire burst forth in several quarters with such fury that in a short time the whole of Lisbon appeared in one vast blaze. It is supposed to have had its origin in the churches which were filled with lighted candles for the celebration of the feast of All Saints, when the earthquake took place.

Of course any attempt to stop the conflagration on the part of the awe-striken citizens was out of the question, and it was not till the close of the sixth day that the progress of the flames was checked. The destruction of property due to the fire was not less than that occasioned by the earthquake itself.

The king, queen, and royal family fled from the palace only a few moments prior to its fall. The Spanish ambassador, with nine members of his family, were buried beneath the ruins of the embassy. The only Englishman of note who is recorded to have lost his life on this occasion, was the Rev. J. Manley, president of the English college. The losses sustained by the different foreign nations on this fatal day were computed at the time to amount to 10.000:000 cruzados, in the following proportion:

Great-Britain	6.400:000
Hamburg	1.660:000
The rest of Germany	80:000
Italy	1.000:000
Holland	400:000
France	160:000
Sweden	120:000
The rest of Europe	320:000
	10.140:000

The losses of the Portuguese were immense. In the Royal palace, the Patriarch's establishment, the customhouse, sete casas, and theater, they are calculated at 10.000:000: in churches and private houses 28.000:000: in furniture stores and other goods 480.000:000, besides 1.230:000 in church ornaments, sacred vessels, marbles, candelabra, statues and paintings: in coined money 1.000:000: in diamonds, jewels and precious stones 4.000:000 besides 2.000:000 in diamonds belonging to the crown. Adding these enormous sums to those lost by foreigners as above stated, the grand total is 536.370:000 cruzados or £ 59.596,000. Out of 20.000 dwelling houses scarcely 3,000 remained that could be inhabited with safety, and beneath the ruins of those that were thrown down, were buried 24,000 to 25,000 persons.

The following particulars were written by an eye-witness a few days after the catastrophe: —

«On the 1.st of November 1755, the barometer standing at 27 inches 8 lines and Reaumur's thermometer at 14 above freezing (63° Fahr.) the weather being fine and serene, at 9.45 A. M. the earth trembled, but so slightly that it was attributed by most to a passing waggon. This agitation lasted 2 minutes: after the lapse of another 2 minutes, the earth shook with so much violence that the houses began to split and crack. This second shock lasted about 10 minutes, and the dust was so great as to obscure the sun. There was then an interval of three minutes and the dust subsided so that people could recognize one another. Then the third and most tremendous shock succeeded. The greater part of the city was in a moment laid in ruins. The sun was perfectly obscured and it seemed as if the earth was about to be reduced to chaos. The screams of the living, the groans of the dying, and the profound darkness, increased the horror. In 20 minutes all had become calm. Every one endeavored to escape into the country; but our misfortunes had not reached their height. As soon as we began to breathe more freely, fires broke out in various parts of the city. The wind blew strongly; no one attempted to stop the progress of the flames: each endeavored to save his own life. Some attempt might perhaps have been made to subdue the conflagration, if the sea had not at the same time threatened to overwhelm Lisbon. On Friday November 7.th at 5. A. M., there was such a severe shock that it seemed as if our misfortunes were about to begin again; no damage, however, was done, for the movement was regular like the heaving of a ship, whereas that which occasioned the mischief consisted of shocks moving in opposite directions. I have observed that the most violent shocks always occurred early in the morning. It is said that the sea rose 9 feet higher than the greatest recorded inundation in Portugal. I saw, with the greatest alarm, on the morning of Sunday, the 2.nd of November that the Tagus, which in some places is more than two leagues broad, was nearly dry on the side next the city. I write this in the fields; I cannot find a single house in which to shelter myself. Lisbon has disappeared. »

The following account of the earthquake is by another eye-witness and was published shortly after the event: —

«There never was a finer morning seen than the 1.st of November 1755: the sun shone out in his full luster; the whole face of the sky was perfectly serene and clear; and there was not the least signal or warning of that approaching event which has made this once flourishing, opulent and populous city a scene of the utmost horror and desolation, except only such as served to alarm, but scarcely left a moment's time to fly from the general destruction.

«It was on the morning of this fatal day, between the hours of nine and ten, that I was sat down in my apartment, just finishing a letter, when the papers and table I was writing on, began to tremble with a gentle motion, which rather surprised me, as I could not perceive a breath of wind stirring: whilst I was reflecting with myself what this could be owing to, but without having the least apprehension of the real cause, the whole house began to shake from the very foundation; which I at first imputed to the rattling of several coaches in the main street, which usually passed that way at this time from Belem to the palace; but, on hearkening more attentively, I was soon undeceived, as I found it was owing to a strange frightful kind of noise under ground, resembling the hollow distant rumbling of thunder. All this passed in less than a minute; and I must confess, I began to be alarmed, as it naturally occurred to me that this noise might possibly be the forerunner of an earthquake, as one I remembered, which had happened about six or seven years ago, in the Island of Madeira, commenced in the same manner, though it did little or no damage.

«Upon this I threw down my pen, and started upon

my feet, remaining for a moment in suspense whether I should stay in the apartment, or run into the street, as the danger in both places seemed equal; and still flattered myself that this tremor might produce no other effects than such inconsiderable ones as had been felt at Madeira; but in a moment I was roused from my dream being instantly stunned with a most horrid crash, as if every edifice in the city had tumbled down at once. The house I was in, shook with such violence, that the upper stories immediately fell; and though my apartment (which was the first floor) did not then share the same fate, yet every thing was thrown out of its place in such a manner, that it was with no small difficulty I kept my feet, and expected nothing less than to be soon crushed to death, as the walls continued rocking to and fro in the most frightful manner, opening in several places, large stones falling down on every side from the cracks, and the ends of most of the rafters starting out from the roof. To add to this terrifying scene, the sky in a moment became so gloomy, that I could now distinguish no particular object: it was an Egyptian darkness indeed, such as might be felt; owing no doubt, to the prodigious clouds of dust and lime, raised from so violent a concussion and as some reported, sulphureous exhalations: but this I cannot affirm: however, it is certain I found myself almost choked for nearly ten minutes.

«As soon as the gloom began to disperse, and the violence of the shock seemed pretty much abated, the first object I perceived in the room, was a woman sitting on the floor, with an infant in her arms, all covered with dust, pale, and trembling; but her consternation was so great, that she could give me no account of her escape. I suppose that, when the tremor first began she ran out of her own house and finding herself in such imminent danger from the falling of stones, retired into the door of mine, which was almost contiguous to hers, for shelter; and when the shock increased, which filled the door with dust and rubbish, ran upstairs into my apartment, which was then open: be it as it might, this was no time for curiosity. I remember the poor creature asked me, in the utmost agony if I did not think the world was at an end? at the same time she complained of being choked and begged for God's sake I would procure her a little drink, on which I went to a closet where I kept a large jar with water, but finding it broken to pieces, I told her she must not now think of quenching her thirst, but saving her life, as the house was just falling on our heads, and if a second shock came, would certainly bury us both. I bade her take hold of my arm, and that I would endeavor to bring her into some place of security.

I shall always look upon it as a particular providence, that I happened on this occasion to be undressed: for had I dressed myself as I proposed when I got out of bed, in order to breakfast with a friend. I should in all probability have run into the street at the beginning of the shock, as the rest of the people in the house did, and consequently have had my brains dashed out, as every one of them had. However, the imminent danger I was in, did not hinder me from considering that my present dress, only a gown and slippers, would render my getting over the ruins almost impracticable: I had, therefore, still presence of mind enough left to put on a pair of shoes and a coat, the first that came in my way, which was every thing I saved; and in this dress I hurried down stairs, the woman with me, holding by my arm; and made directly to that end of the street which opens to the Tagus; but finding the passage this way entirely blocked up with the fallen houses to the height of their second stories, I turned back to the other end which led into the main street (the common thoroughfare to the palace) and having helped the woman over a vast heap of ruins, with no small hazard to my own life, just as we were going into the street, as there was one part I could not well climb over without the assistance of my hands as well as of my feet, I desired her to let go her hold, which she did, remaining two or three feet behind me; at which time there fell a vast stone from a tottering wall, and crushed both her and the child to pieces. So dismal a spectacle, at any other time, would have affected me in the highest degree; but the dread I was in of sharing the same fate myself, and the many instances of the same kind that presented themselves all around, were too shocking to make me dwell a moment on this single object.

« I had now a long narrow street to pass, with the houses on each side four or five stories high; all very old, the greater part already thrown down or continually falling, and threatening the passengers with inevitable death at every step, numbers of whom lay killed before me, or, what I thought far more deplorable, so bruised and wounded, that they could not stir to help themselves. For my own part as destruction appeared to me unavoidable, I only wished I might be made an end of at once, and not have my limbs broken; in which case I could expect nothing else but to be left on the spot, lingering in misery like these poor unhappy wretches, without receiving the least succor from any person.

« As self-preservation, however, is the first law of nature these sad thoughts did not so far prevail as to make me totally despair. I proceeded on as fast as I could, though with the utmost caution, and having at length got clear of this horrid passage, I found myself safe and unhurt in the large open space before St. Paul's church, which had been thrown down a few minutes before and had buried a great part of the congregation, which was generally pretty numerous, this being reckoned one of the most populous parishes in Lisbon. Here I stood some time considering what I should do; and not thinking myself safe in this situation I came to the resolution of climbing over the ruins of the west end of the church in order to get to the river side, that I might be removed as far as possible from the tottering houses, in case of a second shock.

« This with some difficulty I accomplished: and here I found a prodigious concourse of people of both sexes, and of all ranks and conditions; among whom I observed some of the principal canons of the patriarchal church, in their purple robes and rockets, as these all go in the habit of bishops; several priests who had run from the altars in their sacerdotal vestments, in the midst of their celebrating mass; ladies half dressed, and some without shoes; all these, whom their mutual dangers had here assembled as to a place of safety, were on their knees at prayers, with the terrors of death in their countenances, every one striking his breast and crying out incessantly *misericordia meu Deus!*

«In the midst of our devotions, the second great shock came on, little less violent than the first, and completed the ruin of those buildings which had been already much shattered. The consternation now became so universal that the shrieks and cries of *misericordia* could be distinctly heard from the top of St. Catharine's hill, at a considerable distance off, whither a vast number of people had likewise retreated: at the same time we could hear the fall of the parish church there, whereby many persons were killed on the spot and others mortally wounded. You may judge of the force of this shock when I inform you it was so violent that I could scarcely keep on my knees: but it was attended by some circumstances still more dreadful than the former. On a sudden I heard a general outcry.

«The sea is coming in, we shall all be lost!» Upon this turning my eyes towards the river, which in that place is nearly four miles broad I could perceive it heaving and swelling in a most unaccountable manner, as no wind was stirring: in an instant there appeared, at some small distance a large body of water, rising like a mountain: it came on foaming and roaring and rushed towards the shore with such impetuosity, that we all immediately ran for our lives as fast as possible; many were actually swept away, and the rest above their waists in water at a good distance from the banks. For my own part I had the narrowest escape, and should certainly have been lost had I not grasped a large beam that lay on the ground, till the water returned to its channel, which it did almost at the same instant, with equal rapidity. As there now appeared at least as much danger from the sea as from the land, and I scarcely knew where to retire for shelter, I took a sudden resolution of returning, with my clothes all dropping, to the area of St. Paul's: here I stood some time and observed the ships tumbling and tossing about, as in a violent storm; some had broken their cables and were carried to the other side of the Tagus: others were whirled about with incredible swiftness; several large boats were turned keel upwards, and all this without any wind, which seemed the more astonishing. It was at the time of which I am now speaking, that the fine new quay, built of marble at an immense expense, was entirely swallowed up, with all the people on it, who had fled thither for safety, and had reason to think themselves out of danger in such a place: at the same time, a great number of boats and small vessels anchored near it (all likewise full of people, who had retired thither for the same purpose) were all swallowed up, as in a whirlpool, and never more appeared.

«This last dreadful incident I did not see with my own eyes as it passed three or four stones'throw from the spot where I then was: but I had the account, as here given, from several masters of ships, who were anchored within two or three hundred yards of the quay and saw the whole catastrophe. One of them informed me, that when the second shock came on, he could perceive the whole city waving backwards and forwards, like the sea when the wind first begins to rise: that the agitation of the land was so great, even under the river, that it threw up his large anchor from the moorings, which swam, as he termed it, upon the surface of the water: that immediately upon this extraordinary concussion, the river rose at once nearly twenty feet, and in a moment subsided; at which instant he saw the quay, with the whole concourse of people upon it, sink down into the cavity, which he supposes instantly closed upon them, in as much as not the least sign of a wreck was ever seen afterwards. This account you may give full credit to, for as to the loss of the vessels, it is confirmed by every body; and with regard to the quay, I went myself a few days afterwards to convince myself of the truth, and could not find even the ruins of a place, where I had taken so many agreeable walks, as this was the common *rendez-vous* of the factory in the cool of the evening. I found it all deep water, and in some parts scarcely to be fathomed.

«This is the only place which I could learn was swallowed up in or about Lisbon, though I saw many large cracks and fissures in different parts, and one odd phenomenon I must not omit, which was communicated to me by a friend who had a house and wine cellars on the other side of the river: namely that the dwelling house being first terribly shaken, which made all the family run out; there presently fell down a vast high rock near it; that upon this the river rose and subsided in the manner already mentioned and immediately a great number of small fissures appeared in several contiguous pieces of ground, whence there spouted out like a *jet-d'eau* a large quantity of fine white sand to a prodigious height.

«I had not been long in the area of St. Paul's, when I felt the third shock; which though somewhat less violent than the two former, the sea rushed in again and retired with the same rapidity and I remained up to my knees in water though I had got upon a small eminence at some distance from the river, with the ruins of several intervening houses to break its force. At this time I took notice, the water retired so impetuously that some vessels were left quite dry, which rode in seven fathom water. The river thus continued alternately rushing on and retiring several times together, in such sort, that it was justly dreaded Lisbon would now meet the same fate, which in 1746 had befallen the city of Lima.

«Perhaps you may think the present doleful subject here concluded: but alas! the horrors of the 1.st of November are sufficient to fill a volume. As soon as it grew dark, another scene presented itself, little less shocking than those already described. The whole city appeared in a blaze, which was so bright that I could easily see to read by it. It may be said, without exaggeration, it was on fire in at least a hundred places at once, and thus continued burning for six days together without intermission or the least attempt being made to stop its progress.

«I could never learn, that this terrible fire was owing to any subterraneous eruption, as some have reported; but to three causes, which all concurring at the same time, will naturally account for the prodigious havock it made. The 1.st of November being All Saints' day, a high festival among the Portuguese, every altar in every church and chapel, was illuminated with a number of wax tapers, and lamps as customary, these setting fire to the curtains and timber work that fell with the shock, the conflagration soon spread to the neighboring houses and being there joined with the fires in the kitchen chimneys, increased to such a degree that it might easily have destroyed the whole city, though no other cause had concurred, especially as it met with no interruption.

"But what would appear incredible to you, were the fact less public and notorious is that a gang of hardened villains, who had been confined and got out of prison when the wall fell at the first shock, were busily employed in setting fire to those buildings which stood some chance of escaping the general destruction.

"The fire by some means or other, may be said to have destroyed the whole city, at least every thing that was grand or valuable in it, and the damage on this occasion is not to be estimated.

"The whole number of persons that perished, including those who were burnt, or afterwards crushed to death whilst digging in the ruins, is supposed, on the lowest calculation to amount to more than 60,000; and though the damage in other respects cannot be computed, yet you may form some idea of it when I assure you, that this extensive and opulent city is now nothing but a vast heap of ruins; that the rich and poor are at present upon a level, some thousands of families which but the day before had been in easy circumstances, being now scattered about in the fields, wanting every conveniency of life, and finding none able to relieve them.

"A few days after the first consternation was over, I ventured down into the city, by the safest means I could pick out, to see if there was a possibility of getting any thing out of my lodgings: but the ruins were now so augmented by the late fire, that I was so far from being able to distinguish the individual spot where the house stood, that I could not even distinguish the street, amidst the mountains of stone and rubbish which rose on every side. Some days after, I ventured down again with several porters, who having long plied in these parts of the town, were well acquainted with the situation of particular houses: by their assistance I at last discovered the spot; but was soon convinced, that to dig for anything there, besides the danger of such an attempt, would never answer the expense.

« On both the times when I attempted to make this fruitless search, especially the first, there came such an intolerable stench from the dead bodies, that I was ready to faint away: and though it did not seem so great this last time, yet it had nearly been mortal to me, as I contracted a fever by it, but of which (God be praised!) I soon got the better. However this made me so cautious for the future that I avoided passing near certain places, where the stench was so excessive, that people began to dread an infection. A gentleman told me, that going into the town a few days after the earthquake, he saw several bodies lying in the streets, some horribly mangled, as he supposed, by dogs; others half burnt; some quite roasted; and that in certain places, particularly near the doors of churches, they lay in vast heaps, piled one upon another. »

After the earthquake the city was infested with bands of robbers, and for fifteen days it was not safe to return to it. Sebastião José de Carvalho, better known as the Marquis of Pombal, took energetic measures to restore order. Gallowses were erected by his direction in many parts of Lisbon, and whoever could not give a clear account of the property found upon him was hanged on the spot and 350 persons thus perished, including in that number five Irishmen.

The effects of the earthquake were not confined to the capital, but extended themselves more or less over the whole kingdom, but more especially in the south. Indeed the shocks were felt throughout the greater part of Europe, reaching as far north as the Orkneys and as far west as Jamaica. The waters of Loch Lomond and Loch Ness in Scotland were agitated in an uncommon manner. The latter continued ebbing and flowing for the space of an hour, when a wave much greater than the rest terminated the commotion by overflowing the north bank of the lake to the extent of 30 feet. At the same period a singular phenomenon happened at Bristol: the water of the hot well became as red as blood and so turbid as to be unfit for drink. The water also of a common well, which had been remarkably clear, at once turned as black as ink, and continued unfit for use for nearly a fortnight. The tide likewise in the river Avon flowed back, contrary to its natural course; and various other effects of some unknown convulsion in the bowels of the earth were perceived in different places. But all conjecture as to the cause of these extraordinary circumstances was in vain, till the news arrived of the earthquake at Lisbon having happened on the same day, which gave a satisfactory solution to the several phenomena.

Lisbon, like the Phoenix, soon rose again from its ashes. Through the energy of the Marquis of Pombal, the celebrated prime minister of D. José I, those portions of the city which had apparently received the most irreparable damage were reconstructed in a modern and altogether superior style. The prosperous state of the finances, owing to the prodigious sums which were annually drawn from the Brazils and from the Eastern Colonies, enabled the government to repair the ruined edifices in an incredibly short space of time. The wealth of the Court and the devotion of the citizens soon produced rich palaces, spacious churches and splendid monasteries in every quarter; whilst in the center of the city, instead of the irregular houses, among which wound narrow, crooked, and ill-paved streets, might be seen long and symmetrical rows of buildings, intersected by wide and straight thoroughfares bordered by neat foot paths, and laid out with taste and method. Thus a temporary disaster was by the genius of Pombal converted into a source of lasting benefit to the capital.

The close of the year 1808 presented a new and interesting phenomenon in history, the migration of a European court to the western hemisphere. It had long been a topic of serious consideration between the cabinets of Great Britain and Portugal, whether in the case of an actual invasion by France, the Portuguese court might not be advantageously transferred to its dependencies in South America; and the assembling of an army of 40,000 men at Bayonne, for the avowed purpose of invading the territories of the house of Bragança threatened speedily to demand this weighty sacrifice. In vain had Portugal exhausted the royal treasury and made innumerable sacrifices to preserve her neutrality; in vain had she closed her ports to ships of an ancient ally[1]: the French were preparing to march into the interior of the kingdom, and their ambassador, having failed in his endeavor to involve the prince Regent (afterward D. João VI.) in the war against England, had quitted Lisbon. These events were notified to the chamber of commerce for the information of the British residents; and the preparations which had been previously begun by them for settling their affairs and withdrawing from the country were now continued with redoubled urgency. The activity and confusion in the custom house and port of Lisbon were extreme; the most extravagant terms were demanded for the conveyance of residents with their families to England in vessels but ill adapted for their accommodation, or even for security, and towards the end of October, scarcely any thing British, except British feelings remained in the country.

In the meantime the Portuguese navy was equipped with all possible expedition. The preparations were made on a large scale, and stores provided for a long voyage. Lord Strangford, the British Ambassador, was indefatigable in his exertions to confirm the wavering purpose of the court, and effect a speedy embarcation. A strong reluctance, however, to quit his native shores was manifested by the prince, and in proportion as the time approached for a definitive decision, the less inclined did he seem, to make the momentous sacrifice. So far did his wishes to conciliate France prevail, that on the 8.th of November, he signed an order for detaining the few British subjects who still remained in his dominions. On the publication of this decree, Lord Strangford demanded his passports, and presenting a final remonstrance to the Court, proceeded to join the squadron under Sir Sidney Smith, which had been sent to the coast of Portugal to assist in saving the royal family,

---

1. By the decree for the exclusion of British ships, dated Lisbon, 22.nd October 1807.

or in the worst event, to prevent the Portuguese fleet
from falling into the possession of the enemy. A most
stringent blockade of the Tagus was immediately
resolved upon; but after a few days the intercourse of the
British ambassador and the court was resumed, at the
request of the former, who, on his proceeding to Lisbon,
found all the apprehensions of the prince now directed
to a French army, and all his hopes to a British fleet.
To explain this singular change in the politics of the
Portuguese court, it must be observed, that in the
interval between the departure and the return of Lord
Strangford, the prince had received intelligence that
Bonaparte had fulminated against him one of those
edicts which had almost invariably been followed by
the subversion of the throne against which it was
directed. The proclamation «The house of Bragança has
ceased to reign »[1] had gone forth, and to this alarming
denunciation, which cut off all hopes of a compromise,
even by the most humiliating submission, was to be
ascribed the complacency, with which the renewed intercourse with England was accepted. So great was the
panic that prevailed in the Court that it now manifested
as much eagerness to effect a departure, as it had previously shewn hesitation and reluctance towards it. The
interview with the British ambassador took place on the
27.th November and on the morning of the 29.th the Portuguese fleet sailed out of the Tagus with the whole of
the royal family of Bragança, and a considerable number of faithful counsellors and respectable and opulent
adherents. The fleet consisted of eight line-of-battle
ships, four large frigates, and several other vessels of
war, besides a number of merchant ships, amounting in
all to thirty six sail, containing about 18,000 Portuguese
subjects. So critical was the juncture that before the
Portuguese fleet quitted the Tagus, the French army
under general Junot, with their Spanish auxiliaries were
in sight, and on the following day the invaders entered
Lisbon without opposition.

 From the deep rooted aversion of the Portuguese to
the French, Junot soon discovered that all his exertions

---

1. The *Moniteur* of 11.th November 1807.

would be required to preserve the public tranquillity. By the constant blockade of the port the inhabitants experienced much inconvenience: the horrors of famine began to be felt; trade was entirely destroyed; money was so scarce that there was no sale for any goods but those of the most pressing necessity, scarcely any merchants paid their bills, or accepted those that were drawn upon them; the India house was closed; and every thing bore the appearance of gloom and despondency. From all these causes, the minds of the people were excited to an extreme state of irritation; disturbances frequently took place in the city; and in the surrounding country assassinations were daily committed. The hoisting of the French colors aroused the populace against the invaders of their country and the soldiers were obliged to fire repeatedly upon them before they could be compelled to disperse.

There can be no doubt, however, that the French force would have eventually brought the inhabitants of Lisbon under complete subjection, had not the general and determined opposition of the Spaniards to Bonapart's views, the rising in the north of Portugal, the revolt at Oporto, and the disembarcation of a powerful English force under Sir Arthur Wellesley in Mondego bay, fortunately conspired to set them free. The battles of Roliça and Vimeiro were now fought and lost by the French; the disgraceful convention of Cintra was signed, and the invaders and plunderers of Portugal with all their booty were allowed to be transported at an enemy's cost to their native shores. On the 15.th September 1808 Lisbon was completely free from the presence of the execrated French, who for ten months had devastated the country, plundered its wealth, destroyed or carried off its artistic productions, desecrated its temples, and demoralized its inhabitants. The total number of French troops who embarked from Lisbon by virtue of the convention of Cintra amounted in all to 24,035 men.

The French in their progress through the Peninsula had industriously spread revolutionary principles. In the absence of the Court the affairs of government were conducted by a Regency, named by D. João VI., which consisted of five members. Up to this period Portugal had been ruled by hereditary monarchs, whose power was controlled by a National representation consisting of Clergy, Nobility and People, called the Three Estates of the realm. The nobles and higher orders of Clergy were members of the Cortes in virtue of their rank or office. The people sent their deputies elected by the cities and towns. The Cortes were called together and dissolved at the Royal pleasure.

Whatever may have been the evils of the ancient regime, and however liable to occasional abuse the power which it conferred on the sovereign, still it cannot be denied that under it the Portuguese had been on the whole a happy and united people. Under it had passed the palmy days of their history, and with it were linked the glorious feats of their enterprising and chivalrous forefathers. But the new philosophy of France here, as elsewhere, secretly but effectually gained ground. The first attempts at innovation were unsuccessful, and those who prominently engaged in them fell martyrs to the cause. On the 18.th October 1818, general Gomes Freire de Andrade was executed, as were also some others of less note, for conspiring to overthrow the established order of things.

Two years later a fresh attempt was made and succeeded. On the 24.th August 1820 the constitution was first proclaimed at Oporto, and on the 15.th of the following month at Lisbon. The Regency was dissolved, and a provisional junta was established in the name of the king, who was still at Rio de Janeiro. The first efforts of the newly installed government were directed to frame a code in harmony with the new views. It was proclaimed and sworn to on the 11.th of November following. In the year 1822 D. João VI. returned from the Brazils, and on the very day of his landing at Lisbon His bulky and unintellectual Majesty was made to swear himself the First Citizen of the kingdom.

The fundamental change that had taken place in the government was followed by very material alterations in almost all the laws and institutions of the country. These changes were embodied in what was termed the *Nova Lei Fundamental*, which was proclaimed and sworn in 1822. By this code the sovereignty was declared to reside essentially in the people, and the title of Majesty was given to the Cortes. But before these novel experiments in legislation had time to take root in the affections of the people, an end was put to them by a counter revolution brought about by the king's second son, D. Miguel, who was Commander-in-chief of the army.

In the year 1824, was beheld the novel spectacle of the Portuguese king seeking refuge on board an English ship of the line (the Windsor Castle) from a real or feigned conspiracy. How far the Infante D. Miguel was innocent or guilty in the affair, his friends and his foes are not agreed; but before the king left his asylum, he signed a decree for banishing his son, who was conveyed in a Portuguese frigate to Brest, whence he went to Vienna, in which city he continued till after the death of his father, which happened in March 1826.

The next phase of this eventful period was the regency of Dona Izabel Maria, who shortly after received from her brother D. Pedro, then emperor of Brazil, what afterwards proved an apple of discord for this country, the Constitutional Charter, of which the English minister Sir Charles Stuart, was the bearer. Then followed the return of D. Miguel in 1827, and his trampling on the Charter as well as on the claims of his niece Dona Maria, in whose favor her father D. Pedro had abdicated. The war of succession ensued, which commencing in the island of Terceira in 1830, continued with varied success to the contending parties till the year 1833, when the duke of Terceira, having landed in the Algarve with 2,000 men, rapidly marched to Cacilhas, and defeating the Miguelites on the S. bank of the Tagus, crossed over on the 24.ᵗʰ July to Lisbon, which the duke of Cadaval, the timid commander of the forces in the city, had precipitately abandoned on the previous night. Then came the final defeat of the Miguelites and the convention of Evora Monte, by which D. Miguel resigned the kingdom; the accession of Dona Maria II in 1833, who reigned till 1853, when she died in child birth, and was succeeded by her son D. Pedro V.

In 1859 Lisbon was afflicted by an awful epidemic, the yellow fever, thousands upon thousands of its inhabitants perished in a few days: the city was almost deserted, and those stricken with the malady were abandoned by their nearest friends. D. Pedro V. however, though yet a youth, set a noble example and refused to leave; he visited the sick and dying in the hospitals, and by his courageous conduct, did more than any one else to alleviate the miseries of his suffering subjects. His high cultivation and great intelligence, the interest he took in every thing calculated to promote his country's welfare and encourage her arts, sciences or patriotism, but above all his singleness of heart and the benignity of his disposition endeared him to all men. No sovereign who ever filled the throne of Portugal was more beloved by his subjects, and on his death in November 1861 at the age of 24, the whole city attended his funeral, and the tears and lamentations were universal. The circumstances of his death are somewhat singular. A year previous he had lost his beautiful and beloved wife, queen Estephania, the brightest ornament of his court. He was attacked early in November with a kind of fever, which carried him off in a few days, and in the short space of two months his other three brothers were attacked in a similar manner, the youngest of them alone escaping. It was on account of these melancholy occurrences that the royal family removed from the Necessidades, where they then resided, to the palace of Ajuda.

Lisbon has been the birth place of many illustrious men, amongst whom may be mentioned St. Anthony, surnamed of Padua; Luiz de Camões, the great poet; Padre Vieyra, the distinguished preacher; and Pope John, XXI.

PART II.

DESCRIPTIVE.

1. TABLE

BY WHICH TO ASCERTAIN THE NAME OF THE PRINCIPAL BUILDINGS.

It often happens that the tourist in rambling through a foreign city, passes many buildings which attract his attention and excite his curiosity, but without being able to make out what they are by reason of his unfamiliarity with the native language; and in this way he often passes by objects which would have interested him had he only had a means of ascertaining their existence. This want is easily supplied with regard to Lisbon, for every *public gas lamp* has its own number in black figures near the top, and distinctly visible both by day and night.

By the help of these numbers the visitor can at once ascertain the name of any of the principal buildings. He has only to observe the number of the *gas lamp nearest to the entrance* thereof and on referring to the following table he will find the designation of the edifice and the page where it is mentioned in the guide.

LISBON.

N.º of Lamp.		Page.
19	Convento dos Santos o Novo..................	156
21	Convento de Lazaro Leitão.	
27	Convento dos Barbadinhos. Santa Engracia.	
38	Abarracamento da Cruz dos Quatro Caminhos. —Barracks.........................	233

N.º of Lamp.		Page.
91	Estação de mercadorias do caminho de ferro.—Goods station of Northern Railway.	
97, 99	Estação do caminho de ferro do norte e leste.—North Eastern Railway station..	284
103	Arsenal do Exercito.—Military arsenal....	225
104	Ermida da Boa Nova.	
125	Hospital da Marinha.—Naval Hospital....	223
126	Fundição de Cima.—Artillery Foundry.	
128, 129	Palacio do Marquez de Lavradio.	
141	Santa Engracia.— Unfinished church......	161
141	Convento do Desaggravo...............	165
144	Fundição de Baixo.—Artillery Foundry.	
152, 153	Igreja de S. Vicente de Fóra.—St. Vincent's church......................	134
161	Convento das Monicas..................	166
204	Igreja de Santo Estevão.—St. Stephen's...	166
209	Igreja de S. Thomé.—St. Thomas's......	166
239	Armazem da alfandega.	
243	Bomba da companhia das aguas.— Pumping engine of waterworks.	
245	Mercado do azeite.—Oil-market.	
249, 252	Terreiro do Trigo e alfandega municipal.—Corn-market and municipal custom-house............................	247
261, 262	Igreja de S. Miguel.—St. Michael's...	166
290	Igreja de Santo André.—St. Andrew's.	
300, 301	Igreja da Graça.—Church of our Lady of Grace.........................	140
302	Ruinas do Palacio do duque de Loulé.—Ruined palace of the duke of Loulé.	
309	Quartel da Graça.—Convent of Graça, now barracks...........................	233
360	Igreja de Nossa Senhora do Monte.—Church of our Lady of the Mount............	156
387	Igreja da Santa Cruz do Castello.—Church of the Holy Cross...................	166
398	Igreja de Santa Luzia.—St. Lucy's......	166
399	Igreja de S. Thiago.—St. James's.......	166
404, 405	Limoeiro.—The Gaol................	126
429	Igreja de S. Lourenço.—St. Lawrence's...	266
457	Igreja de S. Christovão.—St. Christopher's.	166

OF THE PRINCIPAL BUILDINGS. 75

| N.º of Lamp. | | Page. |

465A Palacio do Marquez de Penafiel.
466 Collegio de S. Patricio.................. 165
478, 479 Real casa de Santo Antonio.—Birth place of St. Anthony.................. 146
483, 484 Santa Maria Mayor.—The Cathedral.. 113
487 Aljube.—Prison for women............. 227
499 Igreja de S. João da Praça.— St. John's.. 166
528 Casa da fructa.
548 Igreja da Conceição Velha.—Old church of the Conception.................... 159
549, 550 Alfandega grande.—Custom-house... 241
558 Casa dos bicos.—The spiked house...... 249
570 Igreja da Magdalena.—St. Magdalen's... 163
589, 590 Igreja de Nossa Senhora da Saude.—Church of our Lady of Health.
619, 1044 Theatro do Principe Real.—Prince Royal's theater...................... 199
674, 694 Igreja de S. Nicolau.—St. Nicholas's.. 163
817, 818 Igreja de S. Domingos.—St. Dominic's 155
902, 1963 Igreja de S. Julião.—St. Julian's... 162
956, 967 Passeio publico.—Public walk...... 229
970 Theatro da rua dos Condes.—Theater.... 199
976, 980 Ruinas de S. José.—Ruins of St. Joseph's church.
979 Lyceu nacional de Lisboa.—Lyceum..... 233
1014, 1015, 1016, 1017 Theatro de Donã Maria Segunda.—Theater.................. 198
1038, 1050 Hospital Real de S. José.—St. Joseph's Hospital........................ 222
1044 Theatro do Principe Real.............. 199
1045 Igreja do Soccorro.—Church of Soccorro.. 165
1050, 1038 Hospital Real de S. José.—St. Joseph's hospital......................... 222
1052 Hospital de S. Lazaro.—St. Lazarus' hospital............................. 223
1083 Praça dos Touros.—Bull-ring.......... 189
1087 Convento de Santa Anna.—St. Anne's Con. 166
1088 Igreja de Nossa Senhora da Pena.—Church of our Lady of the Pena............ 166
1091 Convento da Encarnação.—Convent of the Incarnation...................... 166

N.º of Lamp.		Page.
1145	Asylo de Mendicidade.—Poor-house.	
1149	Hospital de Rilhafolles.—Lunatic asylum.	
1164	Palacio e Capella Real de Bemposta	187
1180	Palacio do Conde da Lapa.	
1194, 1195	Convento do Desterro.—Convent of Desterro, now a hospital	223
1261, 1262	Igreja dos Anjos.—Church of the Angels	166
1269	Ermida de N. S.ª do Resgate das Almas.	
1298	Igreja de S. Jorge.—St. George's church.	166
1321	Instituto agricola.—Agricultural Institute.	231
1329, 1330	Matadouro.—Slaughter-house	248
1364	Igreja de S. Sebastião.—St. Sebastian's	166
1370	Convento de S.ª Rita.—Conv. of St. Rita.	
1382	Convento de Santa Joanna.—Convent of St. Joanna.	
1385	Palacio do marquez de Borba.—Palace of the marquis of Borba.	
1387	Igreja do Coração de Jesus.—Church of the Sacred Heart of Jesus	166
1387	Convento de Santa Martha.—Convent of St. Martha	166
1414, 1415	Quartel de caçadores 2.—Barracks.	233
1432	Convento das Trinas ao Rato.—Convent of Trinas	167
1433	Palacio do marquez de Vianna.—Marquis of Vianna's palace.	
1464	Mãe de Agua.—Reservoir for water supply	217
1466	Arco das Aguas Livres.—Arch of aqueduct	216
1470, 1482	Palacio da condessa de Anadia.—Countess of Annadia's palace.	
1530	Imprensa Nacional.—National printing-office	249
1541	Palacio do duque de Palmella.—Duke of Palmella's palace.	
1545	Igreja de S. Mamede.	
1552	Escola Polytechnica.—Polytechnic school.	231
1617, 1618	Passeio Publico.—Public walk	229
1621	Circo Price.—Price's circus.	
1621	Theatro das Variedades.—Theater	200
1640	Igreja de S. José.—St. Joseph's church.	154
1649, 1673	Passeio de S. Pedro de Alcantara.	230

N.º of Lamp.		Page.
1674	Convento de S. Pedro de Alcantara.—Convent of St. Peter of Alcantara	167
1697	Palacio do marquez de Pombal.	
1712	Collegio dos Inglezinhos.—English college	129
1713	Conservatorio real.—Royal conservatory	232
1749	Palacio do duque de Palmella.—Duke of Palmella's palace.	
1807, 1808	Igreja da Encarnação.—Church of the Incarnation	150
1809, 1810	Igreja do Loreto.—Ch. of Loretto	152
1814	Igreja dos Martyres.—Ch. of the Martyrs	150
1818	Palacio do barão de Barcellinhos.—Baron Barcellinho's palace.	
1831	Convento do Carmo.—Conv. of the Carmo.	144
1857	Ruinas da igreja do Carmo.—Ruined church of the Carmo	144
1860	Club Lisbonense.—Lisbon club	7
1862	Igreja do Santissimo Sacramento.—Church of the Most Blessed Sacrament	166
1866	Casino.	
1870, 1873	Theatro da Trindade.—Theater	198
1872	Theatro do Gymnasio.—Theater	199
1875	Igreja de S. Roque.—St. Roch's church	125
1892	Gremio litterario.—Literary club	7
1920	Theatro de S. Carlos.—Opera	196
1941	Governo civil.—Chief police-office	1
1945	Bibliotheca nacional.—National library	200
1945	Academia das bellas artes.—Academy of fine arts	204
1955	Boa Hora.—Court-house	223
1957	Igreja da Conceição Nova	166
1963	Igreja de S. Julião.—St. Julian's	162
1968	Camara municipal.—Town-Hall.	
1974	Telegrapho.—Chief telegraph-Office	280
1976	Arsenal da marinha.—Naval Arsenal	224
1978	Museu de productos coloniaes.—Museum of colonial products	225
1990	Igreja do Corpo Santo.—Irish church	130
2026, 2040	Mercado do peixe.—Fish market	228
2033, 2034	Igreja de S. Paulo.—St. Paul's	163
2077	Instituto industrial.—Industrial institute	232

N.º of Lamp.		Page.
2115A	Casa da Moeda.—The Mint	246
2148	Igreja das Chagas.—Church of the Chagas	164
2158	Correio geral.—General post-office	281
2162	Igreja dos Paulistas, Santa Catharina.—Church of the Paulists.	
2202A	Igreja e convento de Jesus.—Church and convent of Jesus	143
2210	Academia das Sciencias.—Acad. of Sciences	144
2341	Convento da Esperança.—Conv. of Hope	167
2364, 2365	Convento de S. Bento, palacio das Cortes.—Conv. of St. Bento, now Houses of parliament, and national archives	136
2368	Convento das Francezinhas.—French conv.	166
2369D	Camara dos pares.—Part of St. Bento.—House of peers	136
2405	Igreja de Santa Izabel.—St. Elisabeth's	166
2410, 2437	Cemiterio e igreja dos inglezes.—English protestant cemetery and church.	233
2413, 2425	Quartel de infanteria.—Barracks	233
2437, 2462, 2463, 2465, 2466	Passeio da Estrella.—Public walk called Estrella	230
2461, 2464	Igreja da Estrella.—Ch. of Estrella.	139
2467	Hospital Militar.—Military hospital	223
2498	Convento das Inglezinhas.—English Brigittine convent	131
2512	Palacio do marquez de Abrantes.—Marquis of Abrantes's palace.	
2514, 2515	Igreja dos Santos o Velho.—Church of the Saints	157
2532	Igreja dos Marianos.—Now presbyterian ch.	
2541, 2546	Palacio do marquez de Pombal.—Marquis of Pombal's palace.	
2553	Quartel de infanteria 2.—Barracks	233
2556	Igreja de S. Francisco de Paula.—Church of St. Francis de Paul	164
2571	Convento do Santissimo Sacramento.—Convent of the Blessed Sacrament	166
2574	Quartel de cavallaria municipal.—Barracks	
2576	Quartel de invalidos da marinha.—Hospital for disabled seamen	233
2585	Ermida de Nossa Senhora do Livramento.	

OF THE PRINCIPAL BUILDINGS. 79

N.º of Lamp.		Page.
2624	Igreja das Necessidades	185
2627, 2650	Palacio das Necessidades.—Royal Palace of Necessidades	185
2724	British legation	1
2738	Igreja da Lapa.—Church of the Lapa	166
2739	Asylo de infancia desvalida.—Asylum for poor children.	

BELEM.

1	Estatua de S. João Nepomuceno e Ponte de Alcantara.—Statue of St. John Nepumocene	247
13	Igreja de S. Pedro em Alcantara	166
19	Escola normal.—Normal college.	
20	Convento das flamengas.—Flemish conv.	
30	Palacio do marquez da Ribeira.—Marquis of Ribeira's Palace.	
32	Palacio do Infante de Hespanha.—Spanish Infante's Palace.	
35	Palacio do Marquez de Valladas.—Marquis of Vallada's Palace.	
40	Cordoaria.—Rope walk	241
68	Igreja de Santo Amaro.—St. Amaro's.	
70, 71, 78	Palacio de Belem.—Palace of Belem	186
78	Igreja da Memoria.—Church called *Memoria*	159
91, 93	Jardim botanico.—Botanical garden	230
109	Santa Maria de Belem, *vulgo*, S. Jeronymo.—St. Jerome's church	117
111, 112	Casa Pia.—Charitable institution	124
118	Convento do Bom Successo.—Irish convent	164
126, 145	Palacio de Belem.—Palace of Belem	186
136	Convento das Salessias.—Conv. of Salessias	167
147	Quartel de Artilheria, 1.—Artillery Barracks	233
147	Cocheira real.—Royal coach-house	236
152	Quartel de lanceiros, 2.—Cavalry Barracks	233
155	Quartel de infanteria, 1.—Infantry Barracks	233
181	Bibliotheca de Ajuda.—Ajuda Library	184
182, 183	Palacio da Ajuda.—Palace of Ajuda	167
192	Igreja da Boa Hora.—Church of Boa Hora.	

2. GEOGRAPHICAL POSITION,

POPULATION, AND GENERAL VIEW.

The situation of Lisbon is unsurpassed in beauty by that of any other city in Europe, unless it be Constantinople. Naples and Lisbon in this respect are rivals, the beautiful bay of the former vying with the noble river of the latter, and both seem to be condemned by nature to pay dearly for the advantages she has accorded them, for Naples lives in constant dread of Vesuvius, while Lisbon is ever tormented by the fears of an earthquake[1].

Lisbon is situated in latitude 38° 42' N. and longitude 9° 5' W. of Greenwich, on the N. bank of the Tagus where the river spreads itself into a lake, 9 miles before entering the Atlantic ocean. It is the capital of the kingdom, see of a patriarch, seat of the government, of the supreme civil and military tribunals, and one of the 17 civil districts into which the kingdom is divided. Its population according to the census of 1864 amounted to 163,763, intra-muros: reckoning the suburbs it reaches about 200,000. A slight glance at the map shews that Lisbon is destined to become one of the busiest, as it is one of the best ports in the world.

The traffic between South America and Europe is increasing with amazing rapidity and the commercial relations with Africa are daily becoming of greater importance. Lisbon is already connected by rail with all the countries of Europe, and it only requires a little less apathy on the part of the several companies to shorten the time at present taken, to one half, so that passengers and mails from the whole of Europe to South America and Africa, might be embarked at Lisbon not only with a great saving of time, but also with increased safety, from the avoidance of the dangers of the northern seas. The port of Lisbon affords secure anchorage for any number of ships and its bar is easily

---

1. Lisbon has suffered from earthquakes in the years 1009, 1117, 1146, 1344, 1356, 1531, 1579, 1699, 1722 and 1755.

entered in rough weather. The construction of docks projected by government will be an addition to the advantages it already possesses.

> Nota de embarcações a variedade,
> Humas de tratos da maior riqueza:
> Outras que tem maior felicidade
> Em sujeitar do mundo a redondeza.
> Se advertes d'esse porto a magestade,
> Conhecerás que o autor da natureza
> O fez capaz do muito que antevia
> Que o largo mar aqui tributaria.
> (ULYSSIPPO, cant. XIV — XXII.)

The city is generally described as built like ancient Rome on seven hills, but the skeptical inquirer will find it as difficult to ascertain their names as those of the seven sages of Greece. No doubt the description was correct in former times, but at present the city has outgrown its classical proportions and covers a greater number. The Castello de S. Jorge, Graça, Nossa Senhora do Monte, Penha de França, Campo de Sant'Anna, Buenos Ayres, Chagas, Santa Catharina, S. Vicente, and S. Roque are now all within its walls.

The panorama which presents itself to view on entering the Tagus is acknowledged by all to be of surpassing beauty, and its effect may be said to be magical on the poor voyager who has for days previously been deprived of the sight of land and gazed upon nothing but sky and water.

On rounding cape Rock, the villages of Cascaes, Carcavellos, Oeiras, and Paço d'Arcos, nestling in orange groves of emerald and gold, successively come into view, with the rugged mountains of Cintra in the distant background, crowned with the fairy-like palace of D. Fernando, whilst on the opposite side of the river are the blue bleak Arrabida mountains streaching along the horizon to cape Espichel and in the foreground the fishing village of Trafaria.

Approaching Belem the first view of Lisbon is obtained. The graceful tower of Belem, which marks the spot where Vasco da Gama landed on his return from the Indies, at once attracts attention. A little further on is the famous Jeronymite convent founded by Dom Manuel the Great, in commemoration of Vasco's discoveries; higher up is the church of the *Memoria*, and the huge unfinished palace of Ajuda (now the residence of the Royal family), backed by verdant hills covered with a host of busy windmills.

Proceeding up the Tagus we pass successively the Astronomical Observatory, standing in the midst of a large enclosure or *cerca* of olive trees; the industrial suburb of Alcantara, with a few tall mill chimneys of brick suggestive of England; the asylum for disabled sailors, standing prominently forward, while further back on the brow of the hill is the palace of Necessidades, occupied by the king's father Dom Fernando. Next comes the palace of the Marquises of Pombal, lately the residence of the Empress of the Brazils, and rising above the roofs of the houses, the dome of the Estrella is plainly visible.

Passing the new boulevard called *Aterro da Boa Vista*, over which in bold relief stands the church of the Chagas, we come to the very heart of the city the Praça do Commercio, or Black Horse Square, surrounded by the government offices of uniform architecture, built over a spacious arcade. Facing the water is the triumphal arch of Rua Augusta, and in the center the splendid equestrian statue of Dom José I. On the right of this principal square is the Custom-house, and on the left the Naval Arsenal. Further E., on the acclivity of a hill, appear the square towers of the old Cathedral, and on the summit of the hill is the Castle of St. George, while still further east may be seen the church and convent of St. Vincent, the incomplete *obras de Santa Engracia* and the Railway station.

It is impossible to describe the charming effect produced by the *tout ensemble*, especially when viewed from the middle of the river at early morn. When the sun rises the whole city appears lit up with ten thousand sparkling lights, the reflection of the *azulejos* or glazed tiles, with which the exteriors of many houses are lined, and which present the appearance of being studded with gems.

The S. side of the Tagus or *Outra Banda* has quite another aspect, and consists of a chain of vine clad hills extending as far as Cacilhas, opposite the Arsenal, where the bank makes a bend towards the SE. forming a spacious bay called *Cōra da Piedade*, but known to English tars by the less euphonious title of «Jackass Bay». The river here is some 4 miles wide, and four gun boats are moored in front of the Custom-house to form a square within which all vessels having *pratique* must anchor and nobody is allowed to visit them without an order from the customs authorities. Vessels arriving from infected ports have to anchor in front of the Lazareto, opposite the tower of Belem.

The best general views of Lisboa are obtained from St. George's Castle, N. S. do Monte, the Penha de França, the Graça, the dome of the Estrella, or from Almada.

3. THE STREETS OF LISBON.

The generic names applied to the thoroughfares of the capital are *Rua* a street, *Travessa* a cross street, *Calçada*, a steep street, and *Beco* a street without any outlet or *cul-de-sac*. As a rule the streets are tortuous and narrow, especially in the ancient quarter of *Alfama*. A striking exception in this respect is the lower part of the city called the *Baixa*, where the streets are all of a fair width, perfectly straight, and intersecting each other at right angles. This distinction is owing to the fact that the great earthquake of 1755 so utterly ruined the whole of this district that every house had to be rebuilt from its foundation, and the Marquis of Pombal, at that time the all powerful minister of D. José 1, availed himself of this circumstance to improve and widen the streets and introduce uniformity into their architecture, though it is much to be lamented that he did not pay more attention to sanitary requirements. Indeed the *Baixa* may be pointed to as a true exemplification of Pombal's character.

In the hard straight lines and rectangles, in the uniformity of the elevations, and in the celerity with which the work was accomplished, are evinced the energetic despotism of the unbending ruler, combined with the statesman's sense of public utility, but when we closely analyze the internal construction of the houses we find them wanting in those sanitary arrangements which conduce to the health and happiness of the individual families, shewing that while Pombal effected great public improvements, he lost sight of those higher and more important interests on which depend the real prosperity and happiness of a nation.

Long and tortuous as are many of the streets themselves, they are not more so than the names by which they are known, tho' in inverse proportion, that is to say, the shortest streets have the longest names e. g. *Rua da Porta do Carro do Hospital Real de S. José, Travessa do Abarracamento da Cruz do Taboado, Rua de Santo Antonio da Praça do Convento do Coração de Jesus.*

Nor do the Lisbonites rest satisfied with the elongated nature of the names, but still further to puzzle the unfortunate foreigner, they never fail to speak of their streets by the vulgar names, and not by the official names written up at the corners. Thus *Rua Bella da Rainha* is invariably called *Rua da Prata*. *Rua Nova de El-Rei* is much better known as *Rua dos Capellistas*, indeed the majority of the inhabitants are acquainted only with the vulgar name. The following are the principal streets and squares rejoicing in this double nomenclature:

Official name.	Vulgar name.
Rua Nova da Princeza.	Rua dos Fanqueiros.
Rua Bella da Rainha.	Rua da Prata.
Rua Aurea.	Rua do Ouro.
Rua Nova de El-Rei.	Rua dos Capellistas.
Rua de S. Julião.	Rua dos Algibebes.
Rua da Conceição.	Rua dos Retrozeiros.
Rua dos Correeiros.	Travessa da Palha.
Rua dos Sapateiros.	Rua do Arco do Bandeira
Praça de D. Pedro.	Rocio.
Praça do Commercio.	Terreiro do Paço.
Praça de Alcantara.	Praça de Armas.

Most of the vulgar names are the names of trades and had their origin in the regulations of former times when persons carrying on a certain trade were compelled to occupy shops in a certain street. Thus the goldsmiths were exclusively in the *Rua do Ouro* and the silversmiths in the *Rua da Prata*, etc.

Nearly all the streets are paved with small hard stones which render thick soles essential to the comfort of the pedestrian. The *Calçadas* are mostly macadamized to prevent the horses slipping and it is astonishing to see how safely they are driven at full speed down the steep inclines.

A few streets, principally in the *Baixa*, have flagged causeways for foot passengers but they are of little use in wet weather, none of the houses having fall pipes, but being constructed so as to drip the eaves water on to the heads of the passers by.

The architecture of the dwellings is in general plain and inelegant. The too numerous windows are invariably surrounded by clumsy stone frames projecting slightly from the walls and appearing to form part of the window rather than of the wall, so that the piers look much narrower than the openings, producing an unpleasant effect; and in some buildings the windows are so close to each other that the whole front seems one immense window. *Asulejo*, a kind of Dutch tile, generally blue and white (whence the name) is also extensively employed for lining the exteriors and presents a very neat appearance, besides having the advantage of keeping the walls cool by reflecting the rays of the sun: in fact the whole construction of the houses in Lisbon is with a view to lessen the inconvenience arising from the tropical heats of summer, so that during the short interval of winterly weather they are cold and comfortless.

On comparing the houses built two or three centuries ago with those of to day, little difference will be found except in details: they are constructed with greater solidity than in England and (what may appear paradoxical to strangers) it is not uncommon to see a house roofed in before the walls are built. On account of its liability to earthquakes the houses of Lisbon are first erected in skeleton composed of timber on which the roof rests, so that in the event of a violent shaking the

outer walls can fall to the ground and still leave the
house standing. They are generally three or four stories
high, sometimes even five or six: the dwellings are in
flats with a common staircase for 6 or 8 families and
the rents decrease as the elevation increases. This system
brings the different classes of society into constant contact, for it is not unusual to see a fidalgo occupying the
first floor, a doctor the second, a tradesman the third,
a clerk the fourth and a seamstress the fifth, with a
cobbler in the staircase.

There is no fashionable quarter occupied solely by the
rich as in England: the nobleman's palace and the poor
man's cottage stand side by side. The system of letting
is somewhat peculiar. Houses are uniformly let by the
semestre or half year, from the 1.st of January to the 30.th
of June, and from the 1.st of July to the end of December. The rents are often paid in advance, but even this
is not considered sufficient security by some landlords
who insist on having a *fiador* or bondsman, to answer
for any damage the tenant may do to the property during his occupancy. When the tenant wishes to leave,
instead of giving a written notice to his landlord, he
sticks square pieces of white paper called *escriptos* in
all his windows on the 20.th May or Dec. On these
dias de pôr escriptos all the people in the streets may
be seen walking about with upturned faces, and running
against each other, so intent are they on satisfying their
curiosity as to who is removing and who is not.

Many of the streets are so narrow that carriages cannot pass each other and a notice is posted up at the
entrance prohibiting the transit of vehicles, except in
one direction, and the opposite neighbors can sit at
their windows and talk scandal with the greatest facility.

A general opinion prevails amongst untraveled Englishmen that Lisbon is preëminently a dirty place, and
nothing has done more to perpetuate this erroneous belief than Lord Byron's reference to it in «Childe Harold»:

> But whose entereth within this town,
> That sheening far celestial seems to be,
> Disconsolate will wander up and down
> Mid many things unsigthly to strange ee.

Whatever foundation for this charge there might have been in the poet's time, it certainly cannot be brought against the Lisbon of the present day. The streets are well drained and clean; the scavenger's cart going round every morning to remove the refuse from the houses. No doubt before these sanitary measures were introduced it was not very safe to venture along a narrow street at night, for the only means of getting rid of the refuse was by pitching it out of the window, and woe to the unhappy pedestrian who neglected the warning, often too tardily given, of *agua vae*, to apprise him of the coming shower of solids and liquids mixed, emitting an odor less agreeable than powerful and characteristic.

The thoroughfares are all lighted with gas, and the tourist may wander about at all hours of the night with as much or more safety than in any other capital in Europe, and without being subjected to those importunities which he would be liable to in the large cities of England.

The police force consists of three bodies independent of each other: the *guarda municipal* is a military force composed of infantry and cavalry selected from the flower of the army, and is at the orders of the *ministro do reino*, or Home Secretary. Next comes the *policia civil*, corresponding in organisation with our *bobby*, a body of civil policemen armed with a short saber and an *apito*, or whistle wherewith to summon the assistance of their companions: these are under the orders of the *governador civil*. Lastly come the *cabos de policia*, similar to our Constable, who are appointed by the *regedor de parochia*, an authority elected by the parishioners.

One of the dangers aggravated by very high houses and the system of flats, is that of fires, which are of constant occurrence and often prove disastrous from the rapidity with which they spread owing to the large amount of wood employed in the buildings and the difficulty of escape from the top stories. Indeed the casualties would be deplorably great were it not for the admirable organisation of the fire brigade. Should the tourist remain some time in Lisbon he is sure to be startled from his sleep by the hurried tolling of the church bells. The city is divided into 22 districts, each represented by a certain number of strokes varying from 11 to 32. On the first alarm of fire, the police hasten to the nearest church, and ring the prescribed number of strokes by means of a rope fastened to one of the bells and terminating outside in a small box, to which they have access at all hours. This signal is repeated thrice and the other churches take up the alarm, so that in a few minutes the whole capital is made aware of the existence of the fire and the precise district in which it has broken out. The fire brigade is composed entirely of *aguadeiros* or water-carriers, who are nearly all *gallegos* or natives of Galicia in Spain. A certain number of them are attached to each *chafariz* or fountain, and no one else is allowed to sell water. In consideration for this monopoly they are obliged to appear at the fire with their barrels on the first alarm, under pain of fine. They are also obliged to have their barrels full of water on retiring to rest, to be ready in case of need. The first 30 who arrive at the scene of action receive an extra reward, and the whole of them must continue their services as long as the fire lasts, running backwards and forwards with ant-like industry. In many parts of the city *bombas* or fire engines are stationed, worked also by the *aguadeiros,* and there is a 1.st and 2.nd prize for those which are earliest on the spot, and a picket is sent by each regiment quartered in the capital. The signal is repeated at intervals for a small fire, but when the conflagration assumes vigorous proportions the bells after tolling the number of the district continue with an indefinite number of strokes in quick succession which is termed *repicar*. When the fire has been subdued three strokes are given as a signal that no further assistance is required.

    The *gallegos* are not only the water carriers and fire extinguishers, but also the general drudges of the capital, and meet with the same unmerited contempt which is bestowed on the poor Irish laborer in England. They are a most hard working and frugal race of men, literally the « hewers of stone and drawers of water ». Many of them are small landed proprietors in their own country, possessing a patch of ground with a cow and pig. To escape liability to military service and be allowed to emigrate they get married and quit their country a few days after the ceremony, leaving their wives to look after the home concerns. After years of toil in foreign cities they manage to scrape together a small pittance, and then return to their native village were they spend the remainder of their lives in agricultural pursuits. The number of *gallegos* in Lisbon is upwards of 3,000, and they do most of the hard work, especially porterage. It is surprising to see what heavy weights they can carry suspended by a rope from a strong wooden bar resting on a horse-shoe-shaped collar called a *chinguiço*, placed on their sholders, as they trudge along in pairs, out of step, to neutralize the oscillation of their bodies. This mode of transport is called *a pau e corda,* and two men in this way can carry half a ton. The Portuguese as a rule have an inveterate prejudice against carrying burdens, and it is recounted that when the inhabitants of Coimbra deserted the city on the approach of the French army, the women took what they could, but the men preferred losing every thing, rather than disgrace themselves by becoming porters! They also say « God made first the Portuguese and then the Gallego to wait on him ».

Another mode of transport common in Lisbon tho' not to be seen in English towns, is the cart drawn by a yoke of oxen. These vehicles of antideluvian appearance are made in a most primitive manner: the wheels have no spokes, but are plain disks of wood fixed on to an axis which revolves along with them. The stranger must not condemn their construction before he has had an opportunity of seeing the kind of roads on which they have to travel. A genuine Portuguese road of the old school resembles the dried up bed of a mountain torrent. Nor is this a mere figure of speech for in many parts of the interior, what are roads in summer are streams in winter. The fixing of the wheels to the axis has the advantage of not allowing the cart to swerve from its course when passing a road half a yard higher at one side than at the other, and affords also a convenient method of breaking the wheels by means of a rope tightened round the axis.

Portugal is rapidly improving in means of communication, and within the last twenty years government have made upwards of 3,000 miles of good macadamized roads.

Every kind of eatable, except butcher's meat, is to be bought in the streets, hawked about by barefooted men and women who vie with each other in the loudness of their unintelligible and discordant cries. The fishwomen are the most picturesque, wearing a broad brimmed felt hat, indigo blue closely plaited short woolen skirt, a loose jacket and bare legs. Many of them are further adorned with a profusion of gold ornaments.

One of the commonest street cries is *quem quer uma cautela,* « who wants a cautela », the latter word signifying a division of a lottery ticket. Lotteries in Lisbon take place every week, the amount of the prizes varies: the first prize is usually about £ 1,500, but sometimes £ 10,000; a whole ticket costs about £ 1, but *cautelas* or subdivisions are issued by the *cambistas* at all prices down to 30 réis. These lotteries, conducted with every guarantee as to fairness in the drawing, are a privilege granted by government to the *Misericordia,* or foundling hospital, and other charitable institutions, 15 per cent of the proceeds of the lottery is deducted for them, the rest being given away in prizes.

The Lisbonites have a peculiar way of calling any one's attention in the street by means of a prolonged hissing sound like *pish-sh,* and foreigners at first feel somewhat uncomfortable at being thus deliberately hissed, but they soon discover the cause, and learn to hiss other people quite as loudly as any of the natives.

In Lisbon, as in other capitals, the national costumes are rarely to be seen, the despotic rule of Fashion having extended itself to every country and become a kind of test of civilization.

The dress of the *saloios* or peasantry of the neighborhood is wanting in the picturesqueness to be observed in the northern provinces. The men wear a dark cloth jacket with *alamares* or fasteners of silver, broad brimmed felt hat, and cloth trowsers with a long crimson sash or *cinta* wrapped many times round the waist. The women indulge in gaudy colored dresses and kerchiefs together with massive gold chains and earrings. In the city are still to be seen a few specimens of the once universal *capote e lenço* formerly worn by all classes of women out of doors and especially at church. The *capote* is a dark blue or brown cloth cloak reaching to the heels and completely eclipsing the other garments; the *lenço* is a white kerchief placed on the head so as to leave nothing visible but the face. The Portuguese cloak for men is now an object of great rarity, but the *capa hespanhola* or Spanish cloak is by no means uncommon in winter.

One of the striking sights of the streets of Lisbon used to be the religious processions, but since the abolition of the monastic orders they have been much reduced in number, as well as in magnitude and splendor. At present the chief processions are *Corpus Christi*, on the feast of the Body of our Lord, which starts from the Cathedral and makes a circuit of several of the streets of the *Baixa*, accompanied by the king, ministers, high officers of state and principal members of the aristocracy. *Da saude*, on the fourth Thursday in April, starts from the chapel of *Nossa Senhora da Saude*, proceeds along the Rocio, Rua Augusta, etc., to the Cathedral and on its return calls at St. Domingos': all the regiments in the capital with their bands of music take part in this procession. *Dos Passos*, on the second Friday in Lent, leaves the church of São Roque and passing along the Chiado, Rua Nova do Carmo, Rocio, etc., goes to the church of the Graça. *Do Coração de Jesus* in June. From the church of Jesus making a detour of the principal streets in the *bairro alto*.

The *Viaticum* is also often carried in procession through the streets to the sick and dying. The brotherhood and attendants necessary to form the cortege are called together by the ringing of a bell at the church door. The priest carries the Blessed Sacrament, called by the Portuguese on this occasion *Nosso Pae*, under a canopy preceded by the guild in scarlet capes bearing lights. The approach of the procession is announced by the sound of a bell and every head is uncovered and every knee bent as it moves along. If it take place at night all the windows are illuminated as it passes and an appropriate hymn is sung by the attendants. The effect produced as it slowly and solemnly winds through the streets in the still hour of midnight is touching and sublime.

The tourist will often notice a scarlet curtain hanging at the doors of the churches: this is to apprise the passers-by that the Exposition or devotion of « Forty hours prayer » is going forward within. The Blessed Sacrament is placed for adoration on a high throne amid a radiance of lights and flowers and the interior of the temple is hung with richly embroidered silks. This devotion lasts two days and two nights and is taken up in succession by all the principal churches in Lisbon, so that before it ceases in one it has already commenced in another. Hence it is called *Laus perennis* or perpetual praise.

In promenading the streets of Lisbon in winter time the tourist is advised to keep on the shade side: in summer there is no need for this caution, the scorching rays of the sun being sufficient monitors. In winter, however, tho' the rays of the sun and their chemical action are very powerful they do not incommode, on account of the surrounding cold air, so that the pedestrian gets imperceptibly heated and on crossing to the shade side the difference of temperature is very marked and often results in a severe catarrh.

In choosing an appartment always prefer a S. aspect in winter, as the rays of the sun not only render a fire unnecessary, but are also a great assistance to ventilation. Rooms in which the sunshine never enters are decidedly unhealthy, as is truly said by the Italian proverb « *Dove non entra il sole entra il medico* » « Where the sun does not enter the Doctor does ».

4. CLIMATE.

The climate of Lisbon is invigorating and healthy in winter, but excessively hot in summer, indeed the absolute maximum heat in the sun in July and August is higher than at Rio de Janeiro, reaching 135° Fahr., though the mean temperature of the latter city is much above that of the former which throughout the year is 60°. The N. wind predominates in summer and even on the hottest and most sultry days a cool breeze springs up after sunset. The sudden variations of temperature during the day cannot be favorable to pulmonary invalids, though Lisbon is sometimes recommended by English medical men as a place of residence for consumptive patients. The winters are very mild and snow rarely falls. In 1815, 1829, and 1836 it fell abundantly causing much consternation among the ignorant classes who flocked to the churches to pray. The year may be thus divided: winter, December to March both inclusive; Spring, April and May; Summer, June, July, August, September; and Autumn, October and November. The seasons are much earlier for equal latitudes in Portugal than in America, thus the apricot, peach and cherry bloom at Lisbon the first week in February, while at Lexington U.S. which is in the same latitude, they are not in flower till the beginning of April. Green peas and new potatoes are plentiful at Lisbon in March. The autumnal rains begin in October and between them and the winter rains there is always an interval of fine weather, which from its generally commencing about St. Martin's day (11.th of November) is called *Verãosinho de São Martinho*, or St. Martin's little summer. Heavy rain falls during the months of December, January and February. The weather in March is very changeable

        Março marçagão
        De manhã cara de inverno,
        A tarde cara de verão.

and in April fine showers prevail

        Abr 1 aguas mil.

May is generally fine, and the traveler may reckon with almost certainty on dry weather and a cloudless sky from the middle of June to the end of September.

The following weather statistics are taken from the last published observations of the Observatorio do Infante Dom Luiz for 1872, the results being reduced to the English standards.

Month	Temperature In degrees Fahrenheit				Diurnal variation of temperature. Fahrenheit		
	Mean in shade	Maximum in shade	Minimum in shade	Maximum in sun	Mean in shade	Max. in shade	Min. in shade
December 1871...	47.97	60.44	35.42	101.66	9.83	16.29	4.14
January 1872....	52.57	60.26	39.92	106.52	7.16	12.78	3.60
February........	52.48	63.32	43.24	110.48	8.28	16.02	3.60
March..........	55.11	71.24	43.16	116.96	11.47	19.26	7.56
April...........	58.12	78.44	46.40	122.36	12.17	20.52	6.84
May............	59.13	76.64	48.92	125.06	11.99	18.90	5.76
June............	67.42	87.44	53.60	132.98	16.38	26.10	8.10
July............	69.22	89.24	58.82	133.16	14.04	23.22	5.94
August..........	71.76	90.32	59.54	135.14	16.54	24.12	11.16
September.......	67.89	88.52	54.68	129.74	13.95	23.04	8.46
October.........	58.51	70.70	48.56	116.96	10.51	16.74	6.30
November.......	55.33	72.50	41.72	114.44	10.40	20.52	3.42
The whole year..	59.54	90.32	35.42	135.14	—	—	—

CLIMATE.

Month	Rain — Quantity in inches	Rain — Number of rainy days	Thunder — Number of days	Fog — Number of days	Wind — Prevailing direction	Wind — Very gentle	Wind — Gentle	Wind — Moderate	Wind — Fresh	Wind — Strong	Wind — Tempestuous
December, 1871	2.61	10	1	2	NNE. NNW.	—	4	10	7	—	—
January, 1872	6.97	25	3	5	NW. WNW.	2	5	9	9	1	2
February	8.62	17	1	8	SW. SSW. S.	3	10	9	6	1	—
March	3.32	12	1	1	N. NW.	1	3	12	11	4	1
April	1.96	11	1	—	WSW. N. NNE.	1	5	8	13	3	—
May	1.18	9	6	—	N. NNW.	5	—	16	12	3	—
June	—	—	1	—	N. NNW.	5	2	10	10	2	—
July	0.23	2	1	1	N. NNW.	2	2	9	15	2	—
August	0.13	2	1	—	N. NNW.	2	1	18	10	2	—
September	0.87	8	—	—	NNW. N.	1	4	17	5	2	—
October	1.24	16	1	—	N. NNW.	2	2	17	10	2	—
November	2.69	15	—	3	N.	—	8	11	9	2	—
The whole year	32.82	127	12	20	N. NNW.						

Dead calm on the 19th of December.

5. SQUARES.

PRAÇA DO COMMERCIO.

Often called *Terreiro do Paço* (Palace Yard) because before the great earthquake the king's palace occupied the N. side. This fine square, the principal one in Lisbon, is well known to English residents by the name of «Black Horse Square». From E. to W. it measures 585 feet and from N. to S. 536. On the S. it is bounded by the Tagus having on this side a low wall of white marble, with numerous seats and in the middle a semicircular landing place from which a noble flight of marble steps gracefully descend into the limpid waters, terminating in two majestic columns. This is called the *Caes das Columnas*. The other three sides are bounded by two storied buildings of uniform architecture, resting on lofty arcades or piazzas, well flagged and lighted affording a pleasant promenade in wet weather. The building on the E. side is the custom-house (alfandega) having at the southern extremity an elegant square pavilion surmounted by a balustrade and trophies, the ground floor of which serves as an exchange *(Bolsa* or *Praça)*, where the merchants of the city meet from 2 to 4. The western building is occupied by the ministries of Foreign Affairs, Public Works, and other government offices, and terminates in a pavilion similar to the opposite one, where the ministry of War is located. On the N. side, which is divided by the three chief streets of the lower city *(cidade baixa) Rua do Ouro, Rua Augusta,* and *Rua da Prata,* are the ministries of the Interior, Justice, Supreme Tribunal of Justice and the *Junta do Credito Publico*.

In the center of the square is the famous equestrian statue of Dom José 1, acknowledged by all to be unsurpassed in elegance by any other in Europe. It was erected in 1775 by the inhabitants as a testimony of gratitude to the king and to the Marquez de Pombal for their energy and solicitude in succoring the needy and rebuilding the city after the calamitous earthquake of 1755. Considering the backward state of art in Portugal at the time, this monument may be pointed to as a triumph of genius, and the names of the artists who, surrounded by difficulties of every kind, succeeded in accomplishing their arduous task, justly deserve to be blazoned on the scroll of fame. They are Joaquim Machado de Castro, a native of Coimbra, the sculptor, and General Bartholomeu da Costa, the engineer who superintended the casting and collocation of the bronze statue.

The statue was cast in one piece on the 15.th Oct. 1774 in the *Fundição do Exercito*. Its height is 21 feet, and its weight after being dressed, 80,640 lbs. It was conveyed to its present position by means of a machine invented by Bartholomeu da Costa, a representation of which may be seen on a porcelain medal which is in the Numismatic Cabinet at the Ajuda Palace.

Dom José, dressed in uniform with helmet and plume, having a military cape thrown over his shoulders, is seated on his charger which is trampling on serpents and noxious plants, symbolic of the vices. The attitude of both horse and rider is graceful and natural. The statue stands on an oblong pedestal 21 feet high, 18 feet long and 12 feet wide which is itself placed on an elevated base. On the W. side of the pedestal is an allegorical group, denoting Victory trampling upon the enemy and winning the trophies of war. On the opposite side is another group representing Fame trumpeting abroad the achievements of Victory in Asia and Africa. These two groups are splendid specimens of Castro's skill as a sculptor. He has been much criticized for making the elephant the same height as the horse. If he had preserved the unequal proportions of the two animals when full grown, the effect would have been unpleasant in the extreme. As the groups now stand the harmony of the two sides has been preserved without violating fidelity to nature, for the animal represented is a *cub elephant* as is plainly evident from the shortness of its tusks which are only just making their appearance.

On the front of the pedestal are the arms of Portugal and underneath them a medallion with the effigy of the Marquez de Pombal, the great promoter of this work who thereby intended not only to honor his Royal master, but at the same time to add a feather to his own cap. When he lost his master and his place, his likeness was torn down by the very persons who a few days previously had paid homage to the original. On learning this, the Marquis then in banishment at Pombal, cooly observed. «I am glad of it, for it was not like me». A ship, the city arms, was put in the place of the Marquis's effigy; but on the 12.th Oct. 1833 the former was removed and the latter reinstated in its former position. On the base is the following inscription:

JOSEPHO I.
AUGUSTO PIO FELICI PATRI PATRIAE
QUOD REGIIS, JURIBUS, ADSERTIS
LEGIBUS EMENDATIS
COMMERCIO PROPAGATO MILITIA
ET BONIS ARTIBUS RESTITUTIS
URBEM FUNDITUS EVERSAM TERRAEMOTU
ELEGANTIOREM RESTAURAVIT
AUSPICE ADMINISTRO EJUS MARCHIONE POMBALIO
ET COLLEGIO NEGOTIATORUM CURANTE
S. P. Q. O.
BENEFICIORUM MEMOR
A. MDCCLXXV
P.
JOAQUIMUS MACHADIUS CASTRIUS PINXIT
ET SCULPSIT
BARTHOLOMAEUS COSTIUS STATUAM EQUESTREM
EX AERE FUDIT

On the N. face of the pedestal is a *basso relievo* intended to celebrate the king's liberality. Royal Generosity is represented by a female with a crown upon her head and clothed in royal robes. She is descending from the throne and is in the act of granting her protection to the city of Lisbon also figured by a female in a swoon, clinging for support with her left hand to an escutcheon on which are emblazoned the arms of the Senate. Generosity has her symbol the lion at her feet. On her right appears a man clad in mail, armed with a lance and holding in his hand a branch of olive by which is denoted State Government endeavoring to raise the fallen city. Virtue is represented by a genius crowned with laurel having a star over his head and holding three crowns of laurel in his left hand, while with his right he conducts State Government to the presence of Royal Generosity to whom he communicates the design he has formed of raising the city. Royal Generosity seems to approve the design and with her left hand points out the site, while with her right she discloses the means which are Commerce, Industry and Architecture. Commerce is personified by a man richly habited, who on his knees presents Royal Generosity with an open coffer filled with riches, and near him are his attributes the stork and millstones. Industry is represented by a female crowned with ripe ears of wheat holding in her hand the rudder of a ship and two keys. She is addressing herself to Commerce, to whom by an inelegant gesture of the thumb she discovers Architecture also figured by a female having in her right hand a square and compass, and holding with both the plan of the city.

This *basso relievo* is considered a master-piece of art. It is not, however, exempt from grave defects: notice for instance, the hands of Commerce; their extraordinary size suggests the idea that he is suffering from elephantiasis.

On the N. side of the square, over the *rua Augusta* is an ornamental arch generally called *arco da rua Augusta*. Its origin dates from the rebuilding of the city in 1755, but its completion was only effected in 1873, the work, or rather the delays, having occupied more than a century. During its construction successive ministries have so altered and modified the primitive design that scarcely any traces of it have survived. It was to have been a belfry, but has turned out a triumphal arch with windows at one side and a clock at the other! The height from the crown of the arch to the cornice is much too great, and imparts an appearance of heaviness to the whole structure. This space is filled by the Royal arms of Portugal surrounded by fantastic ornamentations much batter in execution than design. The six columns tho' well proportioned are dwarfed by the immense amount of stone above them. They are some 36 feet high, while the distance from their capitals to the top cornice is 60 feet. The span is 33 feet and the height of the crown above the street 70 feet.

The subject of the magnificent allegorical group at the top is Glory rewarding Valor and Genius. Glory is represented by a draped female figure standing on a throne composed of three steps, and wearing the *peplum* or Greek robe of state. A wreath of laurel encircles her brow and on her forehead is a star. With outstretched arms she holds in her hands two crowns suspended over the heads of Valor and Genius sitting at her feet, on the second step of the throne. Valor, on the right of Glory, is personified by an amazon partially covered with the *Chlamys,* or ancient greek military dress, and wearing a high crested helmet with a dragon on each side, the symbols of Vigilance and of the noble house of Bragança. Her right hand rests on the head of a lion lying at her feet, the emblem of Force and Magnanimity. Her left grasps the *Parazonium* or girdle dagger, as a symbol of her past victories, which are further symbolized by a trophy of flags at her back, which serve also to connect the two figures. Genius is personified by the nude figure of a youth with wings partially spread, the right serving to connect the figure with the rest of the group, and the left encompassing a statue of Jupiter, the supreme god of the Greeks. At his side are the attributes of Letters and Arts, and his right hand rests on the angle of the second step while his left reposes on the Lyre to signify that Harmony should preside over the products of Intelligence.

This group is by the distinguished French sculptor M. Calmels, who has now for many years resided in Portugal, laboring constantly for the advancement of his noble art. As early as 1839 M. Calmels obtained the prize at the Paris *concours annuel,* and has since executed many important works, including the equestrian statue of Dom Pedro IV. at Oporto. In the group here described M. Calmels has been especially felicitous in the gracefulness of the attitudes, the expression of the faces, and symmetry of the whole, as well as in the appropriateness with which he has allegorized his subject. There is a refined grace in the whole composition which calls to mind the exquisite subtilities of ancient Greek art.

On account of the great height (over 100 feet) of the top cornice, the group had to be made of colossal proportions, and is perhaps the largest in Europe. The height from the lower step of the throne to the summit is 29 feet 6 in., and the width at the base 30 feet. The figure of Glory measures 23 feet, and that of Jupiter, scarcely visible from the square 8 ft. 2 in. Under the group is the following inscription:

VIRTUTIBUS MAIORUM UT SIT OMNIBUS
DOCUMENTO P. P. D.

The four statues over the columns are of four national heros, and are due to the chisel of the Portuguese sculptor Victor Bastos, as well as the two recumbent figures representing the rivers Tagus and Douro. The statue nearest the center on the right (looking at the arch) is the Marquez de Pombal and the one at his left Nuno Alvares Pereira. The corresponding statues on the left side are of Dom Vasco da Gama and Viriatus.

A rapid sketch of the lives of these worthies may not be unacceptable to the reader.

MARQUIS OF POMBAL. Sebastião José de Carvalho, born in Lisbon in 1699, was educated for the magistrature and army, both of which he abandoned to enter the diplomatic service. Dom José I. on ascending the throne, named him Foreign minister in 1750 and Prime minister in 1755, which post he retained till the death of the king in 1777. He was created Count of Oeiras in 1758 and Marquis of Pombal in 1770. On the death of his nominal master, he fell into disgrace and was exiled to Pombal, where he died in 1782. He owes his celebrity to the energy he displayed in rebuilding the city after the great earthquake, to his administrative reforms, and to the protection he granted to trade and manufactures. But his expulsion of the Jesuits and the cruelty with which he persecuted the aristocracy, procured for him many enemies and brought about his ruin.

NUNO ALVARES PEREIRA, a famous warrior, who may be styled the Achilles of Portugal. Born near Certan in

1360, he exhibited in his youth a taste for chivalric deeds and the adventures of knighterrantry. He first distinguished himself in the wars of Dom Fernando against Castile, but his fame may be said to commence in 1383 when he espoused the cause of the *Mestre d'Aviz*, afterwards Dom João I. He was the terror of the Castilians and by his personal courage, joined to a military instinct, was always successful in his encounters with them. He vanquished them at Atoleiros in Alemtejo in 1384, and next year at the famous battle of Aljubarrota after which he was named Lord High Constable of the kingdom. He then marched into Castile with 6,000 men and defeated an army of 33,000 at Valverde near the Guadiana. On the termination of the war of Independence this Paladin of Portuguese history set out with the African expedition to Ceuta. Having accomplished so much for this world he now turned his attention to the next, and resolved on spending the remainder of his live in religious seclusion, for which purpose he entered the Convent of Carmo, founded by himself at Lisbon and here he breathed his last in 1431, with the reputation of a saint. His character may be said to be a combination of the valor of the warrior with the meekness of the monk.

Dom Vasco da Gama, the descoverer of the Indies, was born at Sines, a port of the Algarve, in 1469. When only 28 years of age he was appointed by king Manuel to command the expedition sent out to discover the Indies. On the 3.rd of July 1497, with a small fleet of 4 ships and 128 men, he set sail from Lisbon, and after encountering many perils, doubled the Cape of Good Hope and landed at Calicut on the Malabar coast on the 20.th of May 1498. He returned to Lisbon where he arrived on the 29.th of August 1499, having lost the third part of his crew.

In 1502 Vasco again returned to the Indies with a fleet of 16 ships and 3,000 soldiers, and having subdued the king of Calicut and made alliance with those of Cochim and Cananor, he reduced to vassalage the Scheik of Quilôa.

Dom Manuel rewarded these services by granting him the title of Dom, naming him Count of Vidigueira, and

Admiral of the Indian seas, with a pension of 1,000 cruzados (about £ 90).

He was afterwards treated with neglect, till Dom João III having succeeded to the throne, nominated him Vice Roy of India in 1524. He did not, however, long enjoy his new dignity, for having reached India in September, he expired on Christmas day of the same year.

In 1538 his remains were translated to Lisbon where they were received with the utmost pomp, and thence taken to the Carmelite Church at Vidigueira, where they now repose in a magnificent mausoleum erected to the memory of the renowned Discoverer of the Indies.

VIRIATUS, the Vercingetorix of Portugal. The Lusitanians, like the other peoples of the Peninsula, were writhing under the iron rule of Rome. They had been conquered, but not subdued, and although obliged to submit to the Roman sway, they still preserved an ardent love of their former independence, and only awaited some favorable opportunity to throw off the hated yoke.

Viriatus at one time a peaceful pastor, deprived of his flocks by the injustice of a Roman pretor, had fled to the mountains and become the chief of a band of robbers. The Lusitanians no longer able to bear the oppression of their conquerors raised the standard of revolt, but were defeated by Caius Vitellius. Viriatus now came to the front and was chosen leader by his country-men B. C. 149; and by his astute strategy turned the scale against the Romans. Everywhere their skilful leaders were outgeneraled. Vitellius was beaten near Tribola. 5,000 legionaries on their way to Tartasso were intercepted and cut to pieces. Caius Plancius was defeated in a pitched battle at Evora, and Viriatus entered triumphantly into Hispania citerior. Pretor after pretor was defeated. Caius Nigidius who had brought large reënforcements was completely routed near Viseu. Caius Lelius, at first successful, was joined by Fabius Emilianus, who had come from Rome with 15,000 infantry and 2,000 cavalry, but their united forces were vanquished at Ossuna by the valiant Lusitanian. Fabius obtained a temporary advantage at Beja, but was unable to stay the triumphant march of his adversaries, who penetrated as far as Granada and Murcia. Rome then sent two of her best generals to the Peninsula, Quintus Metellus against the Celtiberi and Servilianus against the Lusitanians: after two defeats the proud consul was compelled to make a treaty acknowledging the power of Viriatus, which treaty however was not ratified by the Senate who dispatched Scipio to the scene of action. This wily general discovered in two of Viriatus's ambassadors, two vile traitors, whom he bribed to assassinate their master, and thus ended the career of the brave Viriatus, B. C. 142, vanquished by treachery, but unsubdued by force.

> Quando rendida Italia ao forte Peno
> Nelle ha de ver hum Lusitano Marte:
> Quando de Cezaron, e de Concheno
> Veja glorioso Hespanha o estandarte.
> Quando, do Tejo rico ao Turia ameno,
> Se mostre victorioso em qualquer parte
> Hum novo Alcides, digo hum Viriato,
> E o Romano ardiloso á patria ingrato.
> *Ulyssipo,* cant. 14–7.

PRAÇA DE D. PEDRO.

COMMONLY CALLED THE ROCIO.

A fine open space oblong in shape, measuring 200^{yds} by 60, paved with small black and white stones in a peculiar undulating pattern which produces a singular and on the whole disagreeable effect on the eye. This square, in point of importance the second in Lisbon, is surrounded by trees and numerous seats. On the N. side is the theater of D. Maria II, and on the other three sides lofty regular houses four stories high, the res-de-chaussé being occupied as shops.

In the center is a monument in memory of D. Pedro IV, the «Soldier King». It consists of four parts: base, pedestal, column, and statue. The total height is 92 feet. At the corners of the base, which is square with the angles chamfered, are seated four figures representing Prudence, Justice, Fortitude and Moderation, between which are sixteen shields, four on each face, bearing the arms of the principal Portuguese cities. The pedestal is also square with chamfered angles, having on the E. side the date of D. Pedro's birth «*Nasceu em 12 de outubro de 1798*» on the W. the date of his death «*Falleceu em 14 de Setembro de 1834*», on the N. the date of his granting the constitutional charter «*Outorgou a carta constitucional em 29 de abril de 1826*» and on the S. the date of the inauguration of the monument «*A D. Pedro IV os portuguezes 1870*».

The lower third of the shaft of the column is encircled by a wreath of laurel and four figures of Fame in *basso-relievo* connected by festoons, which they hold in their hands. The rest of the column is fluted and surmounted by a corinthian capital with the arms of Portugal at each face. Standing erect on a hemisphere is a colossal bronze statue of his Majesty D. Pedro IV, of Portugal and first Emperor of Brazil, in the uniform of a general and crowned with laurel, holding in his right hand the constitutional charter, and his left hand resting on the hilt of his sword. This monument is the work of two Frenchmen, M. Gabriel Davioud, architect and M. Robert, sculptor.

PRAÇA DE LUIZ DE CAMÕES.

A moderate sized square near the *largo das duas igrejas*, at the top of the *Chiado*.

Encircled by neat iron railings and rows of evergreen trees, it has in the center a monument in honor of the great Portuguese poet Camões.

For many years influential men had been lamenting the apathy and ingratitude of their fellow country-men in allowing near three centuries to pass away without a mark of honor to the genius who had imparted so much luster to the literature of Portugal, but it was not till 1862 that their persistent efforts were so far crowned with success as to be able, by means of a public subscription, to commence the realization of their patriotic design. On the 28.th June of that year, the foundation stone was laid with great pomp and ceremony by his Majesty, Dom Luiz I, in presence of the whole court and an immense and brilliant assemblage. The inscription on the stone is as follows:

NOMINI IMMORTALI
ALOISII DE CAMOENS
LUSITANORUM POETARUM
PRINCIPI
HOC MONUMENTUM
VOLUNTARIIS ELARGITIONIBUS
FUIT ERECTUM
CUJUS LAPIDEM AUSPICALEM
IN TANTI OPERIS MOLITIONEM
LUDOVICUS I
PORTUGALIAE ET ALGARBIORUM REX
QUARTO KALENDAS MENSIS JULII
ANNO MDCCCLXII
PLAUDENTIBUS CIVIBUS UNIVERSIS
SOLEMNITER FIXIT

The monument was inaugurated in 1867. It was designed and modeled by the Portuguese sculptor Victor Bastos, and consists of a colossal bronze statue of Camões 13 feet in height, holding in one hand his famous poem the *Lusiadas* and the other resting on his sword to denote his twofold character of Warrior and Poet. This figure is supported by an octagonal pedestal surrounded by eight marble statues, 8 feet high, of the following literary worthies: Fernão Lopes, the earliest Portuguese historian; Pedro Nunes, cosmographer; Gomes Eannes de Azurara, João de Barros, and Fernão Lopes de Castanheda, historians of the Portuguese discoveries; Vasco Mousinho de Quevedo, Jeronymo Corte Real and Francisco de Menezes, epic poets who have celebrated the Lusitanian conquests.

The puny appearance of these eight subordinate figures in presence of the heroic dimensions of the principal statue detracts very much from the honor which it was intended to do them, by suggesting the idea that in comparison with the glorious poet they were mere Pigmies, and thus the splendor of their talents appears reduced to a feeble glimmer by the vivid brilliancy of a godlike genius.

A sketch of the life of this remarkable man may not be out of place.

Luiz de Camões, son of Simão Vaz de Camões and Anna de Sá de Macedo, was born in Lisbon in the year 1524. He evinced from an early age, an ardent love of letters, and great aptitude for poetry, and though he had the misfortune to lose his father by shipwreck, when still a youth, yet his mother, notwithstanding her straitened circumstances, sent him to the university which had been transferred to Coimbra by John III. Such were his talents that he completed his studies at the university before attaining his 20.th year. Returning to Lisbon his poetic genius and agreeable manners gained him admission to the best society, but his success at court was of short duration for he fell in love with D. Catharina de Athayde a lady of high station, and her relations not approving of the connection, intrigued against the poet and obtained his banishment to Santarem, and it was during his retirement there that he commenced his famous epic poem the *Lusiadas*. His ardent temperament ill brooking the prosaic and monotonous life of a provincial town, he entered the army and joined the expedition sent to the relief of Ceuta in Africa, and he lost his right eye in a naval engagement near the straits of Gibraltar. On his return to Lisbon seeing his services unrequited, he resolved to sail for India in 1553, bidding adieu to his native land in the words of Scipio Africanus's epitaph: «*Ingrata patria non possidebis ossa mea!*»

Camões distinguished himself by the valor he displayed, especially in the battles fought against the king of Chembé on the Malabar coast, but his poetic genius soon got him into trouble, for he published a satire entitled *Disparates da India*, censuring the vices of the governor, for which he was banished to China, where he passed three years. A quondam friend of the poet's having been appointed governor of India in 1558 his banishment ceased, and he was nominated administrator, at Macau, of the effects of the dead and absent. It was here that he wrote the greater part of the Lusiad, in a grotto overlooking the sea, whither he used to repair to commune with the muses, and which bears the poet's name to the present day. In 1561, having accumulated a small fortune, he sailed for Goa, but as ill luck would have it, the ship in which he embarked was wrecked at the bar of the river Mecon, the poet with difficulty saving his life and his precious manuscript, which like Caesar, he held above the waves with his right hand while with his left he swam to the shore. Nor did this disaster come single, for soon afterwards he again fell a victim to the malice of his enemies, and was falsely accused of malversation of the funds intrusted to him as administrator, cast into prison, and when, having proved his innocence, he was about to emerge from his dungeon, his body was seized for debt and only liberated at length through the influence of the Governor Count Redondo. He had now completed his great poem and was preparing to return to Lisbon, when his usual ill luck brought him into contact with Pedro Barreto, governor of Sofala, who by dint of false promises persuaded the poet to accompany him to Moçambique in Africa, at which place he was very ill treated and obliged to live in the greatest wretchedness and privation.

Some of his friends, passengers in the ship *Santa Fé* which chanced to call at Moçambique, took compassion on his wretched plight, paid his debts, and gave him a passage home to Lisbon, where he arrived in 1570 when an awful pest was raging. In 1572 he published the first edition of his poem, dedicated to king Sebastian, who rewarded him with a pension of 15$000 réis (3 *l.* 6 *s.* 8 *d.*) His hopes of better times were however soon destroyed, for Misfortune, having granted the poor poet a short respite such as the cat grants the mouse, pounced upon him again just when he thought he had escaped her clutches. He was reduced to such straits, that were it not for a faithful black servant Antonio, who went about begging in the public streets to support his master, he might have perished from sheer want. As it was, he lingered on in the midst of every privation, till 1580 when he died in the hospital, in abject proverty, neglected and forgotten by his former friends, and was buried as a pauper in the church attached to the convent of Sant'Anna. This church having been destroyed by the great earthquake and afterwards rebuilt, the precise spot where the poet had been interred was lost sight of, but in 1855 a committee of eminent men was appointed by government to examine the place and all documents which could throw any light upon the subject, and after taking up the floor the tomb was discovered. On being opened the bones of more than one skeleton were found, and as it was impossible to distinguish which belonged to the great poet, they were all transferred together to a coffin which was again deposited in the church. It is to be hoped that ere long a respectable covering may be provided for the remains of Portugal's greatest poet, and that more generosity may be shewn towards his mouldering bones than was accorded to him while living!

LARGO DE S. ROQUE.

A small square with garden near the church of the same name. In the center is an inelegant monument erected by the Italian residents of Lisbon to commemorate the marriage of his present majesty D. Luiz, with D. Maria Pia, daughter of Victor Emmanuel of Italy. It consists of a column surmounted by a disk, having on the W. side the following inscription:

PEL FAUSTO CONSORZIO
DELLE LORO MAESTÀ
IL RÉ DON LUIGI DI PORTUGALLO
E LA PRINCIPESSA MARIA PIA DI SAVOIA
A DI 6 OTTOBRE 1862
NUOVO PEGNO DI FRATELLANZA
FRA I DUE POPULI

———

GLI ITALIANI RESIDENTI IN LISBONNA ERESSERO

The inscription on the other face is a Portuguese translation of the above.

LARGO DO PELOURINHO.

A moderate-sized square having on the S. the arsenal, E. the new town-hall in course of erection and which will be, for its size, the finest building in Lisbon. On the N. and W. it is bounded by private property.

The pelourinho is a column cut out of a single stone into the form of three concentric parallel spirals, and surmounted by an armillary sphere. The etymology of this word is easily traced in ancient codices, in which it appears in the forms *piloria, pilorium,* and *pelorinum* It corresponds with the English pillory, and the *columna. Moenia* of the Romans and was introduced by them into the Gallias and copied by the Portuguese from the establishment of the monarchy. These columns are very common in Portuguese towns, and they are generally situated opposite the town-halls, or *casas da camara,* and are provided with four iron branches and a cage of iron, which served to expose criminals to public view and also for the infliction of capital punishment. These iron branches were removed in 1834 and the armillary sphere substituted in its place. The last execution at the pelourinho in Lisbon took place at the beginning of this century in the person of a young nobleman, who was hanged for fratricide. At present these columns only serve as emblems of municipal authority.

From this square start omnibuses to all parts of Lisbon.

LARGO DE BELEM.

A large open space surrounded by trees and seats, bounded on the N. by the Palace of Belem, on the E. by the Royal stables, on the S. by the Tagus and on the W. by private houses. At the river side is a marble quay with steps descending into the water.

This square is famous as having been the spot where the Duke of Aveiro, Marquis and Marchioness of Tavora, Count Atoguia along with several other members of the Portuguese aristocracy were executed in the most ignominious and cruel manner on the 13.th of Jan. 1759, having been falsely accused and found guilty of participation in the pseudo-conspiracy against the king's life ingeniously contrived by the Marquez de Pombal.

After the execution, the bodies were burned and their ashes cast into the Tagus. A little farther to the W. of this square near the *chafariz* or fountain stood the palace of the Duke of Aveiro. The site is now occupied by an eating-house and in the yard behind it, is a marble column, erected to commemorate the razing of the palace, the ground being afterwards strewn with salt in order that nothing whatever might grow on the hated soil, as appears from the following inscription on the column:

> Aqui foram as casas arrasadas e salgadas de José Mascaranhas exauthorado das honras de Duque de Aveiro e outras, e condemnado por sentença proferida na Suprema Junta da Inconfidencia em 12 de Janeiro de 1759, justicado como hum dos chefes do barbaro e execrando desacato que na noute de 3 de Setembro de 1758 se havia commettido contra a Real e Sagrada pessoa d'ElRei Nosso Senhor Dom José Primeiro. N'este terreno infame se não poderá edificar em tempo algum.

The other squares of more importance are:

PRAÇA DO PRINCIPE REAL, also called *Patriarchal Queimada,* being the site of the old Basilica which was reduced to ashes last century. In the center is a large basin of water with a copious fountain. It is surrounded by good houses and laid out as a garden with shady trees and numerous seats.

PRAÇA DA FIGUEIRA, the Covent Garden of Lisboa.

PRAÇA DOS ROMULARES, vulgarly called *Caes do Sodré,* near the river at the bottom of *Rua do Alecrim:* paved with small black and white stones in a neat pattern: it is much resorted to by seamen.

LARGO DE SÃO PAULO, also paved in mosaic with a fountain in the center and planted with trees.

LARGO DO RATO, in which is the Palace of the Marquis of Vianna.

LARGO DAS AMOREIRAS, which derives its names from being planted with mulberry trees and is situated near the *Mãe d'Agua* or great reservoir.

Campo de Sant'Anna, planted with trees: at the N. end is a small public garden and at the S. the bull circus, with private palaces on the W. side. Here is held every Tuesday the *Feira da Ladra* (see Markets).

Largo do Carmo, also planted with trees and having a fountain in the middle; on the E. side is the ruined church of *Carmo* and the *Club Lisbonense*.

Largo do Barão de Quintella, with a fine palm tree in the center. On the E. side is the Palace of Count Farrobo, now occupied by the *Gremio Litterario* or literary club.

Praça das Flores, with a garden in the middle.

Praça de Alegria, besides many others of minor importance.

6. CHURCHES AND CONVENTS.

The ecclesialogist will be sorely disappointed with the churches of Lisbon, especially if he have visited the Eternal city, gazed upon the wonderous fabrics of Spain or feasted his eyes on the stately minsters of England, France and Germany. With the single exception of the Jeronymite convent at Belem there are none which possess any feature in their exterior architecture to excite either admiration or wonder. There are some fair imitations of the italian style such as the *Estrella* and *Memoria*, the rest are common place buildings devoid of elegance, more attention evidently having been given to internal decoration than to external beauty.

Lisbon is divided into 35 parishes each with its parish church; besides which there are many temples devoted to public worship, which do not form part of the parochial system, such as the *Estrella, Santo Antonio, Loreto*, etc., and in addition to these, the churches attached to the convents, and numerous private chapels called *ermidas*, so that altogether there are not fewer than 200 places of worship in the capital.

The best time to see the churches is before nine o'clock in the morning, at which hour they are usually closed except on Sundays and Holidays when they remain open till 12 o'clock.

The following are the *dias santos* at present officially observed in Portugal, on which days all the public offices are closed, viz:—
1.st January — The Circumcision of our Lord.
6.th January — Kings.
2.nd February — The Purification.
25.th March — The Annunciation.
Holy Thursday — Moveable feast.
Good Friday — Moveable feast.
Ascension day — Moveable feast.
Corpus Christi — Moveable feast.
13.th June — Santo Antonio.
24.th June — St. John the Baptist.
29.th June — Sts. Peter and Paul.
25.th August — The Assumption.
8.th December — Nossa Senhora da Conceição, patroness of Portugal.
25.th December — Christmas day.

Visitors will find some difficulty in gaining admission to the churches after the hour for closing, as the sacristans are not always on the spot and moreover cannot understand how any person can wish to inspect a church through mere curiosity, being often shocked and disgusted at the irreverence, not to say profanity, of ill bred people who pay no respect to the feelings of those who differ from them in religious belief.

BASILICA DE SANTA MARIA MAIOR or *Sé de Lisboa*. — The Cathedral, situated half way up the SW. acclivity of the hill crowned by the castle of St. George.

Authorities are divided as to the epoch of the foundation of this church. Some assert that the original edifice was erected by the Emperor Constantine. Others say it was a Moorish mosque and that king Affonso Henriques on capturing the city had it purified and consecrated by our countryman Gilbert, the first bishop of Lisbon nominated by him. Others again affirm that the church was built *a fundamentis* by the aforesaid king soon after 1147. It is however not improbable that the primitive temple existed as the see of a bishop at the beginning of the IV. century. There is positive evidence that Lisbon was a bishopric long before the establishment of the Portuguese monarchy, for in the synodical council held at Toledo A.D. 589 the name of *Paulus* appears as *Olissiponensis ecclesiæ episcopus*, and in like councils held at the same place in 610, 633, 646, 666, 683, 688, the signature of a bishop of Lisbon again appears.

It is beyond doubt that when Affonso wrested the city from the Moors, it contained within its walls many Christians or Mossarabs, and their bishop is spoken of in history as having assisted at a parley during the siege. Add to this the fact that tradition has constantly pointed to this church as the see of a bishop from remote ages and that there is no other building or ruin in the city which furnishes the slightest indication of having served a similar purpose and is it not reasonable to conjecture that the foundation goes back to the primitive times of Christianity?

The fabric has suffered from so many catastrophes in the course of ages that it offers very little clue to its early history. Even in modern times it has undergone great alterations, for in 1344 an earthquake shook down the choir which was rebuilt by king Affonso IV. and destined by him for his last resting place. Again in 1356 an earthquake on St. Bartholomew's day so damaged it that it was taken down and rebuilt by Dom João I., who erected two magnificent tombs on the gospel side in which he placed the remains of Affonso IV. and his queen. On the king's tomb was a figure of Fame holding in her hand a trumpet taken from the Moors at the battle of Salado, where their cause was finally crushed and which was the only trophy his Majesty retained for himself.

HAEC TUBA, QUAM MAURIS ALPHONSUS NOMINE QUARTUS
 ABSTULIT, UT FAMAM PRIMUS IN ORBE FORET
 DUM RESONAT REGEM PARTUMQUE A REGE TRIUMPHUM
 ALPHONSUM AD FAMAM SURGERE, VOCE JUBET

The great earthquake in 1755 brought down the cupola, roof, and south clock tower, which was soon afterwards rebuilt by order of the energetic Pombal. The conflagration which succeeded the earthquake not only did immense damage to the fabric and rich decorations, but also utterly consumed the archives, causing the loss of many ancient documents, which could have thrown light on the origin of the temple.

In its present state the church is gloomy without being grand. To relieve the somber aspect of the interior the massive stone pillars have been plastered over and painted to imitate marble, and look quite out of harmony with the rest of the church. The nave and transept are much too narrow in proportion to their height and length.

Around the back of the choir is a corridor in which are a number of chapels dedicated to different saints, the most celebrated of which is that containing the ashes of the glorious martyr St. Vincent, whose body lay formerly in the choir and was reduced to a cinder by the fire which followed the earthquake of 1755.

In a small caged compartment in the yard are kept a couple of ravens, a practice which dates from 1173 in which year the remains of St. Vincent were deposited in the church. Until recently the *ciceroni* would inform visitors that the ravens thus exhibited were the identical birds which accompanied the ship that brought the saint's body from the cape which bears his name. Many strange stories having been invented by tourists and others in connection with this subject, it may perhaps be well to give the true version.

In the beginning of the fourth century, one of the most illustrious victims of the persecution of Diocletian was the martyr St. Vincent. After he had undergone the most frightful torments, his lifeless body was exposed by order of the pretor Dacian outside the walls of Valentia, but a miraculous interposition of Heaven guarded the remains of the martyr by the agency of a raven which defended them from the attacks of beasts and birds of prey. The fact is attested by St. Augustine and other contemporary writers. Under the dominion of the Moors in Spain the Christians of the province of Valentia suffered violent persecution under Abderamen, and to escape the cruelty of the Saracen they retired to a distant promontory at the extreme west of the peninsula, where pursued by the enemies of their faith and stopped by the

Atlantic ocean they hid the relics of St. Vincent in a secret and inaccessible spot. When Dom Affonso Henriques extended his kingdom beyond the Tagus, the remains of the martyr were brought by sea from the cape, thenceforward called St. Vincent's, to Lisbon, and deposited with great pomp in the Cathedral on the 15.th of September, 1173.

> «.... do Martyre Vicente
> O santissimo corpo venerado
> Do sacro promontorio conhecido
> A cidade Ulyssea foi trazido. »

In that age of faith the translation of the body was considered an event full of interest, worthy of lasting remembrance and likely to bring down upon the city abundant blessings from the God of martyrs. St. Vincent was therefore chosen patron of the metropolis. A legend says that a couple of ravens accompanied the vessel on its voyage, and to commemorate the arrival of the relics and the connection of the birds with the martyr's history, a ship and two ravens were adopted as the arms of the city, and a couple of the same birds were ordered to be perpetually kept at the Cathedral.

The baptismal font at which Santo Antonio received the first sacrament is here preserved and bears the following inscription:

> HIC SACRIS LUSTRATUS AQUIS ANTONIUS ORBEM
> LUCET BEAT. PADUAM CORPORE. MENTE POLUM.

In a neat mausoleum on the gospel side of the choir or *capella mór* are the remains of Dom Affonso IV:

> ALPHONSUS NOMINE QUARTUS
> ORDINE SEPTIMUS PORTUGALIAE REX
> OBIIT XXVIII MAII MCCCLVII
> PRIORI TUMULO TERRAEMOTU EVERSO
> HUC TRANSLATUS MDCCLXXXI

Opposite to this is the tomb of his queen Beatrice:

BEATRIX PORTUGALIAE REGINA
ALPHONSI QUARTI UXOR
OBIIT DIE XXX OCTOBRIS ANNO MCCCLXI
PRIORI TUMULO TERRAEMOTU EVERSO
HUC TRANSLATA MDCCLXXXI

As the above inscriptions shew, the original tombs erected by John I. were overthrown by the great earthquake.

In 1383 Dom Martinho, the then bishop of Lisbon, who was favorable to the claims of the Spanish party, was, while in the act of tolling the tocsin during the insurrection which gave the crown to the Master of Aviz, hurled headlong from the clock tower and his naked body dragged through the streets.

> E como Astinax, precipitado,
> Sem lhe valerem ordens, d'alta Torre
> A quem ordens, nem aras, nem respeito,
> Quem nu por ruas e em pedaços feito...

At the east end of the church is an ancient stone chair in which the earlier kings used to administer justice. The date 1629 is the year of its removal to its present position.

Gilbert, the first bishop appointed by Affonso Henriques to the see of Lisbon was an Englishman. He was consecrated in 1150, and introduced the breviary and missal of the Anglican church of Salisbury which continued in use down to 1536. Lisbon was elevated to an Archbishopric in 1394 and in 1716 to the dignity of a Patriarchate.

IGREJA E MOSTEIRO DE SANTA MARIA DE BELEM, commonly called *Convento dos Jeronymos* — Church and Convent of St. Jerome at Belem.

This venerable pile, in historical interest and architectural merit unrivaled by any other building in Lisbon, stands out in bold relief among the generally common-place structures of the capital.

When the immortal Vasco da Gama and his intrepid companions had prepared every thing ready for embarking on their grand voyage of discovery, being religious as well as brave, they passed the night previous to their departure in a small chapel near the shore, asking God's Blessing on their perilous undertaking and beseeching the patronage of the Blessed Virgin, Star of the Sea, to guide their barques in safety through the unknown wilderness of waters, to the land of their hopes and dreams.

On the 3.rd of July 1497 Vasco and his heroic party of 148 men embarked in 4 small ships which were lying in the Tagus just opposite the spot where St. Jerome's now stands. After two years of toil and danger the gallant crew returned, their ships laden with the richest treasures of the East, and having completed the greatest voyage of discovery that the world has ever known.

King Manuel, in thanksgiving to the Almighty for his protection and to perpetuate the memory of this glorious achievement, founded a church dedicated to St. Mary, devoting the first gold that came from India to this purpose, and sparing no expense to render the monument worthy of himself and of the deed it was to commemorate.

The foundation stone was laid by D. Manuel in 1500, the site chosen being that of the little chapel where Vasco spent the vigil of his embarkation. The first architect engaged on the work was an Italian named Boutaca, who was succeeded by the Portuguese architect João de Castilho in 1517. The building was not completed till the reign of D. Manuel's successor king John III. Over the entrance door of the Monastery was the following inscription said to have been written by the famous André de Rezende:

VASTA MOLE SACRUM DIVINAE IN LITORE MATRI,
REX POSUIT REGUM MAXIMUS EMMANUEL,
AUXIT OPUS HAERES REGNI ET PIETATIS, UTERQUE
STRUCTURA CERTANT, RELIGIONE PARES.

At the time when the church was built it was nearer to the sea than it is at present, the waters having receded on account of sand-banks having been deposited on this side of the river. The tower of Belem built at about the same time, was at first completely surrounded by the sea, but is now joined to the land by an isthmus. Indeed so near to the shore was St. Jerome's that it was built upon piles of pine wood which were driven into the sandy foundation.

The church consists of nave, transept (having a massive wing at each end to act as abutments), and chancel or sanctuary, the latter being of a later period and quite out of harmony with the rest. The nave is entered by two porticos, one at the west end, the other and more richly ornamented one on the south side facing the Tagus. At the W. end which formerly was the principal front, there were two elegant cupolas, one of which has been recently restored. The whole exterior is of limestone called *lioz*, at first white, but by the action of time assuming a rich golden hue. The principal object which strikes the eye of the artist is the magnificent portico, on which the architect seems to have concentrated all his skill. It consists of a high semicircular arch sculptured in *mezzo relievo*. At each side of the portico is a huge buttress reaching up to the roof, so profusely ornamented with statues, niches and grotesque figures that its character is almost lost sight of. The two small medallions over the doors are the effigies of king Manuel and his queen. Over the central shaft is the Infante D. Henrique, dressed in armor, this wise prince having contributed so greatly to the advancement of science and navigation. On either side and at the same level are the twelve apostles placed in niches. On the crown of the large arch is an image of *Nossa Senhora dos Reis*, to whose invocation the church is dedicated, and over it a splendid canopy reaching to the roof: on the top of all is a statue of the archangel St. Michael. Flanking the portico are two large windows with circular heads elaborately carved and ornamented in the *Manueline* style, and farther to the left 4 smaller windows of like design. The cupola at the southwest angle has been recently restored, but is not in keeping with the ancient work. The original cupola was very different and served as a clock tower. After its destruction the present clock with its *azulejo* face was stuck into the window opening which it now occupies to the disfigurement of the general aspect.

The west portico is also deserving of close examination: it has been much damaged by the great earthquake and by that still more destructive agent, man. It is now in course of restoration. On each side are four angels and over the door two cherubim supporting the arms of Portugal. The central group represents the birth of our Lord, the one to the left the Annunciation, and to the right, the Adoration of the Magi. On either side of the door is a statue in a kneeling posture with an attendant. These are D. Manuel and his queen D. Maria. On the pedestal which supports the founder may be observed his distinctive emblem the armillary sphere, and on that of the queen are the arms of Portugal and Castile. The windows at the sides, beautiful specimens of the *Manueline* style, had been walled up and plastered, but are now being uncovered.

On entering the church by the south door the first objects that fix the attention are the 4 pillars supporting the vaulted roof of the nave which is 256 feet long by 60 wide and about 66 feet high. The pillars are of white marble richly carved in the flamboyant style and ornamented with grotesque figures of animals, birds, and foliage. The shafts of the pillars are divided longitudinally into eight parts by as many slender columns in *mezzo relievo,* and again by three bands which encircle them at different heights into four parts, in the second of which are eight niches intended for statues. In the wall opposite the entrance are seven doors surmounted by niches and canopies; these are the confessionals. Turning to the right we come to the transept supported by two massive pillars, each representing a cluster of 4 pillars like those of the nave. The center arch of the nave is horse-shoe-shaped, approaching to the Moorish style of architecture, and the side arches over the ailes are pointed. The best view of these arches is obtained from the choir. Against the large pillars and facing each other, are two pulpits resting on marble pedestals. The pulpits themselves tho' prettily designed, are merely painted wood. The vaulted roof of the transept is admirably constructed and the numerous ribs, radiating from the centers and intersecting each other give an appearance of lightness to what is in reality a stupendous mass of stone. Indeed so slender are the supports compared with the immense weight they have to bear that when the work was finished the architect was obliged to abscond to screen himself from the severe censures that were passed upon him by the critics of the day, who confidently predicted that the roof would fall in as soon as the scaffolding should be taken away and so far did these surmises influence the mind of the king that he ordered the woodwork to be removed by the hands of condemned felons with the promise that if they escaped the presumed danger, they should be set at liberty. The scaffolding was taken down, the building stood and the architect emerged from his hiding place. The criminals built themselves houses with the timber they had removed and became respectable members of society. The winds and storms of near four centuries have buffeted this venerable pile; it has been more than once severely shaken by earthquakes, and yet notwithstanding its sandy foundation it still stands proudly erect in attestation of the piety of its founder and in commemoration of Vasco da Gama's brilliant discoveries.

The floor is flagged with dark grey, pink, and white marble so as to produce a geometrical design. At the extremities of the transept are lofty pointed arches richly carved, which open into the rectangular wings which serve as abutments. In the chapel on the epistle side, now occupied by a wooden *praesepium* of exceedingly bad taste, are the tombs of the children of king John III. In the center is a cenotaph, supposed to contain the ashes of the unfortunate D. Sebastian who died in Africa. There are grave doubts as to this matter, for the remains were brought from Africa and deposited here by the Spanish Philips who were anxious to put an end to the popular superstition of the *Sebastianistas*, who would not believe in the death of the king and who firmly believed that he would return in triumph to take possession of the throne; and so fixed became this idea in their minds that they could not be brought to relinquish their hopes, and even at the present day there are persons in other respects quite sane, who tenaciously adhere to this old superstition of their forefathers. The skepticism of the Portuguese as to the authenticity of the remains here deposited, is expressed in the inscription which runs thus:

CONDITUR HOC TUMULUS, SI VERA EST FAMA, SEBASTUS,
   QUEM TULIT IN LYBICIS MORS PROPERATA PLAGIS
     NEC DICAS FALLI REGEM QUI VIVERE CREDIT,
    PRO LEGE EXTINCTO MORS QUASI VITA FUIT.

In this tomb rests, if report be true, Sebastian,
Whom a premature death snatched away from Afric's plains.
Say not they err who believe him still to live
For dying in defense of right, his death was life.

The chapel opposite is appropriated to the Blessed Sacrament. Behind the four large paintings are the tombs of several royal princes, as also that of the Cardinal king Henrique, who succeeded D. Sebastian.

The high pointed arch which gives access to the sanctuary is elaborately carved and has on either side a curiously sculptured pulpit of no ordinary merit. At the sides of the arch are four small chapels ornamented with Corinthian columns and carved woodwork covered with gold. The two on the gospel side are dedicated to Nossa Senhora de Belem and to St. Jerome; the image of the latter is of porcelain and was a present from one of the Popes. On the epistle side are the chapels of St. Paula and of Nossa Senhora do Carmo.

The sanctuary, separated from the transept by a balustrade of white marble, was built at a later period and plainly marks the influence of Italian art at that time. It was completed in 1551 by the architect of the convent Diogo de Torralva. Around its walls are 16 Ionic columns supporting an entablature and cornice on which rest an equal number of smaller columns of the Corinthian order. The vaulted roof is of red and green marble in panels, producing an unpleasant effect and resembling inverted tombs. At the east end are five paintings representing the passion of our Lord. The high altar was entirely covered with silver, but a great portion of it has been pilfered.

The sacrarium still retains its silver covering. The *mezzo-relievo* on the *porta coeli* represents the adoration of the Magi and was chiseled by a female-artist Josepha d'Obidos. The inscription on it: «O principe D. Pedro que Deus guarde, deu este sacrario a este real Mosteiro de Belem no anno 1675», shews that it was a present from D. Pedro II.

In the recesses at the sides of the sanctuary are 4 white marble sarcophagi, each supported by two elephants of grey Cintra marble. The one nearest the altar on the gospel side contains the remains of D. Manuel the Great. The inscription on it is remarkable and runs thus:

LITTORE AB OCCIDUO QUI PRIMI AD LIMINA SOLIS
EXTENDIT CULTUM NOTITIAMQUE DEI,
TOT REGES DOMITI CUI SUBMISERE THIARAS,
CONDITUR HOC TUMULO MAXIMUS EMMANUEL.

The other tomb on the same side is of D. Maria, daughter of Ferdinand the Catholic, and wife of king Manuel. Facing the founder's tomb is the sarcophagus of his successor king John III. with the following inscription:

PACE DOMI BELLOQUE FORIS MODERAMINI MIRO
AUXIT JOANNES TERTIUS IMPERIUM
DIVINA EXCOLUIT REGNO IMPORTAVIT ATHENAS
HEIC TANDEM SITUS EST REX PATRIAEQUE PARENS.

The adjoining tomb contains the ashes of his wife D. Catharina of Austria, daughter of Philip I. of Spain.

The remains of the unhappy Affonso VI. who after many years of incarceration, expired in the Palace at Cintra, were placed in a small chamber behind the high altar, but have been removed to the Royal mausoleum in St. Vincent's.

Leaving the sanctuary and turning to the right we come to a door that leads to the sacristy, a spacious room with a vaulted roof supported by a pillar in the center. Around its walls are tiers of drawers containing some rich specimens of antique vestments embroidered in gold. An almost incredible quantity of gold and silver plate of great artistic merit used to be kept here, but D. Pedro during the civil war removed it to the mint *for greater security* where most of it was transformed into current coin of the realm. Some few objects escaped such as the Remonstrance made of the first gold brought by Vasco da Gama from Quilôa as a tribute, and which at present occupies a place in the king's museum in the Palace of Ajuda.

The paintings on the panels over the drawers represent various episodes in the life of St. Jerome.

The choir at the W. end is supported by three arches: The larger one was brought down by the earthquake of 1755, but has been rebuilt. The entrance to the choir is from the upper cloister of the *Casa pia*.

The stalls, about 80 in number, are exquisitely carved with delicate arabesque tracery. Over them are 14 paintings of inferior merit representing the apostles, St. Jerome, and St. Augustine. The large organ on the epistle side was never finished, but the one on the gospel side was built in 1781 and was noted for the rich melodious sweetness of its tones: it has been allowed to fall into complete ruin, many of the smaller pipes' having been stolen and sold for the value of the metal they contained. The small organ which at present does duty was transferred from the palace of Ajuda.

Leaving the church by the W. door, and turning to the right we come to the entrance to the Convent, now occupied as an asylum for poor orphans, called the *Casa pia*. Overhead is the following inscription:

EXTITIT ALCYDES GENTIS DOMINATOR IBERAE
FRENAVIT CAESAR GALLICA REGNA JUGO REX PIUS EMANUEL
VICTOR SUPEREMINET INGENS SOLIS
AD USQUE ORTUM QUI TULIT IMPERIUM.

On the right is a bust of Hercules under which is written:

HOC LAPIDE ANTE FORES DEPICTA
ALCYDIS IMAGO REGALIS FIRMUM DENOTAT AEDIS OPUS.

The bust on the other side is of Julius Caesar:

CAESARIS INCISO PRAESENS IN MARMORE VULTUS
INDUAT AUGUSTAE LIMINA FAUSTA DOMUS.

On application to the porter permission to visit the cloisters is readily obtained. With the exception of Alcobaça and Batalha, they are the finest in Portugal. They are built in the form of a square, each side measuring 180 feet and consisting of a piazza with 6 beautifully carved arches or windows. The court in the center is embellished with fountains and statues, and tastefully laid out as a garden. The cloister is two storied, having a second piazza less elaborately carved, built on the top of the principal one.

The refectory, at one corner of the cloister, is a long narrow room lined with *azulejo*, and has on its walls a complete series of likenesses of the kings of Portugal, works of little value.

The dormitory and cells occupied the long wing built on a piazza running W. from the front of the church. This portion is now being restored and is intended to accommodate the orphan girls of the *Casa pia*. The boys who are already installed in other parts of the building number about 350.

The monastery was occupied by the monks of St. Jerome, to whose order D. Manuel presented the church and house, at the same time changing the name of the locality to Belem, which means Bethlehem.

Santo Templo
Que nas praias do mar está assentado,
Que o nome tem da terra para exemplo
Donde Deus foi em carne ao mundo dado.
CAMÕES, c. 4, t. 87.

S. ROQUE, St. Roch, at the top of the *rua larga de S. Roque*.

This church, as well as the adjoining buildings, was formerly in the hands of the Jesuits, to whom it was given in 1533 by king John III. St. Francis Borgia, third general of the society, is said to have preached from one of its pulpits, and his cloak or black gown darned, probably by himself, with white thread, is still preserved here as a relic.

The church contains some good paintings by Bento Coelho, Gaspar Dias, Avellar and Vieira Lusitano. The life of St. Francis Xavier by Diogo Reinoso in the sacristy is worthy of attention. But the great object of attraction to a stranger is the far-famed chapel of St. John the Baptist. It is the richest work of art in Portugal, and probably has no rival out of Rome.

It is needless to ask who was the founder of this chapel. One glance at the costly materials of this miracle of art is enough to satisfy the beholder that it must have been king John V., who by the discovery of the gold mines and brilliants of the Brazils was enabled to vie in magnificence and ostentation with Louis XIV.

It is related that on the feast of St. Ignatius Loyola in 1718, king John V. attended the church of St. Roch and observing that all the chapels, except that of St. John the Baptist, were adorned with a profusion of candles and flowers, he inquired the reason, and being informed that while every other chapel had a brotherhood or guild to provide for its embellishment, St. John's had none. 'Then', said the monarch, 'since the chapel is dedicated to the saint of my name, henceforward it shall be under my care'.

A few days afterwards, he sent the dimensions of the place to his ambassador at Rome, with orders for him to have a chapel made of the richest material and finest workmanship, regardless of expense.

Vanvitelli was the architect chosen to make the design, and a model having been made and sent to Lisbon for the king's approval, he remitted fabulous sums to carry out the work. The chapel, having been completed, was erected in St. Peter's and Pope Benedict XIV. consecrated it, and was the first to officiate on its altar, and he received for this favor, as a present from the king, a solid gold chalice set with brilliants worth £ 10,000.

Having been taken to pieces and packed in cases it was sent to Lisbon accompanied by the celebrated sculptor Alessandro Giusti, who was engaged to superintend the fitting of it up. The poor king, however, did not live to see the result of his generous solicitude, being on his death-bed when the chapel arrived, and it was not till the 13.th of January 1751 that the inauguration took place in the presence of his successor Joseph I. Fortunately it escaped destruction by the great earthquake which happened four years later, and which shook to the ground the façade of St. Roch's.

The chapel is the first adjoining the transept on the gospel side, and is concealed from view by massive curtains. The exterior of the arch is of coral, with the royal arms of Portugal on the key-stone supported by two alabaster angels. The interior of the arch is of alabaster. A balustrade of verd-antique divides the chapel from the body of the church, the entrance to it being by two side doors of bronze delicately worked and with jambs and lintels of verd-antique. The walls are of black marble, jald-antique and alabaster, with pilasters of jald-antique. Over the doors are two mosaics set in porphyry frames. The cornice is of jald-antique relieved with bronze. The vaulted roof is of the same stone and verd-antique ornamented with jasper. Over the altar is a large mosaic with porphyry frame representing the baptism of Christ in the Jordan. The Eternal Father appears in a cloud attended by a group of angels; underneath, the Dove descends over the head of Christ who is standing in the Jordan near the Baptist, ministered to by angels and regarded by the two Marys. The artist has been singularly felicitous in delineating the feet, faintly discernible under the water. The mosaic on the gospel side represents the descent of the Holy Ghost on the Apostles and the B. Virgin; that opposite is the Annunciation. These mosaics are so well executed that many incredulous visitors refuse to believe they are other than oil paintings until they are convinced by running their hands over the chilly surface.

On either side of the principal mosaics are four columns of lapis-lazzuli with bronze capitals and bases of alabaster and jald-antique. The wall at the back of the columns is of alabaster and amethysts: the architrave is of jald and the figures of angels of jasper. The space between the altar and mosaic is filled with coral, amethysts, and lapis-lazzuli. The step on which the cross and candlesticks are placed is of coral with gilded bronze: and the whole of the altar of jasper, with a frontal of lapis-lazzuli and amethysts. The altar steps are porphyry and the suppedaneum of Egyptian granite. The floor is marble mosaic inlaid with porphyry imitating a richly flowered carpet, with a globe in the center.

The mosaics were made in the celebrated Vatican manufactory. They are copies of three *chefs-d'œuvre* by renowned artists. The Baptism is a copy of the painting by Michael Angelo. The Annunciation by Guido Reni, and the descent of the Holy Ghost by Raphael Sanzio da Urbino. The originals were copied for the purpose of being imitated in mosaic, by Agostino Massuci.

From the roof hang 3 large lamps of silver and gilded bronze, and at the sides of the chapel are two massive candelabra of gilded silver 8 feet in height, profusely adorned with statues of apostles, evangelists and other saints and figures in *basso relievo*. Four men are required to move one of them: they cost £ 16,000.

Many other valuables, which are only used on the feast of St. John, are kept in the Treasury of the chapel in three rooms near the sanctuary. Amongst these may be mentioned a frontal of silver and lapis-lazzuli having on each side of it, a silver angel 3 feet in height: it cost upwards of £ 5,000. Four reliquaries weighing 600 lbs. A carpet of gold thread valued at £ 7,000. The total cost of the chapel with its accessories is calculated at £ 200,000.

Under the pulpit near the chapel of St. John is the tomb of an English knight, Sir Francis Trejean. The history of this gentleman is curious and is related in a latin memoir printed shortly after his death. Having been seen at court by queen Elizabeth, she fell deeply in love with him, but finding him indifferent to her advances, her love turned to hatred, and she pursued him with the bitterest resentment. His adherence to the creed of his forefathers furnished her with a pretext, and the knight, after an imprisonment of twenty eight years, escaped to the continent and died at Lisbon with the reputation of a saint.

The inscription on his tomb is as follows:—

Aqui está em pé o corpo de Dom Francisco Trejean. Fidalgo Inglez mui illustre o qual depois de confiscados feus Estados e grandes trabalhos padecidos em 28 annos de prisão pela defesa da fé Catholica em Inglaterra em perseguição da Rainha Izabel no anno de 1608 a 29 de Dezembro morreu nesta cidade de Lisboa com grande fama de santidade. Havendo 17 annos que estava sepultado nesta Igreja de S. Roque da Companhia de I. H. S. no anno de 1626 aos 29 de Abril se achou seu corpo inteiro e incorrupto e foi collocado neste logar pelos Inglefes Catholicos residentes nesta Cidade aos 29 de Abril de 1696.

COLLEGIO INGLEZ, commonly called *Os Inglesinhos*. The English college situated on the rising ground to the W. of the *Passeio de S. Pedro de Alcantara*.

This establishment owes its existence to the persecuting enactments of former times. Excluded in their fatherland from the seats of learning raised by the piety of their ancestors, the British Catholics were for centuries forced to educate their youth in foreign climes. When reared, if vested with the sacerdotal character, they were stealthily introduced to the scene of their future labors, where, branded by the law as felons and traitors they were compelled to skulk for the rest of their lives in hourly dread of the informer and pursuivant, often terminating their career in prison, or on the scaffold. These things have happily passed away. Splendid Catholic establishments, both lay and ecclesiastical are now to be met with in every part of Great Britain: yet as the seminary at Lisbon still answers the end of its original institution, it has been thought proper to maintain it in its present state. It is supported almost entirely from England and spending its income in this country, amply repays the protection that has been afforded to it by all the governments that have ruled in Portugal.

The date of its foundation is 1628: the building is of irregular architecture, having been erected at different periods. It possesses a cabinet of natural philosophy, a library and an astronomical observatory. The view from the latter is one of the finest in the city, commanding the river, and its bar, and the Atlantic Ocean to the W., Palmella and the Arrabida mountains to the S., the famous lines of Torres Vedras to the N., together with a magnificent panorama of the circumjacent town. The college usually numbers about thirty students, and many eminent divines, well known to English Catholics, have received here their training. The Very Revd Dr Baines is President, the 21.st since the foundation of the college. In the neat church attached to the college and dedicated to Saints Peter and Paul, mass may be heard every week-day at 7 and on Sundays and Holidays at 10.

IGREJA DO CORPO SANTO in the *Largo do Corpo Santo*, a short distance to the W. of Black Horse Square.

This church and convent were founded by, and still continue in the possession of the Irish Dominicans.

During the epoch of persecution which followed the overthrow of the church in England, the catholics were subjected to most stringent penal laws, and every measure was taken to extinguish their faith. Not being able to celebrate their religious rites in public and still less to educate priests, they were obliged to have recourse to the expedient of establishing seminaries in foreign countries.

In 1629 the Irish Dominicans, having heard of the success which had attended a similiar institution of the Jesuits, resolved to establish at LISBON a college for the education of youths intended for the Irish priesthood, and with this view communicated with Frey Domingos do Rosario, an Irishman formerly called Dominic O'Daly, one of their order who happened to be at the court of Madrid. Frey Domingos obtained a letter of recommendation from Philip IV. to the governors of Portugal, this country being at that time under the sway of Spain. Leave having been granted by the Portuguese authorities, the Dominicans rented some miserable houses in the locality called *Sitio da Cotovia* where they remained one year, removing then to an equally wretched habitation in the *Calçada do Combro*, where they stayed until 1633 when a Portuguese nobleman, D. Luiz de Castro do Rio, Lord of Barbacena, made them a present of a theater formerly devoted to comedy, attached to his house situated in a street called *Fangas da Farinha,* on the site now occupied by the *Boa Hora* or court-house. The poor friars converted the boxes of the theater into cells in which they lived, and the stage was fitted up as a chapel.

Better times were, however, in store for them, for D. João IV., who had succeeded to the throne of Portugal on the expulsion of the Spaniards, died in 1656 and the regency was conferred on his widowed queen, Dona Luiza de Guzman, with whom Frey Domingos do Rosario, the first rector of the Irish college, was a great favorite. By her influence and munificence the Dominicans were enabled to purchase the site in CORPO SANTO and build a church and convent not unworthy of their merits. This edifice however was shaken to the ground by the great earthquake of 1755, and the present building has since been erected through the generous contributions of catholics in Ireland, assisted by their charitable Portuguese sympathizers.

On the abrogation of the penal laws in the United Kingdom, this college became of less importance and when the monastic orders were prohibited in Portugal, tho' the measure did not extend to themselves, yet they were placed in a very unfavorable position which induced them to dispose of the greater part of their property in Lisbon, and migrate to Tallaght near Dublin, where they purchased land and built a new house. Many illustrious men afterwards promoted to the miter in Ireland and elsewhere have been educated in this convent, not to mention a number of others who by their pious zeal and disinterestedness have merited well of their country and proved an honor to the college in which they received their training.

The Rev.[d] Thomas Smith is the present Rector, and mass is still celebrated in the church every morning.

CONVENTO DE SANTA BRIGIDA. — Brigittine convent near *S. Bento,* half a mile W. of the general post-office. — This convent was until a few years ago occupied by a Community of English nuns, successors of those who at the beginning of the XV. century possessed Sion House, the seat of the Dukes of Northumberland.

Henry V. of England in 1415 founded a convent near his palace at Richmond, and gave it the name of Sion. It was inhabited by 60 nuns, all of noble blood, of the order of St. Bridget. On the suppression of the monasteries by Henry VIII. the nuns fled to Dermond in Flanders, where they took shelter in a convent belonging to the same order. On the accession of queen Mary, Sion was restored to its rightful owners who however enjoyed a very short possession being again driven out by queen Elizabeth. They returned to Flanders whence they migrated to Zurich-zee, in Zealand, to a small convent given to them in 1563 by the duchess of Parma then governess of Flanders, and here they remained till 1568 when finding the place extremely unhealthy and having lost many of their number by death they removed to Mishagan where they were not permitted to dwell more than a few years when their convent was sacked, the poor ladies escaping to Antwerp, and thence to Mechlin were they bought a house. Three years later the city was taken by the prince of Orange and the persecuted community again fled, first to Antwerp and then to Rouen where they arrived in 1580. Their wanderings were however not yet at an end, for Rouen was besieged and taken in 1595 by Henry the IV. and the poor nuns, now reduced in number to 15, took refuge on board a ship by which they were conveyed to Lisbon, where they arrived on the 20.th of May of the same year. Philip II. of Spain, then reigning over Portugal, gave them a pension of 2,5000 réis per diem, which was continued by his successor D. João IV. Misfortune seemed still to cling to the community for in 1650 their convent was reduced to ashes. Having been rebuilt by the generosity of the king and other friends it was completely destroyed by the great earthquake of 1755. They managed again to build a Sion House of their own, where, though driven out for a while by the Peninsular army, they still remained, keeping the original keys of Sion House in token of their continued right to the property. They were visited by a former duke of Northumberland to whom they exhibited these keys.

Over the entrance door was a beautifully carved stone pedestal surmounted by an iron cross which the nuns brought away from Sion House and carried with them through all their peregrinations.

The following history of Sion House from Spelman's work on sacrilege may prove interesting:

«Sion House, with the exception of Shaftesbury, was the most influential nunnery in England. This site was, on the dissolution, kept in the king's hands, and Catharine Howard was confined here for nearly three months, leaving this prison for the scaffold; Henry's body lay here in state; and here it was that Father Peto's prophecy was fulfilled, by the dogs licking his blood. Edward VI. granted the place to the duke of Somerset, who perished on the scaffold: then it reverted to the crown. Next it came to John Dudley, duke of Northumberland; and here it was that Lady Jane Grey was persuaded to accept the crown. In 1557 the nuns, having all this time lived together in community, were recalled and put in possession of the house, and Sir Francis Englefield rebuilt two sides of the monastery. On the re-dissolution by queen Elizabeth, it came again to the crown, and was by James I. granted to Henry Percy, earl of Northumberland, 'one of the most unfortunate, says Augier, of his race'. On a groundless suspicion of having been concerned in the Gunpowder Plot, he was stripped of all his offices, adjudged to pay a fine of £ 30,000, and sentenced to imprisonment in the Tower for life. In 1613 he offered Sion House in lieu of the fine, but it was not accepted. In 1619, after fifteen years' imprisonment, he was set at liberty on payng £ 11,000. In the time of his son, it was used as a prison for the children of king Charles; and his grandson Joseline, eleventh earl, died without issue male. Lady Elizabeth Percy was heiress of this, and of five other of the oldest baronies in England: and before she was sixteen, she had been thrice a wife and twice a widow. She was married at the age of thirteen, to Henry Cavendish, earl of Ogle, only son and heir of the Newcastle family; he died a few months afterwards. Thomas Thyne, of Longleat, Esq. of the family of church-property notoriety, and count Königsmark, were rivals for her hand. She was married to the former; but before the marriage could be consummated, he was assassinated by three ruffians hired by Konigsmark. She was married three months afterwards to Charles the Proud, duke of Somerset. The character of this man is well known. The roads used to be cleared when he rode out; he made his daughters stand while he slept in the afternoon; and left one of them £ 20,000 less than the others for sitting down at that time when tired. He had many children, but one son only survived him. In this son the male line failed again, Sir Hugh Smithson succeeding.»

IGREJA E MOSTEIRO DE S. VICENTE, commonly called *S. Vicente de Fóra.*

In the earlier periods of Portuguese history, in those *dark ages* when men were strongly imbued with love for their country, with eagerness for the propagation of christianity and the acquisition of glory, it was customary to perpetuate the memory of great achievements, by the founding of churches and monasteries. These institutions have proved of the utmost benefit to mankind, for not only did they tend to keep burning the lamp of faith, but also were the retreats of learning and genius, and without them letters, arts and sciences would inevitably have perished in the turmoil of war.

S. Vicente de Fóra was founded by Affonso Henriques to commemorate the taking of Lisbon. The siege having lasted five months, the city was taken by assault on the 21.st of October 1147. Soon after this event the august conqueror laid the first stone of this temple, giving thanks to God for the victory He had vouchsafed to the champions of the Cross. The spot selected was that where the king had erected a temporary chapel, hospital and cemetery. The new church was dedicated to the Blessed Virgin Mary and St. Vincent, but has always been known under the latter name, especially since Affonso Henriques declared St. Vincent patron of Lisbon. The people added the term *de fóra* because it was situated *outside* the walls of the city. The royal founder made a donation of the church to the canons regular of St. Augustine. The first fabric lasted only four centuries, and when the usurper Philip II. of Spain came here in 1581, he found it in a state of ruin and to ingratiate himself with the people of Lisbon, he resolved to rebuild it *a fundamentis*. On demolishing the old edifice the foundation stone was discovered bearing the following inscription:

> HOC TEMPLUM AEDIFICAVIT
> REX PORTUGALIAE ALFHONSUS I IN HONOREM
> BEATAE MARIAE VIRGINIS
> ET SANCTI VICENTI MARTYRIS XI CALEND.
> DECEMBRIS SUB ERA MCLXXXV.

Another stone was found at the same time with a Latin inscription dedicated to the emperor Vespasian.

The new church was commenced on the 25.th December 1582 and completed in 1627, after 45 years of uninterrupted labor. The principal façade, looking W. has three porticos, two small towers and seven statues, six of them representing saints of the order of St. Augustine, one being of St. Anthony, who at first entered this order; the seventh is St. Sebastian who is placed here in compensation for having taken down a church dedicated to him in order to use the stone for this building.

The interior corresponds to the exterior in magnificence. It has the form of a Latin cross, the high altar being in the center, surmounted by a baldachin, the work of the celebrate sculptor Machado de Castro. The statues on it are St. Vincent, St. Sebastian, St. Augustine and St. Theotonio. The floor is flagged with squares of marble, the vaulted roof is of blue and white marble, in fact the whole interior is ornamented with marble of various hues. The organ is at the back of the altar, and on the gospel side of the sanctuary is a small door that leads to the mausoleum of the Patriarchs of Lisbon, a long narrow apartment draped with black cloth. Near the collateral chapel on the same side is the tomb of Nuno Alvares Pereira, the famous Lord High Constable of the kingdom, and progenitor of the reigning family of Bragança. His remains were by D. Maria I. transferred to this place from the ruined convent of the Carmelites, which he had founded and in which his body had lain unmolested from the time of his death. The original monument of alabaster was destroyed by the earthquake; the present one is a fac-simile in wood.

The last resting place of the dynasty of Bragança is at the back of the sanctuary, the entrance to it is from the cloister. All the kings of this house are here, except Affonso VI. and Mary I. In the center are two marble cenotaphs, on one is the coffin of D. Pedro IV. who is to remain there permanently, the other is the temporary resting place of the last sovereign and is now therefore occupied by D. Pedro V. The other coffins are placed in order, each having a sliver plate with the name, date of birth and death of its mouldering tenant, a sad and significant epilogue to all the grandiose titles in which they gloried when living.

The large and noble convent attached to the church is now the residence of the Cardinal Patriarch. It contains the ecclesiastical archives and the office in which the business connected with the church is transacted. The extensive grounds reach nearly to the Graça, containing vases, statues, etc. Part of its walls are the ancient ones with which D. Fernand I. surrounded Lisbon in 1372.

CONVENTO DE S. BENTO, about half a mile to the W. of the post office. This extinct convent of the Benedictines was built by that order as is shewn by the inscription over the entrance to the cloister which ran thus:

CUI TANTUM SACRATUR OPUS CUI NOBILE TEMPLUM
HAEC BENE BIS DICTO DEDICAT ORDO NIGER
QUI PARAT EXPENSAS MONACHUM DITISSIMA PULCHRUM
PAUPERIES PROPRIIS SUMPTIBUS FECIT OPUS

The building was completed in 1598 and is one of the few that escaped injury by the great earthquake. Architecturally however there is nothing to note except its vast size and the solidity of its construction.

The convent at present accommodates the House of Peers, House of Deputies, and *Torre do Tombo,* or national archives.

The *Camara dos Pares* or House of Peers occupies the W. side of the building and has been recently erected at great expense. The façade is of Portuguese marble in a simple but effective style. From the nature of the ground, however, it has the appearance of being buried in a hole. The entrance to it is by the principal door on the E. front. The chamber is in the form of a semi-elliptical amphitheater, having two galleries running round its circumference, the lower one for the Royal Family, Diplomatic Corps, and members of the Peers' families: the upper one for the general public. In front of the galleries are 22 Corinthian columns of white marble with composition capitals. Over the president's chair is a full length portrait of his Majesty Dom Luiz, by José Rodrigues, over which is a crown supported by two angels carved in wood by Portuguese artists. In front of the tribune are two bronze medallions with the effigies of the former presidents, the duke of Palmella and Cardinal Guilherme Patriarch of Lisbon. Over the two entrance doors are Carrara marble allegorical groups by M. Calmels. The ceiling is painted to imitate stucco work, and the room is lighted from the top on the same principal as the English House of Commons. An elegant corridor runs round the outside of the chamber in which are the busts of its former presidents, dukes of Terceira, and Palmella, Cardinal Guilherme and count Lavradio who was for many years Portuguese minister at the court of St. James's.

The peers are nominated by the king without any limit as to number, and there are at present about 140. They are either hereditary or life peerages; in the former case certain conditions are attached to the succession, such as the possession of a certain amount of property and the taking of a degree at the university of Coimbra.

The peerage does not carry with it any title of nobility, but as many members of the aristocracy have been created peers, there are some members of the upper house who have titles, whilst others are simply styled *Dignos Pares do Reino.*

The *Camara dos Deputados* or House of Deputies is situated on the north side of St. Bento. It is a large chamber in the form of a parallelogram surrounded by tribunes for the public, for ladies, Diplomatic Corps and members' friends. The house has no pretensions whatever to elegance. Nor are its acoustic qualities superior to its decorations, so that honorable members have to vociferate with stentorian voices to make themselves heard in all parts of the room.

The number of deputies is 107 elected by ballot by the 107 circles or electoral districts into which the kingdom is divided.

The franchise is limited to householders who have an income of 200$000 (£ 45) per annum. The qualification for a deputy is the possession of an income amounting to 400$000 (£ 90).

Torre do Tombo, or archives of the nation, is open from 9 A. M. to 2 P. M. every day except Sundays and Holidays. Permission to visit it is politely accorded on application to the *Guarda Mór,* who is generally on the spot.

Tombo is a law term meaning the examination and description of the tenures of all kinds of property, boundries of lands and the registration of the deeds by which they are held. The word was afterwards applied in a figurative sense so as to denote the *depôt* in which all public and private papers of great value are registered or lodged. The original copies of the laws, royal grants, ratifications of treaties and state papers of every kind are here deposited. Prior to 1755 these archives were lodged in a building in the castle of St. George, which being destroyed by the terrific earthquake of that year, caused their removal to this convent, though not without the loss of many valuable documents.

The oldest deeds here deposited are of the IX. century, but the great bulk of them may be said to begin with the establishment of the Portuguese monarchy. To the tourist the following may prove of interest:

Treaty of peace made the 29.th December 1652 between Oliver Cromwell and D. João IV., with secret article and ratification exchanged in 1655. — Signed by the Protector and bearing the great seal representing the English parliament.

Commercial Treaty between Portugal and Siam, signed and sealed by the first and second kings of the latter country, with English translation.

Commercial Treaty between Portugal and Japan, written on gold speckled paper and enclosed in a beautiful Japan case.

Diploma of the order of the Garter conferred on D. João VI. by George IV., 1823.

Treaty of Peace (1841) between Turkey and Portugal.

Treaty of the marriage of Dom Pedro V. with Dona Estephania of Hohenzollern-Sigmaringen, a fine specimen of modern caligraphy.

Treaty of the marriage of Dona Antonia with Leopold of Sigmarigen.

Small book of Gospels used in the administration of oaths by the Portuguese Inquisition. Vellum MS. ill.

Several MS. Offices of the Blessed Virgin. Ill. vellum (n.os 16, 17 and 18).

Office of the B. V. beautifully ill., which belonged to Philippa of Lancaster.

Reforma de D. Manuel ou *Livros de leitura nova*, 58 folio vols. MS. vellum. Contains a copy of all documents existing in the archives prior to his reign. There are in it several authentic specimens of Portuguese illumination at the beginning of the xvi. century.

Hydrographic Atlas, made at Goa in 1571 by Fernão Vaz Dourado. MS. folio, vellum.

The Bible, with commentaries by Frei Nicolau de Lira, MS. 2 vols. fol., ill. initials and numerous pictures.

Mestre das Sentenças, Magister Sententiarum. MS. 1 vol. ill. 1594.

Livro da nobreza e perfeição dos reis christãos e nobres linhagens dos reinos e senhorios de Portugal. MS. 1 vol. fol., vellum, xvi. century.

Livro das fortalezas que são situadas no extremo de Portugal e Castella. MS. fol., vel., end of xv. and beginning of xvi. centuries. Contains views and plans of the frontier fortresses.

But by far the most valuable work in an artistic point of view is the famous Jeronymite Bible, which as a specimen of illumination is without a rival in Portugal. It consists of the Bible with annotations by Nicolau de Lira, in 7 large folio volumes MS. vellum and profusely illuminated on almost every page. It was executed in Italy in 1495-97 by order of D. Manuel the Great, and presented by that monarch in 1517 to the convent of St. Jerome at Belem. The beautiful paintings and heraldic emblems are attributed by some to Julio Romano, whilst others refer them to Peter Perugino.

Junot when he invaded Portugal in 1808 took the Bible from the convent and carried it to France, but after the establishment of the general peace, Louis the XVIII. in 1815 purchased it from Junot's widow for 80,000 francs and returned it to its rightful owners, from whom it was agains wrested on the abolition of the monastic orders, and is at present the property of the state.

BASILICA DO CORAÇÃO DE JESUS,

commonly called the *Estrella*, situated on the high ground which forms that part of Lisbon named Buenos Ayres, or the

English quarter, on account of so many English families residing there. From the elevation of the ground and the height of the dome it is one of the most conspicuous objects in the city.

The church owes its origin to a vow made by D. Maria I. for the birth of an heir to the throne, in fulfilment of which it was built, being commenced in 1779 and completed in 1790. The principal architect was Matheus Vicente, the same who built St. Antonio da Sé.

The architecture is in imitation of the famous convent at Mafra, especially the dome and the two towers.

The four colossal figures on the peristyle supported by 4 columns, which adorns the west front, represent Faith, Adoration, Liberality and Gratitude, qualities so conspicuous in the Royal foundress. The images in the niches are St. Thereza, St. Elias and St. Mary Magdalen de Pazzi. The two statues in the vestibule are Our Blessed Lady and St. Joseph. In the sanctuary are two seraphim beautifully executed, and on the epistle side is the Mausoleum of D. Maria I., whose mortal remains were translated from Rio de Janeiro where she died in 1816. Most of the sculpture in the interior is by the celebrated Machado de Castro, author of the equestrian statue of Joseph I. The figures on the outside are by his disciples. The façade which looks towards the enclosure of the convent is considered superior to the west one in point of architecture. The fine view from the cupola will amply repay the trouble of ascending it. The towers contain a ring of eleven bells: the largest weighs upwards of 4 tons.

The church is said to have cost 16 million *cruzados* or about £ 1.400,000.

NOSSA SENHORA DA GRAÇA on the second of the chain of hills which commences with that crowned by St. George's Castle.

The Hermits of St. Augustine came to Lisbon soon after its capture from the Moors by Affonso Henriques, and established themselves at the foot of the hill on which is the church of *Nossa Senhora do Monte*, in a small hermitage with the invocation of St. Gens, first Bishop of Lisbon, who used to preach to the people from that spot. Thence they removed to the top of the hill taking with them the stone chair of St. Gens, which may still be seen in the church of Nossa Senhora do Monte. Finding this situation too bleak and distant from the city they determined in 1271 to remove to the site at present occupied by the church and convent of the Graça, this hill being at that time called Almofala. The church was at first dedicated to St. Augustine and known by that name till 1362, when some fishermen at Cascaes on drawing in their nets found a beautiful image of Our Lady carved in cypress wood which they looked upon as miraculous and deposited in the church of St. Augustine. This image having acquired great fame under the title of *Nossa Senhora da Graça,* the church became widely known by this name, and its invocation was changed by the popular wish. The original fabric having suffered much by the lapse of time was pulled down and the foundation of a new one laid on the 9.th March 1556 by Frey Luiz de Montoya, which however lasted but two centuries, being almost completely destroyed by the great earthquake of 1755.

The present building, erected soon after the earthquake, is uninteresting in an architectural point of view. It is cruciform in shape, having a single nave and transept: the interior decorations are mostly imitations of stone and marble. The painting on the ceiling of the choir or *capella mór*, representing the apparition of Christ to St. Augustine, and the four Evangelists, are by the celebrated Portuguese artist Pedro Alexandrino, as well as the ten pictures representing episodes in the life of St. Augustine.

Among the relics preserved at this church, is an arm of St. Vincent, which being enclosed in a wooden reliquary, escaped the rapacity of the French.

At the S. end of the transept is an image of Our Saviour, sinking under the weight of the cross. This image is well known throughout Portugal, under the name of *Nosso Senhor dos Passos,* and is visited by immense numbers of pilgrims every Friday, in commemoration of our Lord's passion and death, more especially in Lent, when the image is carried in procession to the church of St. Roque, and on the following day brought back accompanied by the various brotherhoods and crowds of people.

The crystal coffer which serves to contain the sacred Host is an object of great merit. It is the work of a celebrated Venitian lapidary, and was made at Venice at the and of the xv. century, of the finest crystal that could be procured. It measures 4 $^1/_2$ palms in length by 3 in width and is 2 $^1/_4$ palms high. Round it are 28 spiral columns, with silver capitals having between them crystal panels of elegant design.

The lapidary brought the coffer to Lisbon and offered it to D. Manuel for 50,000 cruzados, thinking that monarch, on account of the enormous riches he derived from the recently discovered Indies, the most likely customer to purchase so costly an object. D. Manuel however declined to buy it, on which its owner took it to Madrid for the purpose of seeing whether the Emperor Charles V. would become its purchaser. He found the price too high so that the disappointed lapidary had to return with his treasure and after offering it to the king of England and several other princes, and not finding any one in Europe willing to pay so high a figure, he took it to the East and eventually sold it to the king of Ormuz for 37,500 cruzados. It afterwards became the property of a Moorish prince, who in return for some favor, made a present of it to Dom Frey Aleyxo de Menezes, archbishop of Goa, who sent it to Lisbon to be used as a Sacrarium in the church of Nossa Senhora da Graça. Strange to say though the whole of the building, except the belfry, was shaken down by the great earthquake, this fragile object escaped uninjured. The following inscription was under the sacrarium:

MANNA ABSCONDITO FIDEI ARCANO
PENITISSIMO TREMENDO ADORANDO HUMANO
SALUTIS PIGNORI ASSERVANDO
FRATER ALEXIUS DE MENESES HUJUS
CONVENTUS HUMILIS ALUMNUS ET PRIOR,
ARCHIEPISCOPUS BRACHARENSIS, HISPANIAE
ET INDIA PORTUGALIAE PROREX, SUPREMI
CONSILII PROSES
ANNO D. MDCXV.

Within the crystal coffer was a second one of silver and tortoise and within this a third of gold, one palm in length, presented by Dona Philippa de Vilhena, widow of the Vice-Roy of India, Mathias d'Albuquerque. The whole was supported by two silver angels, eleven palms in height. This valuable coffer which if we reckon compound interest has cost the enormous sum of over £ 2,500.000,000, is at present covered with dust and dirt! The famous Affonso d'Albuquerque, the greatest captain of his age, who conquered and reduced to feudatories all the kings of India, is interred in the *casa do capitulo,* without any monument!!

In the sacristy is the mausoleum of Mendes Foyos, secretary of state of Dom Pedro II.

IGREJA E CONVENTO DE JESUS. — The convent of Jesus belonged to the third order of Franciscans, and dates from the 30.th of July 1615. Its church suffered greatly from the violent earthquake of 1755, so much so that early next year the roof fell in, and the whole building became a heap of ruins. The present edifice was erected shortly afterwards from the designs of the architect Joaquim de Oliveira. The monastic orders having been abolished in Portugal, the church is now used as the parish church of *Nossa Senhora das Mercês.* In the corridor which leads from the transept to the sacristy, is a marble mausoleum containing the remains of Antonio de Sousa de Macedo. The walls of the corridor are lined with *azulejo* bearing Latin and Portuguese verses taken from the works of this celebrated writer.

The principal attraction is the library, a noble room 200 feet by 60, well lighted and ventilated. The books are methodically arranged on shelves surmounted by busts, painted to imitate marble, of the most distinguished philosophers, poets, historians, etc., of different nations and ages. The painting on the ceiling represents the Sciences and Virtues presided by Religion. There is a well classified and complete catalogue, and the room is open to the public as a reading room from 10 A. M. to 3 P. M. every day except Sundays and Holidays. The number of volumes is upwards of 40,000, principally on religious subjects. There are a few MSS., amongst which deserve particular notice a Missal richly illuminated by Estevão Gonçalves, canon of Vizeu cathedral. The work was commenced in 1610 and finished soon after 1621. The several feasts are illustrated by exquisitely painted miniatures, and every page is surrounded by a brilliant border. Also a curious hydrographic atlas made shortly after Vasco da Gama's discoveries, as appears from the author's own statement: «*Lazaro Luis fes este liuro de todo o uniuerço e foi feito na era de mil he quinhentos he sesẽta he tres anos*». 1563 of the era of Caesar corresponds with 1525 of the present calendar.

In an adjoining room is the library of the Academy of Sciences; it is not open to the public, but strangers are readily admitted. The library consists principally of the transactions and reports of the chief scientific societies of Europe. The Portuguese Royal Academy of Sciences, *Academia Real das Sciencias*, was established through the exertions of the duque de Latões, a nobleman of great talent who having been banished from Portugal traveled over the whole of Europe during 22 years. On his return to Lisbon in 1778 he undertook the organizing of this society under the patronage of Dona Maria I. to succeed the *Academia Real de Historia* which had died out. Its members are either Honorary, Effective, Free or Corresponding. His Majesty Dom Fernando is president. Its secretary Illmo Sr. José Maria Latino Coelho, ex-minister of Marine, one of the first orators in Portugal and a distinguished writer, is also an accomplished linguist, being familiar with all the languages of Europe, as well as an excellent classical scholar. The society have published many volumes under the title of *Memorias,* containing learned papers on a variety of useful subjects, thus acting up to their motto: «*Nisi utile est quod facimus stulta est gloria*». The meetings of the Society are held in the *Convento de Jesus.*

IGREJA E CONVENTO DO CARMO. — In the square of the same name, near the Chiado.

These ruins are most interesting to lovers of Gothic architecture. The church was founded by the progenitor of the reigning dynasty, Dom Nuno Alvares Pereira, Lord High Constable of Portugal, in fulfilment of a vow for the successful issue of the glorious battle of Aljubarrota. It was commenced in 1389 and completed in 1422, the whole expense being borne by its noble founder. Documents are in existence which shew that the workmen employed in its construction received 13 réis = $3/4^d$ per diem, at that time equivalent to $2 \frac{1}{2}$ alqueires of wheat, about a bushel.

The church was dedicated to *Nossa Senhora do Livramento* and presented to the monks of the Carmelite order, and when Nuno Alvares Pereira, the greatest warrior of his age and the savior of his country, determined to retire from the world and abandon the turmoil of war for the peaceful repose of monastic life, he selected this convent for his abode, and having taken the habit of a Carmelite friar, passed the rest of his days in religious seclusion. He died here on the 12.th of May 1431, and his remains were interred in the church. It was customary for the inhabitants of Lisbon to repair to his tomb on each anniversary, and strewing flowers on it, sing the following verses:

> El gran Condestable
> Nuno Alvares Pereira
> Difendio Portugale
> Con sua bandera
> E con seu pendone
> No me lo digades none
> Que santo es el Conde.

The remains of the Constable were by D. Maria I. translated to the church of *S. Vicente de Fóra*, where they now lie.

The great earthquake and subsequent fire destroyed the major part of the building. The lofty arch of the sanctuary still remains standing, as well as the ribs of several other: the Gothic porch also withstood the shock. The nave was of an immense size, measuring 160 feet in length. The splendid tower is worthy of examination, and permission to gain access to it may be easily obtained by applying to the Commander of the Municipal Cavalry, which occupy the adjoining convert.

The church at present serves for the Museum of the Archaeological Society, and contains many interesting specimens arranged in what was the sanctuary and collateral chapels. Admittance to the public on Sundays and Thursdays from 11 to 3. There is no catalogue published of this collection nor are the objects numbered or placed in any order: it is therefore impossible to describe them in a guide book. The two colossal statues to the right on entering the ruined nave were intended to form a part of the monument erected in honor of D. Pedro IV. The five female figures so conspicuous at the east end of the chancel are part of a monument which was to have been raised to the memory of D. Maria I. These statues were cut at Rome by the Portuguese sculptor Aguiar: the center one represents Her Majesty and the four others Asia, Africa, America and Europe. The iron railing with bronze ornaments is from the convent at Mafra. In the side chapels are plaster models of different works of art, the most notable being that of the exquisitely chaste pulpit of *Santa Cruz* at Coimbra. Also diminutive models of the acropolis, circus maximus and other classical buildings. At the far end of the first chapel is a model of the tomb of the founder of the church, the original in alabaster having been destroyed by the great earthquake. The upright figure in armor represents Nuno Alvares Pereira as Lord High Constable, and the recumbent figure represents him in the habit of a Carmelite friar. In a glass case are a few specimens of flint implements and weapons, as also Roman relics found at Troy, an ancient Roman settlement near Setubal.

IGREJA DA REAL CASA DE SANTO ANTONIO, commonly called *Santo Antonio da Sé,* from its proximity to the Cathedral, in front of which it is built.

King John II. left a legacy to build a church in honor of St. Anthony on the site of the house in which this saint was born in 1195. This bequest was carried out by D. Manuel who erected a splendid church, completed about 1509, but which was destroyed by the great earthquake and succeeding fire, nothing escaping except the image of the saint. The present church was erected in 1787 by the architect who built the church of the *Estrella,* Matheus Vicente. It is of moderate size with handsome fittings, and contains a number of paintings representing the life of the saint. The full-length portrait of St. Anthony is much venerated by the people, who evince their devotion by kissing the feet as they pass. St. Anthony is perhaps the most favorite Saint in Portugal, where he is invariably styled *of Lisbon* tho' in other countries he is better known as *of Padua* where he died. A brief sketch of his life may not be out of place.

Santo Antonio was born in 1195. His parents were of noble descent and distinguished piety. He was first educated in the Sé where he learned the elements of christian doctrine, Latin, and music. At the age of 15 he entered the order of the canons regular of St. Augustine who occupied S. Vicente de Fóra, whence he was transferred to one of their houses at Coimbra. Influenced by the arrival of the relics of five Franciscan martyrs, brought from Morocco by the Infante Dom Pedro, he resolved upon entering that order in 1221. Burning with zeal to become a martyr he visited Morocco, but being attacked by a severe illness he was unable to continue his labors as a missionary and resolved to return to Portugal. Stress of weather, however, drove him to Sicily, and he availed himself of this circumstance to visit the founder of his order at Assis. He became afterwards a professor at Padua and acquired great fame for his eloquence and numerous miracles. He devoted the rest of his life to missionary labors in France and Italy, and died at Padua in 1231 where his remains (except the head which is preserved in a gold casket in his church at Lisbon) are interred in the magnificent church built in his honor. Eleven months after his death, on the 30.th May 1232, he was canonized by Gregory IX, on which day it is said that all the bells in Lisbon rang forth merrily of their own accord and that the inhabitants *bon gré mal gré* were irresistibly lead to dance in the streets:

> En toda la ciudad fiestas se hacian
> Sonando por si mismas las campanas
> Que muy solemnemente se tañian
> Haciendo consonancias mas que humanas

> Muy grande admiracion todos tenian
> Por ver que eram las causas soberanas,
> Pues no habia en todo el pueblo quien supiese
> Porque tal gozo y fiesta se hiciese.

St. Anthony of Lisbon is generally represented as a young man habited as a monk with the infant Saviour in his arms. This refers to an episode in his life when a missionary in France. Having been sheltered by one of the faithful, the master of the house on passing his guest's door to retire to rest, peeped through a chink and saw the saint with the infant Jesus in his arms, and St. Anthony, aware that he had been observed, made his host promise not to reveal what he had seen until after his death:

> O grande Antonio, claro por natureza,
> Famoso em letras, raro em santidade,
> Gloria maior da gloria Portugueza,
> Insigne filho da Ulysséa cidade!
> Tal de tua doutrina he a grandeza,
> Tal de tua virtude a claridade,
> Que, penetrando as aguas, faz que acuda,
> Para te ouvir a geração mais muda.
>   *Ulyssipo*, cant. 14–34.

NOSSA SENHORA DA PENHA DE FRANÇA, situated on the most northerly of the chain of hills forming the east of Lisbon.—A carver in wood named Antonio Simões, who formed one of the unfortunate expedition to Africa in which D. Sebastião lost his life, being in great danger at the battle of Alcaçar-Quibir, made a vow that if he escaped he would make nine images of our Lady under different titles.

Having returned safe to Lisbon, he set about fulfiling his vow and having dedicated eight of the images he was at a loss what name to give the ninth. At the suggestion of a Jesuit, he chose Nossa Senhora da Penha de França, after a celebrated image of this title near Salamanca in Spain. The image was at first lodged in a small chapel in Rua do Ouro, now Nossa Senhora da Victoria, and afterwards removed to a church built by Simões on the summit of the hill where the present one now stands. In 1599 while an awful plague was raging in Lisbon, as many as 600 persons dying per diem, the Spanish troops headed by their Captain-General, Count Portalegre, went in procession to the *ermida*, and the Senate of Lisbon registered a vow to build a new church and make a yearly procession to it from Santo Antonio da Sé, if the pestilence ceased. The plague ended and the senate erected a large church, finished in 1625. This building was thrown down by the great earthquake, more than 300 worshipers perishing beneath its walls, but was rebuilt in three years. The image is the ancient one, which was dug out of the ruins somewhat mutilated. The paintings are said to be the first works of the fertile Pedro Alexandrino. Near the sacristy is a room, *dos Milagres*, in which is a crocodile called by the Lisbonites, *o lagarto da Penha de França*. The legend runs that a pilgrim having toiled up the hill, fell asleep near the church, and was attacked by an immense lizard, but that the Virgin went to the assistance of the exhausted traveler, giving him supernatural strenght and courage to overcome the monster. Outside the sanctuary this legend is represented in *azulejo*. Visitors to the church, who do not see the crocodile, are joked by the Portuguese who say «foi á Penha e não viu o lagarto», which is like saying «to go to Rome and not see the Pope».

This Senhora is held in especial veneration by sailors, who frequently go thither in procession to testify their gratitude for the succor they believe themselves to have received, when in imminent danger, through the intercession of our Blessed Lady. On these occasions they carry part of the sails or masts of their vessel to the church, which is dedicated to Nossa Senhora, and there redeem them for wax candles to be burnt before her shrine, or other appropriate emblems of their respect and gratitude. They also suspend small waxen figures or pictures which they intend to serve as public acknowledgments of cures they believe to have been wrought by the Almighty through the intercession of his glorified servants. Nor can this practice be deemed altogether superstitious by those who believe in the interference of Providence in the affairs of this world, and that the prayer of the just man availeth much and that gratitude is a duth inculcated by Religion.

NOSSA SENHORA DOS MARTYRES, in the *Chiado*. The foundation of this church is the most ancient in the capital. It was here that the English and other crusaders who died in the assault on Lisbon when it was captured from the Moors by Affonso Henriques in 1147, received christian burial, the ground having been consecrated for that purpose by D. João Peculiar, archbishop of Braga, by order of the king. The crusaders erected a small chapel to mark the spot where their companions lay, and placed in it an image of our Lady, which they had brought with them from England. As those who perished in the cause of a Christian king against the hated Sarasen were accounted martyrs, the chapel acquired the name of *Nossa Senhora dos Martyres*. Shortly afterwards, D. Affonso built a handsome church on this site, to perpetuate the memory of those who had rendered him such signal service, and mark the burial-place of his foreign allies. The original fabric was altered and restored in 1598, 1710 and 1750, but the great earthquake reduced it to a heap of ruins. The present building is quite modern, and consists of a single nave with chapels at each side, the paintings in which, are by the celebrated Pedro Alexandrino.

It was in the baptistry of this church that the first Moor received baptism after the taking of the city. The original font was preserved down to the time of the great earthquake and bore the following inscription:

> Eſta he a pia em que ſe baptiſou o primeiro
> Chriſtão n'eſta cidade quando no anno de
> 1147 ſe tomou aos Mouros.

Pedro Julio, afterwards elevated to the papal chair under the name of John XXI., was at one time prior of this parish.

NOSSA SENHORA DA ENCARNAÇÃO, at the top of the *Chiado*, opposite *Nossa Senhora do Loreto*. Owing to the proximity of these two churches, the open space between them is called *Largo das duas Igrejas*.

The original church was built by Dona Elvira de Vilhena, Countess of Pontevel, being commenced in 1698, and completed in 1708. The noble foundress never once entered the church during her life time, lest she should be guilty of vainglory on beholding the result of her munificence; only after death did she cross its threshold for the first and last time, her remains being interred within its sacred precincts.

The great earthquake and subsequent fire destroyed nearly the whole of the old fabric with its precious works of art; the present edifice is of modern construction, being finished within the last few years.

Exteriorly there is nothing to claim admiration. The principal façade is much too high in proportion to its width. It has three doors, the center one flanked by Corinthian columns and pilasters supporting an entablature ornamented with angels, over which is a *basso relievo* representing the Annunciation. The two side images are *Nossa Senhora do Loreto* and *Santa Catharina*. The interior of the church is neatly decorated and contains some fine specimens of Portuguese marble as well as imitations of the same in stucco. Besides the *capella mór* or sanctuary there are 8 chapels, 4 on each side of the nave, ornamented with Corinthian columns of artificial marble and oil paintings of no great merit. On the gospel side are the chapels of the *Blessed Sacrament, Nossa Senhora da Conceição, Santa Anna* and *Santo Antonio*. On the opposite side *Nossa Senhora da Piedade, S. Miguel, Nossa Senhora do Carmo*, and *S. Sebastião*.

Under the choir is a small baptistry lined with marbles of different colors which are scarcely visible, the place being so dark.

The chapel of the Blessed Sacrament is most beautiful. It is entirely lined with rich blue, pink and white marble exquisitely sculptured, and is closed by a pair of elegant gilt bronze gates. The roof is octagonal and embellished with symbols of the New Testament in *alto relievo*. In the center of it, are the Lamb, the Book the seven seals and lamps, surrounded by the heads of a man, of an ox, of a lion and of an eagle, symbolic of the four evangelists. On the narrow panels which form the corners of the chapel are symbols of the Old Testament, the ark with two cherubim, the vase of manna, the tables of the law, a burning heart, a sword and staff on a cushion with a royal crown over it, and the column of fire which guided the Israelites. The painting of the Last Supper between the columns over the altar is not equal in merit to the rest of the work.

The *capella mór* is also lined with fine marbles, as well as the high altar. It has four Brazilwood doors delicately carved. The remains of the foundress rest on the epistle side, and on a black marble tablet edged with white and surmounted by a coronet may be read the following inscription:

CHRISTO SACRUM
OSSA D. ELVIRAE MARIAE
VILLENIAE
COMITIS PONTEVELENSIS
HEIC QUIESCUNT
PRIMO MONUMENTO QUOD
IPSA SIBI PARAVERAT
AEDEQUE QUAM SUA
PECUNIA STRUXERAT
TERRAEMOTU DIRUTIS
NOVUM IN HAC NOVA
AEDE BENEMERENTI
POSUERE

On the gospel side lies her husband Count Pontevel:

CHRISTO SACRUM
NONII CUGNIAE ATAIDII
COMITIS PONTEVELENSIS
PRIMO MONUMENTO
UNA CUM AEDE DIRUTO
OSSA HEIC
REPOSTA SUNT
REQUIESCAT IN PACE
ANNO CIƆIƆCCLXXIIII

The painting on the ceiling representing the Annunciation is attributed to Pedro Alexandrino.

The sacristy contains nothing of interest.

NOSSA SENHORA DO LORETO at the top of the *Chiado*, directly facing the church of the Incarnation.

The Loretto owes its origin to the Italian residents of Lisbon, which city in the XVI. century was one of the great emporiums of commerce in Europe.

Many foreign merchants, especially Italians, took up their residence in it, and wishing to have a church of their own, they subscribed the necessary funds, and having obtained the consent of the Pope and Portuguese authorities, built the original Loretto in which mass was first celebrated on the 8.th of January 1522, in the reign of D. João III. The primitive fabric was reduced to ashes on the 29.th of March 1651, and rebuilt by the Italians in the course of 25 years. The great earthquake of 1755 damaged it to a great extent and the subsequent fire consumed the whole of the valuable works of art which adorned the interior. The principal front looks S. and at the sides of the entrance are the statues of SS. Peter and Paul. In the center at the top placed in a niche is the conventional statue of our Lady of Loretto. The church consists of a single nave with 5 chapels on the epistle side and 4 on the gospel side; the walls are decorated with fine polished marbles. In niches over the chapels are the twelve apostles and the Evangelists St. Luke and St. Mark painted by Cyrillo Wolkmar Machado in imitation of the statues destroyed by the fire. Seen from the entrance, they produce a very good effect and present the appearance of solidity. The painting on the ceiling representing Nossa Senhora do Loreto with angels in the act of transporting her house, is by Pedro Alexandrino. For the benefit of late-risers it may be well to mention that the last mass on Sundays and Holidays is at 1 o'clock P. M.

S. DOMINGOS.—St. Dominic's, near the east end of the theater of Dona Maria II: the most spacious church in the capital. It was founded in 1249 by D. Affonso III., attached to the convent of the Dominicans, the first stone of which had been laid by his predecessor D. Sancho II. in 1241, and was subsequently enlarged by D. Manuel. At the time of the establishment of this church an arm of the sea ran up close to its gates and on several occasions it suffered inundation. The original building was completely destroyed by the great earthquake and was afterwards rebuilt. After the extinction of the monastic orders, the convent was converted into dwelling houses, and the church incorporated into the parochial system as *Santa Justa e Rufina*. It is ornamented by eight columns of red marble at the altars in the transept, and by forty six half columns in the nave. The sanctuary contains four colossal pillars of blue marble with some bold carving by the sculptor Padua.

At the entrance to the sacristy is the tomb of the famous ascetic writer Fr. Luiz de Granada, with the following inscription:

> Frater Ludovicus Granatenſis ex Praedicatorum familia cujus doctrinae maiora extant miracula Gregorii decimi tertii Pontificis Maximi oraculo quam ſi caecis aspectum mortuis vitam impetrasset. Pontificia dignitate ſaepius recuſata clarior mira in Deum pietate et in pauperes miſericordia, inſignumque librorum ac concionum varietate toto orbe illuſtrato aetatis ſuae anno 84 Olyſſipone moritur magno Reipublicae Chriſtianae deſiderio pridie Kalend. Januarii anno 1589.

S. JOSÉ. — In the *Rua de S. José*, which runs parallel to the *Passeio Publico* at a short distance to the E. thereof.

The church of St. Joseph was built in 1509 by the societies or guilds of Carpenters and Masons. The great earthquake seriously damaged the principal façade, which was pulled down and rebuilt by the said societies in 1757 as may be learned from the inscriptions at each side of the entrance, which run thus:

On the gospel side:

> In. A. O. (*In anathema oblivionis.*)
> Por cauſa do lamentavel terramoto do primeiro de Novembro de 1755 ſe arruinou a frontaria d'eſta igreja. A irmandade do Sñr. S. Joſeph, como padroeira da meſma a mandou levantar no eſtado em que ſe acha, no anno de 1767.
>
> Ultra non commovebitur. Liv. 1. Par: 17. 9.

Under this inscription are sculptured the mason's implements with these words:

> Hic eſt Faber. Joſeph faber lapidarius.

The inscription on the other side says:

> Na era de 1537 fe principiou a confraria do Sñr. São Jofeph que foi a primeira d'efte Reino, e na era de 1547 a 7 de abril fe tirou S. Jofeph de Santa Jufta para efta cafa.
> Poffederunt filii Jofeph. Jofue. 16. 4.

Under which are sculptured joiners tools: on the saw is written:

> Jofeph faber lignarius.

The year 1537 of the era of Caesar, corresponds with 1499 of the present calendar.

CONVENTO DE ODIVELLAS, 5 miles to the N. of Lisbon on the road which passes *Campo Grande*.

This convent is celebrated for the excellent marmalade made by the nuns. *Marmelada* properly so called is made from the quince, in Portuguese *marmelo*. The church is the only part of the ancient building which remains and it contains the tomb of its founder D. Diniz, in a small dark chapel. In one of the walls at the entrance is embedded a stone ball more than a yard in circumference, under which is the following inscription:

> Efte pelouro mandou aqui offerecer a San. Bernardo Dom Alvaro de Noronha por fua devoçam, que é dos quom que lhe os turcos combateram a fortaleza Durumuz fendo elle capitam dela, na era de 1557.

« Dom Alvaro de Noronha, out of devotion to St. Bernard, placed here this ball, which is one of those with which the Turks attacked the fortress of Ormuz, while he was its commander, in the era of 1557. »

This date must be the year of its collocation for the siege of Ormuz by the Turks took place in 1552.

Near the convent is a ruined arch popularly called *Monumento de D. Diniz:* its origin is unknown and many conjectures have been made as to the date of its construction, but without clearing up the point, which still continues to excite the curiosity of antiquarians.

CONVENTO DE SANTOS O NOVO, at the extreme E. of the city.

During the reign of the Emperor Diocletian, the Christians were persecuted with the utmost rigor, and among the number of his victims were the sisters Maxima and Julia who together with their brother Verissimus were martyred at Lisbon in the year 303. After the infliction of most atrocious torments, they were beheaded and their bodies cast into the Tagus. Though weighted with heavy stones the corpses miraculously came to shore and were buried in the spot now occupied by the parish church of *Santos o Velho,* a small chapel being built in after years to commemorate the spot. Even the Moors on becoming masters of the city, respected the belief of its inhabitants and permitted christian worship to be continued within its walls. D. Affonso Henriques, on capturing the city, built a church in place of the humble hermitage, and his successor Sancho I. added to it a convent and made a donation of both to the *Commendadores* of the military order of Santiago, who retained possession of it till 1217, when they migrated to Alcaçar-do-Sal. The old convent was now occupied by the wives and female relations of the knights of Santiago, who organised themselves into a religious community, with the title of *Commendadeiras da ordem militar de Santiago.*

In the reign of D. João II. the Commendadeiras built a new house at the extreme east of the city, near where the present convent stands, and removed to it in 1490, taking with them the relics of the martyrs. In course of time the place became too small for them, so that they erected the present spacious building in 1685.

NOSSA SENHORA DO MONTE on the summit of the second hill to the N. of St. George's Castle. A fine view of the city and river is obtained from this spot, which is elevated about 340 feet above the level of the sea. The present church, a small building erected on the ruins of the former one which was completely destroyed by the great earthquake, is surrounded by an enclosure in which are several trees of great antiquity and in the center is a small obelisk bearing the following inscription:

>   ULISSIPONE HIC
>   AUGUSTINENSIUM
>   PRIMA SEDES AB
>   ANNO 1148

from which it appears that the Augustinians settled here soon after the taking of Lisbon by Affonso Henriques. It was formerly called the hermitage of St. Gens, the first bishop of Lisbon, and a rude stone chair in which the saint used to sit while preaching to the people, is still preserved in a closet under the choir on the epistle side within the church. Until some years ago this chair was placed outside the church under the *alpendre* or porch, and was an object of much devotion being visited by many pilgrims, but especially by women in a state which made the ascent of so steep a hill a matter of no small difficulty and who entertained the belief that by seating themselves in the chair of St. Gens they would insure «a good time». One of these devotees was Dona Maria Anna of Austria who made a pilgrimage to this chair in 1723. The primitive building was taken down in 1243 and a new one built which the Augustinians continued to occupy till 1271 when they migrated to the adjoining hill where they had built the magnificent convent of the *Graça*.

IGREJA DE SANTOS O VELHO, at the W. end of the new embankment called *Aterro da Boa Vista*.

In the year 303 the two sisters Maxima and Julia and their brother Verissimus were martyred by order of the infamous Emperor Diocletian. After being subjected to excruciating tortures, they were put to death and their bodies, weighted with stones, cast into the Tagus near Almada. The corpses were soon after washed on shore and religiously buried by the Christians.

>   Mas, não te cegue o resplandor sómente
>   Que a alta casa de Antonio reverbera,
>   Olha tambem cá outro, que excellente
>   N'esta cidade o mesmo Ceo venera.

> Quando da grande Roma a cega gente
> Persiga á nova ley que o mundo espera,
> Verissimo, com Maxima e com Julia,
> Ganharão n'este sitio sacra dulia.
>
> Irmãos em sangue como em fortaleza,
> E de Lisboa filhos esforçados.
> Depois de mortos com a maior firmeza,
> Com huma pedra ao mar serão lançados;
> Porém, vencendo as leis da natureza,
> A terra tornarão mais illustrados,
> Mostrando tal poder sua virtude
> Que o peso natural das pedras mude.
>   *Ulyssipo,* cant. 14-38.

On the advance of the Moors, the relics of the martyrs were transferred to the opposite bank of the river and deposited in the spot where the church of Santos now stands. When Affonso Henriques captured the city in 1147 he built a church on the site, in place of the small hermitage originally erected and dedicated it to the *Santos gloriosos Martyres.*

His son and successor Sancho 1, founded a convent contiguous to the church and made a donation of both to the Commendadores of the military order of Santiago. The Commendadores remained here till 1217, when, the Moors having been driven from a great part of the Alemtejo, they removed their house to Alcaçar-do-Sal. The old convent was now occupied by the wives and female relations of the knights of Santiago who lived in community like nuns. In the reign of D. João II. they built a new convent at the extreme east of Lisbon called *Convento de Santos o Novo,* to which they removed in 1490 taking with them the relics of the martyrs. The fabric was little damaged by the great earthquake and is now used as a parish church. A legend says that on the shore near this spot pebbles used to be found stained with a blood-red cross:

> FACTI SUNT LAQUEIS, SAXA PER ASPERA
> EXSCULPSIT FLUIDAS SAGUIS IMAGINEM
> NON VI, NEC MANIBUS, SED CRUCE FULGIDA
> TESTANTUR LAPIDES FIDEM

On the right side of the entrance is a small chapel of the Martyrs, and under it in a vault lined with *azu-*

lejo is the spot where they were buried prior to their removal to Santos o Novo.

In the sacristy is a curious crucifix, of silver and *pau santo*, presented by Dom João V. The figure of our Lord, represented as still alive with up turned face, is carved out of the tusk of a hippopotamus, as well as the other figures standing at the foot of the cross, of our Lady and St. John the Evangelist.

IGREJA DA CONCEIÇÃO VELHA, the old church of the Conception in the *Rua nova da Alfandega*, opposite the custom-house.

A society or brotherhood was established in 1498 for the protection of orphans, and occupied a part of the cathedral till king Manuel, seeing the great utility of the institution, determined to build this church and house for their use, but it was not completed till the reign of his successor John III.

The original fabric was destroyed by the great earthquake, except the side portico and two windows which remain standing and now form the front of the small church at present existing. The portico is a good specimen of the *Manueline* style of architecture, but has been frightfully disfigured by taking away a group which represented N. Senhora da Misericordia, D. Manuel, his queen and children, from over the door and substituting an ugly iron grating. This act of vandalism was perpetrated with the object of admitting more light into the church. The figures thus removed are to be seen in the sacristy. The interior possesses no works of art worthy of mention.

It has been often stated that this church occupies the site of the ancient Jewish Synagogue, this mistake arising from the fact that before the great earthquake there was a church called *Conceição Velha*, in the street now called da Conceição, which was formerly the Jewish temple, having been purified and adapted to Christian worship in the reign of D. Manuel.

IGREJA DE NOSSA SENHORA DO LIVRAMENTO E S. JOSÉ, commonly called *Igreja da Memoria*, near the palace of Ajuda.

This beautiful little church was erected to commemorate the providential escape from attempted assassination of king Joseph I. on the 3.rd of September 1758. The king was proceeding in his carriage late at night to the palace of Ajuda and on reaching this spot a volley of shots was fired at the carriage, and its occupant severely wounded. It is not known who were the authors of this attempt, but the king's Prime minister Sebastião José Carvalho, afterwards so notorious under the title of Marquis of Pombal, made it a pretext for wreaking most cruel vengeance on his own enemies, and persuaded the king that the attack was the result of a conspiracy against his person. In consequence of this, many noble families, obnoxious to the crafty minister, beheld their principal members, of both sexes, either exiled or imprisoned, their estates confiscated, and their names declared infamous. Tortures were employed to wring from the noble victims a confession of guilt, and when this did not succeed, false evidence was fabricated and the ill-fated nobles condemned to the scaffold. They were executed with the utmost barbarity in the Largo de Belem, on the 13.th of January 1759. The foundation stone was laid the year after by the king himself as may be seen from the following inscriptions engraved on it:

JOSEPHUS I
LUSITANIAE REX
FIDELISSIMUS
DEIPARAE LIBERATRICIS
PROTECTIONE
III NONAS SEPTEMBRIS ·
ANNI MDCCLVIII
HIC INTER DENSOS GLOBOS PLUMBEOS
SOSPENS EVADENS
CONSPIRATORUM INSIDIAS
IN EUM
GEMINA SCLOPORUM DISPLOSIONE
IRRUENTIUM
TEMPLUM HOC
IN PERPETUUM TANTI BENEFICII
MONUMENTUM
AEDIFICARI FECIT

HUJUS TEMPLI IN HONOREM
DEI ET BEATISSIMAE VIRGINIS MARIAE
LIBERATRICIS AC IPSIUS SPONSI
SANCTI JOSEPH DICANDI
LAPIDEM HUNC PRIMUM
AB IPSO REGE DELATUM
BENEDIXIT AC IMPOSUIT
EM.^{mus} D. FRANCISCUS I
S. R. E. CARDINALIS DE SALDANHA
PATRIARCHA LISBONENSIS
SUMMO PONTIFICE CLEMENTE XIII
DIE III SEPTEMBRIS
ANNO DOMINI MDCCLX
POST TERRAEMOTU V

The church was built in the reign of D. Maria I., and is in imitation of the Estrella. The architect was João Carlos Ribiena.

SANTA ENGRACIA, near St. Vincent's, a short distance to the NE. of the cathedral.

The original church of this name was built by the Infanta Dona Maria in 1568. On the stormy night of the 15.th of January 1630 sacrilegious robbers entered the church and stole the sacred vessels not even respecting the consecrated particles. The indignation felt at this unprecedented outrage caused a society to be formed consisting of 100 members of the aristocracy, who every year made a feast in honor of the Blessed Sacrament, and who provided funds for the erection of a splendid temple. When however it was nearly finished, the walls gave way and the whole fabric fell to the ground. A fresh beginning was made and the foundation stone of the present unfinished edifice was laid in 1682 by king Pedro II. and has on it the following explanatory inscription:

> Cum ineunte trigefimo fupra milefimum fexcen-
> tefimum falutis anno ex D. Engratiae Æde quidam
> nefarius homo per tenebras procellofae noctis San-
> ctiffimum corpus Domini furatus effet, Nobilitas
> Lufitana in tanti facrilegii expiationem centum-
> virale foladitium conftituit et eodem in loco ma-
> gnificum Templum propriis fumptibus confruere
> decrevit, ut ubi impia manus Sacrofanctam Eu-
> chariftiam temerare fuerat aufa, ibi a piis animis
> aeternum colenda foret. At opere jam perfectioni
> proximo forte colapfo iterum Nobilitas Lufitana,
> impellente ac magnifice adjuvante Sereniffimo
> Petro Portugalliae Principe et Moderatore aliud
> Templum, fed elegantioris ftructurae erigere fta-
> tuit, cujus primum fundamentorum lapidem idem
> Sereniffimus Princeps pro infita Lufitanis Regibus
> pietate propria manu jecit. Ann. Dni. MDCLXXXII.

It was intended to have been the largest rotunda known, with a single altar in the center. The architects however, fearing the walls would not bear the pressure of the dome desisted from the work and left it in its present unfinished state.

A legend says that one Simão Peres Solis, condemned to death as a participator in the act of sacrilege above referred to, declared on the scaffold that in proof of his innocence the church would never be finished. Considering, however, that the execution took place half a century before the foundation stone of the building was laid, it appears that Solis must have been a prophet as well as a martyr!

Como as obras de Santa Engracia has become a proverb in Portugal, and is applied to anything which is never likely to be finished.

The building is now used as a dépôt for artillery.

S. JULIÃO, at the N. side of the Camara Municipal.—The parish of St. Julian existed prior to 1200, but the exact date of its foundation is unknown. The ancient church in which Pope John XXI, one of the two Portuguese who have occupied the chair of St. Peter, was baptized, was completely destroyed by the great earthquake. Having been shortly afterwards rebuilt it was reduced to ashes on the 4.th of October 1816, on the occasion of the funeral ceremonies of Dona Maria I. The present building, recently completed, contains some fine marbles, two superb columns in the choir or capella mór and some beautiful carving work.

S. NICOLAU. — St. Nicholas's in the *Rua da Prata,* the most easterly of the three streets which terminate in Black Horse Square. — The foundation dates from 1280, the present church is of recent construction and possesses no features which call for special mention. In the sacristy are some rich ancient vestments acquired from the extinct monasteries.

S. PAULO at the W. end of the *Largo de S. Paulo,* half a mile to the W. of Black Horse Square.

The original church, according to the following verses which were enscribed over the door, was founded in 1388.

Numen adest intus Paulo maiora canamus
    Regia dum mirum munera pandit opus.
Aera salutis habet septem saecula Phoebi
    Bis sex annorum si tam excipias.

The awful earthquake of 1755 however entirely destroyed the old building, the present church being erected shortly after the catastrophe.

SANTA MARIA MAGDALENA, at the E. end of the *Rua da Conceição,* one of the streets which intersect Rua Augusta.

The foundation of this church is as old as the Portuguese monarchy, its exact date is not known, but it was prior to 1164 in which year the death of one of its priests is recorded in the register. It resisted the great earthquake, but the succeeding fire reduced it to ashes. The portico still remains as a sample of its former architecture. The present structure was built in 1783.

In a narrow street running N. and parallel with the front of St. Magdalen's are some Roman inscriptions which deserve inspection. See article on Roman antiquities.

S. FRANCISCO DE PAULA.—Built soon after the earthquake by queen Marianna Victoria, daughter of Philip V. of Spain and wife of Joseph I. of Portugal. Her remains are deposited in a mausoleum in this church. The painting over the high altar, representing S. Francis de Paul is by Vieira Lusitano, one of the most celebrated painters of his day. Also the 3 paintings in the chapels of N.S. da Conceição, Holy Family, and St. Anthony, are by this artist. They were finished in 1765.

IGREJA DAS CHAGAS.—One of the most conspicuous from its position. The original church was built by a confraternity or guild called *Chagas de Jesus* (the wounds of Jesus), consisting of mariners who sailed to the Indies and Brazil. The first mass was celebrated on the 30.th of November 1542. The great earthquake brought it down, but it was shortly afterwards rebuilt. It contains the remains of Saint Urbano.

From the church-yard a splendid view is obtained of the Tagus as far as its bar, as well as of a great part of Lisbon.

CONVENTO DE S. DOMINGOS at Bemfica, a small village, 4 miles to the NW. of Lisbon.

King John I. gave the site to the order of St. Dominic in 1399. The church, built in 1624, was destroyed by the great earthquake, the sacristy only remaining standing. It was, however, soon rebuilt, and on the abolition of the monastic orders in 1833 was purchased by her Highness Dona Izabel Maria and converted into an asylum for the poor. It is chiefly interesting as being the last resting place of the great Vice Roy of India, D. João de Castro. His remains are deposited in a tomb in the chapel called *capella dos Castros*.

The distinguished Portuguese classic Frei Luiz de Sousa lived, died, and is buried in this convent.

CONVENTO DE NOSSA SENHORA DO BOM SUCCESSO, at the extreme W. of *Belem*.

The convent was founded in 1626, and was at first occupied by nuns of the order of St. Jerome but was afterwards given to the Irish nuns of the order of St. Dominic by queen Luiza de Gusman. It is still inhabited by Irish nuns who devote themselves to the education of young ladies.

COLLEGIO DE S. PATRICIO.—St. Patric's college, for the education of youths intended for the Irish priesthood, was founded by the Jesuits of S. Roque in 1593, in a house which they rented in that part of the city called *Mouraria*. After several removals they settled down on the present site in 1611, the land being given to them by Antonio Fernandes Ximenes, a Portuguese nobleman. Several bishops and archbishops received here their first training, one of whom, Dennicio Herleo, was martyred on the 7.th of June 1684. The house now belongs to the Irish dominicans of Corpo Santo; the Rev.d D.r Russel is Rector.

MADRE DE DEUS.—This convent of Franciscan nuns was founded by Dona Leonor of the House of Lancaster, queen of John II. and sister of Dom Manuel. Notwithstanding the damage done to it by the great earthquake, and the patches of modern architecture by which it was subsequently disfigured, it is yet a curious monument of antiquity. Its principal attraction consists in several paintings by Portuguese and foreign artists of eminence, such as Grão Vasco, Bento Coelho, André Gonçalves, Christovão de Utrecht. The best are in the sacristy. The church is now being restored in a most judicious manner.

CONVENTINHO DO DESAGGRAVO.—This little convent, adjoining the unfinished church of St. Engracia, was founded by Dona Maria Anna, daughter of D. José I., in 1783, on the ruins of the famous convent of St. Clare. Dona Maria Anna died in 1813 at Rio de Janeiro and her remains were translated to Lisbon in 1822, and deposited in a tomb under the choir of this convent where they now rest.

OTHER CHURCHES.—Besides the foregoing there are also the following churches:

Nossa Senhora do Soccorro, founded in 1646.
S. Sebastião, founded in 1652.
S. Pedro d'Alcantara.
Santissimo Sacramento, founded in 1671.
S. Miguel, foundation unknown, rebuilt in 1674.
Santo Estevão, founded prior to 1295.
Santa Izabel, queen of Portugal, founded 1742.
S. João da Praça, founded anterior to 1317.
S. Jorge, founded in the reign of D. Diniz 1279.
Santa Cruz do Castello.
Nossa Senhora da Ajuda.
Santa Luzia, under the invocation of S. Braz.
S. Lourenço.
S. Thiago.
S. Thomé e Salvador.
Nossa Senhora dos Anjos.
Santissimo Coração de Jesus.
Nossa Senhora da Pena.
S. Christovão.
Nossa Senhora da Conceição, Nova.
Nossa Senhora da Lapa.
S. Luiz, Rei de França, the French church.

Besides the convents of nuns mentioned in the preceding pages, the following are still in existence as such:

Santa Anna, of Religious of the third order of St. Francis, founded in 1562. In its church rest the ashes of the immortal poet Camões.

Santa Martha, founded in 1571 by king Sebastian.

Santa Monica, founded in 1586 by D. Maria Abranches.

Do Santissimo Sacramento, near Alcantara, of the order of St. Dominic; founded in 1607 by the Count and Countess of Vimioso.

Da Encarnação, of the military order of S. Bento d'Aviz, founded in 1617 by the Infanta Dona Maria, daughter of king Manuel the Great.

Da Invocação da Santa Cruz, commonly called Das Francezinhas, French nuns of the order called *Capuchinhas*, founded in 1667 by Dona Maria Francisca, wife of Affonso VI.

Das Salessias, at Belem, of the order of St. Francisco de Sales.

Da Esperança.

De S. Pedro d'Alcantara.

Das Trinas.

Das Albertas.

De Chellas, about 2 miles NE. of Lisbon, containing many antiquities, especially Roman remains: said to be the site of the ancient Temple of Vesta.

7. PALACES.

PALACIO DA AJUDA. (PALACE OF AJUDA.)

Situate near the summit of a hill above the suburb called *Belem,* and is one of the conspicuous objects which strike the eye on coming up the Tagus.

This palace, at present the residence of the king and queen of Portugal, is a vast unfinished building, erected on the site of a temporary edifice of wood hastily raised to receive the royal family after the calamitous earthquake of 1755. The foundation stone was laid by D. João VI., and were the palace to be finished on the gigantic scale of the original plan it would certainly be one of the largest in the world. Only a third however has been built, which is more than sufficient to accommodate a monarch. On account of its unfinished state it presents the appearance of a ruin without the charm of antiquity. Prince Licknowsky somewhat too severely observes, in his «Recollections of 1842»:

«What interest can I take in this enormous and cold mass of stone, abandoned to loneliness, without a past and without a present! Unfinished modern ruins which offer nothing and recall nothing to recollection! The wretched style of the last century, the ugly statues, the cold marble, all this cannot please merely because eighty millions of cruzados were spent on the work, and because it would be a great work if it were to be completed.»

The S. side was to be the principal façade, with the state entrance in the middle, but the E. side only being yet finished, it is considered the front of the palace. It consists of a central peristyle forming the entrance, having three arches between six Tuscan columns, supporting a balcony over which are 6 columns of the Composite order with architrave, frieze, and cornice and three windows corresponding with the arches below. At the top are two allegorical figures, but this part is not yet finished.

On each side of the peristyle runs a wing terminating in a square pavilion of similar architecture but a story higher and crowned with a balustrade and trophies. Between the windows of both wings and pavilions are tiers of pilasters corresponding in order with the columns of the peristyle. What is finished on the S. side is identical with the wings here described. The whole of the building is of a kind of white marble called *lioz*. The appearance of the finished façade is much marred by having immediately in front of the N. pavilion, a lot of wretched looking houses and the ruined foundation of the former patriarchal church. Entering under the three arches we come to two circular vestibules adjoining each other and surrounded by columns and intervening niches in which are placed statues representing Perseverance, Love of Virtue, Love of country, Clemency, Affability, Innocence, Humanity, Good Tidings, Virtuous action, Desire, Diligence, Decorum, Gratitude, Generosity, Constancy, Liberality, Counsel, Consideration, Honesty, Intrepidity, Liberty, and Providence.

These allegorical figures bear the names of the Portuguese sculptors Machado de Castro, Barros, Aguiar, Faustino José Rodrigues and others, but the works do no great credit to their authors.

The parts of the interior which offer any interest to the visitor are: $1.^{st}$, the State apartments; $2.^{nd}$, the Royal private apartments; $3.^{rd}$, the Picture Gallery; $4.^{th}$, the Numismatic Cabinet, and $5.^{th}$ the Library, which however is not in the palace itself but in a building contiguous.

THE STATE APARTMENTS.

Are situate at the E. front and consist of large lofty rooms painted in fresco and decorated at the beginning of this century. The principal saloon called the *Sala da tocha* has painted on its walls and ceiling the acclamation of D. João IV., by the Portuguese artist Taborda. The *Sala de audiencia* is decorated in a similar manner. The next saloon is the *Sala do beijamão* so called from the ancient custom of kissing the king's hand at the lévées held on gala days. Formerly the Monarchs of Portugal were treated with the utmost deference by their subjects, who used to fall down on their knees to kiss their sovereign's hand. The ceremony of *beijamão* is now abolished in the case of the king, being substituted by a profound inclination of the body. In paying homage to the queen, however, the ladies still continue the ancient practice.

Now follow a long suit of rooms terminating in a small chapel, but which contain nothing that demands special notice.

THE ROYAL APARTMENTS.

Occupy the first floor at the W. end of the S. front, with windows opening on to a terrace and enjoying a splendid view of the Tagus. They were fitted up shortly after the marriage of his Majesty D. Luiz, with her Royal Highness the Princess Maria Pia, daughter of king Victor Emmanuel of Italy.

In the center of the suit is a marble hall, called the *Sala de marmore,* which separates the apartments of the king from those of the queen. Its ceiling is divided into 64 panels composed of different varieties of agate presented to the king by the Vice-Roy of Egypt. Running round the room is a Doric entablature of wine-colored marble having between the triglyphs metopes of agate corresponding with the panels of the ceiling, but having the center ornaments guilded. From the architrave down to the plinth, some 15 feet, the walls are also lined with agate, the window jambs and plinths being of marble like the entablature. An agate arch with crystal sliding doors gives access to the apartments of the king. The total space covered with agate is 1,900 sq. ft. The floor is a mosaic of Portuguese marble and agate. A secret door formed of a single agate opens by a spring on applying the foot to a certain part of the mosaic. In the middle of the room is a fountain, being a large basin on a pedestal with a group of dolphins and two genii of Carrara marble. State dinners are sometimes given in this hall, in which case the table is placed over the fountain. The adjoining apartment is the king's smoke-room and is fitted up and furnished with american oak and green silk. The ceiling is of paneled oak in the style of the xv. century.

The stems and sterns of ships, carved on the octagonal medallions, represent the war ships commanded by his Majesty before his accession or launched during his reign. There are also four pictures of the principal Portuguese men of war, by Sr. Pedroso. The floor is inlaid with wood of various hues.

The next room, intended as a private reception room, is lined with rich blue silk. The marble statue on a pedestal surrounded by a divan, represents «Resignation» and was offered to the queen by the city of Naples. It is by the Italian sculptor Solari. A number of pictures adorn the walls. The one opposite the statue, representing an attack of Arab horsemen, is by Fasini. The interior of a room with mountebanks awaiting day-break is by Volterra. An episode of the Italian war, by Germano Induno. The magnificent vase of Sèvres china in the center of the room is a present from Napoleon III.

Another vase from the Royal Berlin manufactory, and presented by the king of Prussia, is admirably painted. At one side of the mirror is a silver gilt tête-à-tête, a gift of the emperor of the French, and on the mantel-piece two urns formerly belonging to Frederic Augustus, king of Poland.

Returning to the marble hall and proceeding W., we come to the apartments of her Majesty the queen. The first is a small cabinet lined with rose colored velvet and the furniture ornamented with exquisitely painted porcelain and the ceiling with richly gilt stucco, Asiatic birds and butterflies. Around it are twelve medallions with views of Italy and of Lisbon painted by Signori

Cinatti and Rambois, talented Italian artists resident in the capital. The floor is of inlaid woodwork.

In this room are two gilt bronze statues worthy of notice. One represents a Punchinello, the other «The man with the Iron Mask». The latter is a miracle of nature and art combined. He is dressed à Louis XIV. with knee-breeches fringed with gold, white silk stockings, buckled shoes, a slouched hat with one side looped up with brilliants and a velvet cape thrown over his shoulders. He holds in his hands a guitar studded with brilliants and having strings of gold. To represent the silk stockings, the satin breeches, the lining of the cape, the brim of the hat, the hands, and the part of the face not concealed by the mask, *single pearls* are employed, having been secreted by the oysters in the exact shape required to imitate the different objects above specified, and in this consists the extreme rarity of the statue.

In the next apartment, lined with green silk, is a beautiful marble bust of the queen's sister, princess Clotilde, by Santo Varni. There are also some good portraits of D. Pedro IV., of D. Amelia, late empress of the Brazils, of D. Maria II., of D. Luiz while an infante, painted by Winteralter. Also the portraits of the king's father D. Fernando and of Victor Emmanuel of Italy. Another picture, the interior of Milan Cathedral by Luigi Bisi, was presented by that city to the queen: the opposite painting, representing an island of Venice, is by Sr. Fiena.

There is also a silver model of the third and last tomb erected to the memory of Italy's great poet Dante Alighieri. It is a quadrangle crowned with a dome. The cornice is in imitation of that on the tomb of Cæcilia Metella in the *Via Appia* at Rome. Over a Tuscan door is engraved the simple epitaph:

DANTIS POETAE SEPULCHRUM

This model is a present from the inhabitants of Ravena, where the author of the *Divina Comedia* died in 1321.

The splendid album presented to the queen by the city of Turin contains 24 water-color paintings by distinguished Italian artists. The marble statue representing «Innocence» is by Benedetti di Lize and is a present from the city of Palermo.

In the oratory is a most ingenious genuflexorium made by Martinetti & Son of Turin and offered to the queen by the workpeople of that city. The large painting over the altar is a copy of Murillo. There is also a small Madonna by Perugino valued at £ 7,000.

THE PICTURE GALLERY.

Open to the public on Sundays from 1 to 4, consists of two well lighted and ventilated rooms on the third floor of the palace.

This collection of oil paintings is entirely due to the efforts of his Majesty D. Luiz, ever anxious to contribute to the advancement of art, and though its origin is thus recent it is already the best of its kind in the country. The first room is devoted to modern pictures; the second to the old masters. A third room is about to be added for statuary. There are very few specimens of Portuguese art prior to the present century. There seems to have been absolutely no demand for paintings (except for the churches), as Camões says:

> Outros muitos verias que os pintores
> Aqui tambem por certo pintariam,
> Mas falta-lhes pincel, faltam-lhes cores,
> Honra, premio, favor que as artes criam;
> Culpa dos viciosos successores
> Que degeneram certo e se desviam
> Do lustre e do valor dos seus passados
> Em gostos e vaidades atolados.

FIRST ROOM.

MODERN PAINTINGS.

1	The Portuguese Royal family leaving the Tagus, accompanied by the French war ships «Magenta», «Flandre» and «Heroine».	João Pedroso, Port.
2	Episode of the battle of Marino.	F. Vittori, Italian.
3	The trombador of the village.	Visconde de Menezes, Port.
4	Moonlight view.	F. A. Nickel, German.

PALACIO DA AJUDA. 173

5 A Moor. — M. H. da Silva. Port.
6 A Warrior. — Miguel Angelo Lupi, Port.
7 Naval combat. — I. d'Ivernois, Suisse.
8 Landscape. — I. Newton, Port.
9 An eagle. — João Baptista Ribeiro, Port.
10 Landscape — I. Newton, Port.
11 Landing at Villa Franca de Nisa of the Princess Beatrice, daughter of D. Manuel and wife of the Prince of Savoy. — H. Gamba, Italian.
12 Calf's head. — Palizzi.
13 A «muleta». — L. Ascencio Tomazini, Port.
14 An Odalisk. — P. Pommayrac, French.
15 Cascade at Tivoli. — Massimo d'Azeglio, Italian.
16 A Beggar. — José Rodrigues, Port.
17 A country lad. — José Rodrigues, Port.
18 Portrait of Napoleon III. — A. Ivon, French.
19 A procession. — M. Tedesco, Italian.
20 A hermit. — Visconde de Menezes, Port.
21 Guido taking the portrait of Beatrice Cenci on the eve of her execution — John Lewis Reilly, English.
22 Returning from the pasture. — Thomás José d'Annunciação, Port.
23 View of an ancient castle. — Ferri, Senior, Italian.
24 Meditation by moonlight. — Miguel Angelo Lupi, Port.
25 Landscape. — C. Hugard, French.
26 Study of a head. — A. Zona, Italian.
26 A family scene. — G. Gonin, French.
28 Portrait of J. Rossini. — Cosselli, Italian.
29 Tinturetto interrupting the painting of his daughter's portrait to contemplate her corpse. — Miguel Angelo Lupi, Port.
30 Naval combat off Cape St. Vincent. — Morel Fatio, French.
31 A market. — Francisco José Rezende, Port.
32 Embarcation of Catharina Cornaro. — Italian.
33 Castle of Sigmaringen. — A. Lasinsky, German.
34 Interior of the cathedral at Monza. — M. Bianchi, Italian.
35 Marriage of His Majesty D. Luiz with Dona Maria Pia, in the church of St. Domingos, Lisbon. — Antonio Manuel da Fonseca, Port.
36 Dutch scene. — P. Tetar Van Elven, Dutch.
37 The Princess of Lamballe, episode of the French revolution. — C. Ferri, Italian.

38 Faithful unto death. John Lewis Reilly, English.
39 Landscape. Kalekreuth, German.
40 Landscape. Castle of Hohenzollern. A. Lasinsky, German.
41 Landscape. E. Bertea, Italian.
42 A philosopher. M. H. da Silva, Port.
43 D. Martinho, subject taken from the poem entitled D. Jayme. Bordallo Pinheiro, Port.
44 Portrait of Bulhão Pato. M. H. da Silva, Port.
45 A bitch suckling her pups. Henriette Ronner, Belgian.
46 Study of a head. M. H. da Silva, Port.
47 A market. Leonel Marques Pereira, Port.
48 Landscape. Kalekreuth, German.
49 A Beggar. Esteves, Port.
50 Arabian hunters. Pasini, Italian.
51 Christ at Emmaus. French school.
52 A view in Switzerland. C. Hugard, French.
53 Landscape. C. Bernyer, French.
54 Tasso on the eve of his death contemplating the Capitol. M. H. da Silva, Port.
55 Innocence. Gastaldi, Italian.
56 Episode of the Italian war of 1859. Italian.
57 Landscape. French school.
58 Landscape. C. Bernyer, French.
59 Italian customs. Italian.
60 Episode of the Italian war of 1859. Italian.

SECOND ROOM.

OLD PAINTINGS.

1 St. Francis of Assis receiving the Cross. Bolognese school.
2 Landscape. Jacopo de Ponte Bassano, Venetian.
3 Bambochata. Adrian Van Ostade, Dutch.
4 Virgin and Child. Venetian school.
5 A village feast. Flemish school.
6 St. Francis of Assis. Spanish school.
7 A sketch. Trevisani.
8 A portrait. French.
9 Study of a head. Bolognese school.
10 The fortune teller. Moise Valentin, French.
11 Portrait of one of the Medici. Venetian school.
12 A Pietà. German school.
13 St. Magdalen. Attrib. to Francisco Mola.
14 Nymphs. Cornelis Poelenburg, Flemish.

PALACIO DA AJUDA.

15	Lo with his daughters.	Attributed to Parmigiano.
16	Sketch of Abraham and his son.	Bolognese school.
17	Two children playing at cards.	J. B. de Faria Barros, Port.
18	Madonna	Bolognese school.
19	Lucrecia.	Lucas Hranack, German.
20	The Holy Family.	Lombard school.
21	Cain killing Abel.	Bolognese school.
22	Meleagrus offering to Atalante the head of the Calydonian boar.	Peter Paul Rubens, Flemish.
23	Portrait of Domenico Pisani.	Giovanni Bellini, Venitian.
24	The Head of our Lord.	German school.
25	St. Francis of Assis receiving the protection of the Blessed Virgin.	German school.
26	Turkish embassy.	Diego Velasquez, Spanish.
27	Virgin and Child with St. John.	Leonardo da Vinci, Lombard.
28	Portrait of an old man.	Flemish school.
29	A philosopher.	Gerard Dow, Dutch.
30	Portrait of the celebrated Francis Ajolle.	Andrea del Sarto.
31	St. Bruno receiving the protection of the Virgin.	Anthony Van Dyck.
32	Portrait of a young lady.	Ferdinand Bol, Dutch.
33	Portrait of a Venetian personage.	Gio. Battista Moroni.
34	Portrait.	Thomas Gainsborough.
35	A family scene.	Dutch school.
36	A nymph in the garden of the Hesperides.	Paulo Veronese.
37	Fruit.	Jan Davidze de Heem, Fl.
38	The descent from the cross.	Quintin de Matzis, German.
39	Aurora.	Bolognese school.
40	Landscape.	Paul Bril, Flemish.
41	The descent of the Holy Ghost.	German school.
42	St. Luke.	German school.
43	Judith.	Bolognese school.
44	A hermit.	Spanish school, attributed to Murillo.
45	St. Stephen.	Bolognese school.
46	Portrait.	Flemish school.
47	Study of a head.	Dutch school, attributed to Adrian Van Ostade.
48	The descent from the cross.	Florentine school.
49	Portrait of D. Olimpia Pamphili Doria.	Flemish school.
50	St. Sebastian.	Florentine school.
51	Our Lord.	Bolognese school.
52	The Transfiguration.	Copy of Raphael by Giulio Romano.
53	Pietà.	A. Allegri Corregio. Lomb.

PALACES.

54 Virgin and Child with St. Anne. — Lombard school.
55 Virgin and Child. — Roman school attributed to Giulio Romano.
56 Virgin and Child with St. John. — Bolognese school.
57 Martyrdom of St. Stephen. — Andrea Sacchi, Roman.
58 Mystical marriage of St. Catharine. — Murillo.
59 Virgin and Child. — Composed by Raphael, painted by Bagnacavallo.
60 Pietà. — Hans Memling.
61 The B. Virgin with her divine Son. — Jacques Stella, French.
62 Virgin and Child. — Francesco Francia, Bologn.
63 S. Bartholomew. — Spanish school.
64 — French school.
65 St. George killing the dragon. — German school.
66 Country scene. — Klengl, Flemish.
67 Mystical marriage of St. Catharine. — German school.
68 St. Mary Magdalen. — Tiziano Vecellio.
69 St. Sebastian. — Anthony Van Dyck.
70 St. Jerome. — Parmezan school.
71 The Infant Jesus. — Josepha d'Obidos, Port.
72 The adoration of the shepherds. — Roman school.
73 Cato tearing out his entrails. — José Ribera Spagnuoletto.
74 Mystical marriage of St. Catharine. — Guercino.
75 Works of charity. — Flemish school.
76 Military scene. — Philip Wouverman, Flem.
77 The Nativity. — Florentine school.
78 Give unto Caesar that which is Caesar's. — Flemish school.
79 Portrait of Charles I. of England. — Anthony Van Dyck.
80 St. Jerome. — Flemish sch. att. to Teniers.
81 Portrait of William IV. of England. — Sir Godfrey Kneller.
82 St. Matthew. — Subleyras, Bolognese.
83 A young lady. — French school.
84 Christ bound to the column. — Domingos A. Sequeira, Port.
85 A philosopher. — Neapolitan school.
86 Landscape. — Salvator Rosa.
87 St. Magdalen. — Spanish school.
88 Landscape. — Petit, French.
89 Crucifixion. — Bolognese school, attributed to Guido Reni.
90 St. Anthony receiving the lily. — Carlo Maratti, Roman.
91 St. John the Baptist preaching in the desert. — D. Antonio Sequeira, Port.
92 Likeness of a nun. — Hans Holbein, German.
93 Portrait of Paulo Visconti's daughter. — Paris Bordone, Venetian.

94	Marine.	Vanderweld, Dutch.
95	Religious subject.	Venetian school.
96	The good Samaritan.	Flemish School.
97	St. Jerome.	Guercino, Bolognese.
98	Virgin and Child.	Italian school.
99	Negro's head.	Study, French school, Gericault.
100	Abraham expelling Agar and Ismael.	Bassano, Venetian.
101	The Virgin with her divine Son.	Carlo Maratti, Italian.
102	Portrait of Louis XIV. in his infancy.	French school.
103	A philosopher.	Spanish school, attributed to Spagnoletto.
104	A view of Venice.	Venetian school.
105	A village.	Dutch school.
106	Crucifixion.	Giaquinto Corrado.
107	Portrait.	French school.
108	Sea piece.	Dutch school.
109	Crucifixion.	Hans Memling, German.
110	Portrait.	Maes, French.
111	Sea piece.	Dutch school.
112	Jesus on his way to Calvary.	Wofmat, German.
113	Portrait.	Anthony Van Dyck.
114	Sea piece.	Flemish school.
115	Fruit.	Dutch school.
116	Portrait of D. João V.	Attrib. to Pompeo Batoni.
117	Portrait of D. Marianna of Austria, João V's queen.	Attrib. to Pompeo Batoni.
118	Christ bearing the Cross.	Attrib. to Andrea del Sarto.
119	Portrait.	Bolognese school.
120	Christ.	Bolognese school.
121	Christ tormented.	Albrecht Durer, German.
122	Portrait of queen Maria de Medici.	Rubens.
123	The Holy Family.	Andrea del Sarto.
124	David.	Salvator Rosa.
125	Virgin and Child.	Att. to sch. of Grão Vasco.

GABINETE NUMISMATICO.

The Numismatic cabinet contains a fine collection of ancient and modern coins and medals, together with a number of valuable works of art in gold and silver.

Of ancient coins, the best and most complete collection is the Roman, consisting of 2,653 gold, silver and copper coins. The Republic is represented by 519; the Empire by 1,840, and the Byzantine empire by 294.

A few words on Roman money during the two former periods may not be out of place. In primitive ages when exchanges were made in kind, there was no one article which served as a standard of value for the rest, but in course of time cattle, and especially sheep and oxen, in consequence of their value and universal necessity to man, as well as of the facility of transfering them from one place to another, being found the most convenient article of exchange, gradually became the measure of value for other commodities, and from the Latin name *pecus*, cattle, was derived the term *pecunia*, money, wealth.

Later on, the Romans made use of pieces of copper, at first without any fixed weight or shape, but afterwards a uniform weight, a pound, was adopted and Servius Tullius began in the sixth century B.C. to cast copper money in the shape of animals, generally the ox or the sheep. The pound of copper called *as libralis* retained its weight till the beginning of the first Punic war B.C. 264 during which, on account of the necessities of the treasury, it was gradually reduced to 2 oz. and in the second Punic war to 1 oz. and subsequently by the *Lex Papiria* B.C. 191 to $1/2$ an ounce which continued to be the standard down to the Empire, retaining its original name *as* as well as its subdivisions *semis, triens, quadrans, sextans*, and *uncia*, respectively the half, third, fourth, sixth and twelfth of an *as*.

It is not known with certainty when the practice of coining silver was first introduced, some authorities go back as far as Servius Tullius while others assert that there was no silver coin till B.C. 269. The silver coins in use during the Republic were the *denarius* = 10 copper asses, the *quinarius* = 5 asses and the *sestercius* = $2 1/2$ asses. The silver remained virgin till the reign of Septimius Severus who began to introduce alloy and this debasement continued to increase till the intrinsic value had been reduced to a minimum when Diocletianus restored the coinage to its pristine purity.

Gold coin first appears in the consulship of C. Clodius Nero and Licinius Salinator B.C. 207, prior to which period gold payments were made in bars or ingots. The gold *denarius* was equivalent to 25 silver *denarii* = 100 *sestercii* or 250 *asses*. The *quinarius* was half this value or 125 *asses*. There were also other gold coins of 60, 40, and 20 sesterces, but very few of these have come down to us. During the Republic and the begining of the Empire, the weight of the gold *denarius* remained constant, there being 40 to the pound. Nero augmented the number to 45; Constantine the Great, to 58 and at the division of the Empire there were 72, and the name of the coin was changed to *soldus* or *solidus*. The purity of the gold was not tampered with, no alloy being used. The Romans however fabricated coin of lead or other base metal covered with a thin plate of gold or silver; this was done either by false coiners or to supply a deficiency in hard times. For the latter purpose coins or counters called *tesserae* were also issued of leather, wood and other substances with a nominal value stamped thereon.

During the Republic many families had the privilege of coining money on which they were allowed to stamp the likenesses of their ancestors and representations of their achievements. This right called *jus imaginis* was conceded only to those who had filled the office of *aedilis, praetor,* or *consul* and to their descendants, who alone possessed the privilege of keeping in their houses the *imagines* of their forefathers. These *imagines* were masks of wax made to represent the deceased both in features and complexion and were placed in wooden boxes ranged round the *atrium* or court in order of consanguinity and each box had marked on it the titles of honor gained by the departed. Of the consular families who enjoyed this right of coining money there are no fewer than 185 represented in this collection. On the establishment of the Empire, Augustus reserved to himself the right of coining gold and silver, leaving copper to the Senate, and henceforward each coin bears the effigy of an emperor, which served to protect it from being dishonestly lightened, since to efface the likeness of the sovereign was a crime of leze-majesty, punishable with death. Indeed such was the respect paid to the coin of the realm during the reign of Tiberius that a master was condemned for beating his slave while the latter held in his hand a coin bearing the effigy of the emperor.

These ancient coins are well worth a close examination: they are not only interesting to the numismatologist, but also to the general student, who will find among them many curious records of antiquity. Not only do they present authentic likenesses of all the Roman emperors and of the eminent men during the Republic, but also furnish many highly interesting particulars as to the lives, habits, manners, customs, dress and deities of the Romans and representations of ancient monuments of art, such as triumphal arches, columns, statues, bridges, palaces, aqueducts, basilicas, temples, circuses and an infinity of other details.

Those who wish for a full description of this collection are referred to the work by Dr. A. C. Teixeira de Aragão entitled *Descripção historica das moedas romanas existentes no gabinete numismatico de Sua Magestade D. Luiz I.*

The collection of coins referring to Portugal is without doubt the most complete in existence. It may be divided into two categories viz. coins current in the country prior to the establishment of the Portuguese monarchy, and those coined by the Portuguese kings.

Of the former class the most interesting are those coined in various parts of the peninsula during the Roman occupation, by virtue of decrees of the Senate at Rome, and generally bearing the letters S. C. (Senatus Consulto). Also the gold coins of the Visigothic kings, beginning with Leovigildus A. D. 572, and ending with the last ruler Rodrigo 711: this series is most complete, and the specimens in a fine state of preservation.

Coming now to the Portuguese monarchs we find no authentic specimen earlier than the reign of Sancho I. There is a gold coin bearing the legend MONETA DOMINI ALFONSI which is attributed to Affonso I., but it more probably belongs to the third king of that name.

In the present monetary system the *real* (plural *réis*) is the unit of value in which all accounts are kept; its value is now about $\frac{1}{10}$ of a penny which at first sight seems an extraordinarily diminutive standard to have been adopted, but this is due to the great depreciation which has taken place in the coinage, and it is interesting to see how the original *real* of Fernando I., a silver coin about the size of a shilling, has degenerated into its present minute proportions. This has been effected in three ways; by reducing the weight, by debasing the metal, and by increasing the nominal value.

D. João I. affords a conspicuous example of the two first processes.

During the reign of his predecessor D. Fernando I. the *real* was all silver and weighed 70 grains (port.), but D. João, to raise money for carrying on the war with Spain gradually reduced its weight to 49 grs. and the quality of the metal to $\frac{1}{12}$ silver and $\frac{11}{12}$ alloy. In consequence of the great diversity in the intrinsic value of the different réis, some being pure silver while others were nearly all copper, much confusion was caused, and to prevent this D. Affonso V. began to coin réis entirely of copper and in 1462 he passed a law enacting that for the future all contracts should be made in copper réis *(real preto)*.

He however coined also silver réis of 68 grs. worth abouts 30 of the copper. In the next reign the silver *real* was reduced to 40 grs. and was worth 20 copper ones for which reason it acquired the name of *vintem* to distinguish it from its copper namesake. So that the original *real* branches off here into two coins, one of silver, thenceforward called *vintem,* and the other of copper which retained its parent's name. Let us now trace the *vintem*. We find its weight gradually diminishing till the time of D. João IV. when it weighed only 23 grs. and the next king, D. Affonso VI, being very hard up, hit upon a plan of enriching himself and his people at one and the same time. In 1663 he issued a decree raising the nominal value of the silver coins 25 per cent. and ordering that the money be brought to the mint to be stamped with the augmented value, so that for instance the *cruzado*, whose nominal value was 400 réis became 500 réis, the king retaining the lion's share or 80 réis for himself and giving the remainder or 20 réis to the owner!

The smaller coins however such as the *vintem* were called in and recoined with a corresponding diminution of weight and thus the *vintem* fell to 18 grs.

In 1688 D. Pedro II. more modest than his predecessor was content to raise the nominal value of the gold and silver coinage 20 per cent, but without going to the trouble of stamping the coins, and thus the *cruzado* was reckoned 480 réis though it continued to be marked 400. The silver *vintem* had now arrived at 15 grs. and was again reduced by D. João V. to $12\frac{1}{3}$ grs. and so it remained till the reign of D. Maria II., when it was substituted by the copper *vintem* of 512 grs., the silver one being found highly inconvenient on account of its microscopic dimensions.

During the foregoing vicissitudes of the silver *vintem*, the copper *real* was proportionately reduced so as to continue one twentieth of its value, and eventually became so small that three of them were required to make a coin equal to half a farthing. Thus it appears that in the XIV. century the original *real* was of silver and weighed 70 grains, while the last silver real (having changed its name to *vintem*) weighed only $12\frac{1}{3}$ grs. and was equal to 20 réis copper, in other words the standard *real* has been reduced to the $\frac{1}{112}$ of its value.

The effect of the Brazilian gold mines is plainly visible in the number and size of the gold pieces coined during the reign of D. João V., indeed such was the plentifulness of the precious metal that most of the coins of that period are found to exceed their legal weight.

Amongst the artistic treasures may be mentioned a processional gold cross weighing 12 marks 4 oz., beautifully wrought and presented by D. Sancho I. to the church of the Holy Cross at Coimbra. The principal face is studded with 17 rubies and sapphires, and 56 pearls. The former were taken from the crown of a Moorish king and each has engraved on it a talismanic sign. At the back of the cross are the symbols of the four evangelists with an *Agnus Dei* in the center. The following inscription runs from the top to the bottom:

DNS — SANCIUS — REX — IUSSIT — FIERI — HAC — X
ANO — ICARNATIOIS — MCC XII

«King Sancius ordered this cross to be made in the year of the Incarnation 1212.»

But by far the most interesting object in this museum is the Remonstrance, formerly the property of the Convent of St. Jerome at Belem. It is a *chef-d'œuvre* of the Manueline style of Portuguese art. It was made in Lisbon by order of king Manuel out of the first gold received in tribute from India consequent on its discovery and vassalage by Vasco da Gama, as may be seen from the white enamel inscription round the rim of the base:

O MUITO ALTO PRINCIPE PODEROSO
SENHOR REI DÕ MANUEL A MANDOU FAZER
DO OURO E DAS PARIAS DE QUILOA
AQUABOU EM CCCCCVI

«The most high and powerful king Dom Manuel ordered this remonstrance to be made out of the gold and tributes from Quiloa Aquabou in 1506.»

The upper part of the base is divided by blue enamel chains into six compartments filled with flowers and birds in *alto relievo* brilliantly enameled.

The knob of the stem is surrounded by six armillary spheres. The main body is flanked by two open pillars, ornamented with angels in niches, playing various instruments. In the center is a circular receptacle for the sacred Host under which are keeling in adoration the twelve apostles, with seraphim hovering over their heads. The upper part, supported by columns *à jour* forms a kind of canopy on the summit of which is a cross. In the center of the canopy are two niches: in the upper one is the Eternal Father holding in His left hand the globe and cross while with His right He is giving His blessing. In the lower one is suspended a dove to represent the Holy Ghost. This *chef-d'œuvre* is unsurpassed for artistic merit, for historic interest, for the richness of the materials and the celebrity of its author. It was chiseled by the famous Gil Vicente, the father of the Portuguese theater, who though victorious in the field of literature, carried on the business of a goldsmith. It is made entirely of gold and enamel and by the originality of the design, the extreme delicacy of the ornamentation, the brilliancy of the colors, and the gracefulness of the outlines it captivates the attention, satisfies the exigencies, and excites the admiration of the most fastidious critic.

In glass cases round the cabinet are many valuable pieces of silver-gilt plate, some Polish tankards of beautiful workmanship, a curious baptismal font set with 138 Roman coins, and which has served at the christening of the sovereigns of Portugal for many generations; Thomason's illustrations of the Holy Scriptures, being a series of medals in five vols., and many other articles of *vertu*.

THE LIBRARY.

Occupies a mean looking building in front of the N. pavilion of the palace. Part of this house serves as an occasional residence for the learned librarian Alexandro Herculano, who wrote here his famous history of Portugal.

This library consists of about 25,000 volumes nearly all old works including many taken from the Jesuits, especially from the extinct *Collegio dos Nobres*. Amongst them are many rare books such as:

The *Cancioneiro*, or collection of Portuguese ballads, a large folio MS. attributed to the reign of D. Diniz, 1279–1325.
Symmicta Lusitanica ex MSS. Codicibus Bibliothecae Apostolicae Vaticanae aliarumque urbis, 222 vols. folio MSS. 1744. Written by order of the magnificent D. João V., and contains a copy of every document referring to Portugal which could be found in the Vatican and other archives and libraries in Rome.
Letters written from India, China and Japan by the Jesuit Missionaries to their Superior in Portugal down to the beginning of the XVIII. century, 50 vols. folio MSS. on Japanese and Indian paper.
Several MSS. Bibles and Breviaries of the xv. century.
The works of the Jesuit father Jacome Gonçalves in Chingalese, a language of the Island of Ceylon, 6 vols. MSS. 1725.
Many specimens of early printing, amongst which *Missal Bracharense* de D. Jorge da Costa, Lisbon, 1498. Gothic.
Ordenações do reino, 1521.
Decades of João de Barros, 1553.
Also a splendid edition of the Lusiad of Camões printed by the Morgado de Matheus.

The library is not open to the public, permission to visit it must be obtained from the Librarian or his substitute.

PALACIO DAS NECESSIDADES.

Situate at the extreme west of the city on the rising ground above the *Praça de Alcantara*, commanding a magnificent view of the Tagus and its bar. It may be divided into three parts, viz., the palace properly so called, which faces the S.; the church adjoining the same; and the upper palace, formerly a convent, which faces E. and W.

The name of «Necessities» is certainly not the most appropriate appellation for the residence of a Monarch and especially of its founder, king John V. who gave it this name, and who, enriched by the constant flow of gold from the Brazils, vied with Louis XIV. in the splendor of his court and in the profuse magnificence of his entertainments.

A short history of the origin of the palace will clear up this apparent incongruity and explain the true signification of the ominous title.

In 1598, a poor weaver who lived at Ericeira, a small village on the W. coast, to escape a plague which broke out in the neighborhood, fled with his family to Lisbon and took up his quarters at Alcantara, bringing with him an image of our Lady of Health *(Nossa Senhora da Saude)*, which he held in great estimation. By the assistance of some friends, and the alms of the faithful, he was enabled to erect a small chapel for its reception, which he dedicated to our Lady under the title of Reliever of our Necessities. The image soon became famous and was much resorted to by the people under the impression that many wonderful cures had been effected through the intercession of Christ's Holy Mother. Among others D. João V. entertained a particular veneration for this image and attributed to the prayers of her whom it represented, his recovery from a dangerous illness in 1742. In gratitude for this cure he bought the whole of the land which forms the site of the present edifice and built a beautiful church in place of the humble chapel, as well as a convent which he gave to the congregation of St. Philip Neri, commonly called Oratorians, whose members besides their sacred duties, devoted themselves to the instruction of youth.

That he might himself be near the shrine, his Majesty ordered a palace to be erected adjoining the church and it was called by the same name of Necessities. The work was completed in 1747 and is one of the few buildings that escaped destruction by the terrific earthquake of 1755. Admission to the lower palace and grounds is readily granted on applying to the *Vedoria,* but to visit the interior of the convent, now occupied by D. Fernando, and containing many rare works of art collected by him, permission must be obtained from some officer of his household, which is not usually granted except when his Majesty is from home.

The gardens are tastefully laid out and well stocked with flowering shrubs and trees, fountains, aviaries, etc. The church in an artistic point of view possesses but few attractions. The statues of Saints Peter and Paul, of S. Carlo Borromeo and S. Camillo de Lellis deserve attention.

PALACIO DE BELEM.

(On the N. side of the Praça de D. Fernando, commonly called Largo de Belem.)

This palace formerly belonged to count Aveiras, and was bought by D. John V. in 1726. It is intended for a summer residence, but the present royal family rarely occupy it. It is now principally used to lodge foreign sovereigns and princes who may come to visit his Most Faithful Majesty.

The palace contains some fine rooms comfortably furnished, but there are few works of art to call the visitor's attention. The entrance hall, paved with squares of blue and white marble, contains the busts of Roman emperors in jasper, and in the central apartment is a magnificent bust of king John V., in Carrara marble on an elegant pedestal.

The palace is surrounded by a garden and an orange grove with shady walks. There are two delightful terraces. That in front of the palace commands a fine view of the Tagus, and has an elegant fountain in the center. The upper terrace on the W. of the palace, is embellished with fountains and statues, and contains two pavilions converted into aviaries, between which is a cascade surmounted by a colossal marble group representing Hercules beheading the Hydra of Lerna.

There are two other marble statues brought from Italy. One of them represents the death of Cleopatra, and has the following inscription:

IMPROBE AMOR QUID NON MORTALIA PECTORA COGIS.
(Virgil.)

Jofé Mazzuoli Senenfi fecit Roma anno MDCCXVII.

The other symbolizes charity, being a young matron suckling her captive father. On the pedestal is written:

QUO NON PENETRAT AUT QUID NON EXCOGITAT PIETAS.
Val. Max. Liv. v. cap. IV)

This statue was made at Rome in 1737 by Bernardino Ludovici.

Adjoining the palace is a splendid riding school, called *o picadeiro*, completed by Joseph I.: it is one of the finest in Europe, and it is here that the young princes are taught to ride.

PALACIO DE BEMPOSTA.

(Commonly called Palacio da Rainha, near the Campo de Santa Anna on the road to Arroios.)

This palace was built about 1700 by queen Catharine of Bragança, daughter of John IV. of Portugal, and widow of Charles II. of England. A treasure of great value is supposed to be concealed in some part of the estate. On the site of the palace was formerly a house occupied by a gentleman named Telles, who affirmed that his father repeatedly declared that he had concealed a large sum of money on the premises during a riot and that after his death, the stone of a ring which he constantly wore was to be taken out and that on the back of it letters were engraved which would point out the spot. On his death, however, the ring was not forthcoming and the disappointed heir was unable to discover the hiding place, but sold the property to the queen with the proviso that should ever the treasure be found, it should be given up to the vendor's family *in solidum*.

King John VI. died in this palace on the 10.th of March 1826: in point of architecture it has nothing notable. The chapel is dedicated to Nossa Senhora da Conceição, who is represented in the painting over the high altar by an Italian, Giuseppi Trono, but the likenesses of D. Maria I. and of the young princes which form part of the same picture, as well as of Santa Izabel (queen) and of S. John the Baptist are by an English artist named F. Hichey, who having called at Lisbon on his way to India, was induced to remain to execute these paintings. The paintings in the Sacristy are by André Gonçalves, who died in 1736. There is also a Madonna with a number of virgins attributed to Grão Vasco.

The grounds attached to the Palace are at present used by the agricultural Society for experimenting with new instruments. It is here also that the new hospital called D. Estephania is being erected, founded by the lamented D. Pedro V. in memory of his virtuous and beautiful queen. The palace is now used for the military school.

PALACIO DE QUELUZ.

At a small village of the same name, about 6 miles north of Lisbon. This palace, commenced in the reign of D. Pedro III. at the end of the last century, is an irregular pile of buildings, overcharged with ornamentation. It was formerly a favorite residence of the Royal family, especially of D. João VI. and of D. Miguel, of whom a very good full length likeness, as a youth of 20, is here exhibited. Many valuable works of art used to adorn this Palace but of late it has been almost entirely abandoned and allowed to fall into utter disrepair. The noble rooms which were decorated with immense mirrors, excellent paintings, beautiful tapestries and huge China vases are now almost empty and present an aspect of discomfort, damp, and moth. One of the rooms is considered an object of historical interest, because D. Pedro IV. happened to die there, and the bed in which he breathed his last, is shown to the visitor with the assurance that it is in exactly the identical same state as on the fatal 24.th of September 1834.

In the oratory is a Doric column made of a single piece of agate which was taken from the excavations at Herculaneum and sent by Pope Leo XII. as a present to D. Miguel.

The extensive gardens and pleasure grounds, with their numerous shady walks, offer a most agreeable promenade during the hot summer weather.

A high cascade and several fountains with marble basins and statues add to the attractions of the luxuriant vegetation and enliven the sylvan solitude.

A good Hotel in the village affords accommodation to visitors who go to spend the day. Admission to the Palace and grounds is readily granted on the spot.

PALACIO DE CAXIAS.

About 6 miles to the W. of Lisbon. This palace is situate near the shore, and is only occupied by the Royal family during the bathing season. Attached to it is a pleasure ground having a magnificent cascade and a *mirante*, which commands a fine view of the Ocean and the bar of the Tagus. The road to Caxias, Paço de Arcos and Cascaes is by far the pleasantest drive in the neighborhood of Lisbon, and runs close to the banks of the river.

The king has several other palaces not far from Lisbon, such as *Alfeite* on the south bank of the Tagus, where his Majesty goes to shoot, *Cintra, Mafra,* etc.

8. PUBLIC AMUSEMENTS.

PRAÇA DOS TOUROS, Bull-ring. In the *Campo de Sant'Anna*.

The bull-fight is generally characterized a cruel and brutalizing amusement, but these epithets, however justly applied in former times, are scarcely applicable to the *touradas* of the present day at Lisbon, and no visitor who has the opportunity, should miss witnessing this national sport of the Portuguese, which though not possessing the life-and-death interest of the Spanish original, yet never fails to produce a thrill of excitement unaccompanied by the barbarous cruelty and disgusting brutality which disgrace the bull-fights of Spain.

The *praça* is a large open circus, in form a twelve-sided polygon, with two tiers of about 200 boxes extending half way round its circumference, on the shade side. Under these boxes but extending nearer to the center and encircling the whole *praça*, are rows of seats forming the *galleria*, which cost 500 réis on the shade side, and 240 réis in the sun. The price of the boxes varies according to size and tier, from 2$500 réis to 4$500 réis. The bull-ring or arena is separated from the gallery by two barriers 5 feet high leaving between them a space 3 feet wide, called the *trincheira*.

The center box, with the royal arms over it, belongs to the king; the one beneath it, to the commissioner of police.

Opposite the royal box, on the other side of the circus, is the door by which the horsemen enter, and on the left is a large folding door flanked by two wickets: from the latter the bulls alternately issue, and by the former make their exit after having been fought.

To the enthusiasts of this sport the entertainment begins on the vigil of the fight. In Lisbon the bull-fights are generally held on Sundays and Holidays during the summer months. The number of bulls in each performance is usually 13, which, however tame they may be, are always announced as *bravissimos*. They are driven in a herd along with trained oxen called *cabrestos*, into Lisbon on the night previous to the fight, by the road which passes *Campo Grande*. and to this place large numbers of carriages, occupied by amateurs and the fast life of the capital, repair to pay their respects to the horned quadrupeds and satisfy their curiosity as to the quality of the animals. So long as the bulls are driven in a herd and accompanied by the *cabrestos*, they are not dangerous, but if one of them get separated from the rest, he immediately becomes infuriated and rushes through the streets attacking anything that comes in his way, and his mad career is rarely brought to a close without serious damage and often loss of life.

The bulls having been at length safely conducted to the *praça*, the next operation is that of *embolar* or placing wooden balls on the tips of their horns. This ceremony begins at 10 o'clock on the morning of the fight and may be witnessed by ticket holders. Poor taurus is driven into a small cage in which he is securely pinioned and his head fastened so as to admit of the balls, attached to leather sheaths, being placed on his horns, which is only accomplished after a hard struggle.

The bull is now ready to enter the arena. The best age for bulls to be fought is from 5 to 7 years. Their age is easily known by the number of rings on the lower part of the horns; the first ring represents 3 years, and each succeeding ring one year, so that a bull with four rings is 6 years old. There is a great difference in the quality of the bulls, the best are those that are well bred, having fine glossy coats, thin legs and long tails, bright black eyes, and restless velvety ears. Those that have been fought before are very cunning and dangerous, as also those that are long-sighted, short-sighted or see more with one eye than with the other.

Bulls are divided into seven classes according to their behavior in the ring: 1.st *boiantes* or those that are very wild and unsophisticated, easily dazzled, and rush to the attack with blind fury; these are the best and safest to fight. 2.nd *Revoltosos* are like the first with this difference that they turn round very quick and take more notice of any object which is placed before them, following it up with eagerness. 3.rd *Que se cingem* or bulls that are not easily deceived by the colored cape with which the bull-fighter seeks to dazzle them, but follow him up closely. 4.th *Que ganham terreno* or those that instead of stopping to toss their adversary continue their course and chase him out of the ring. 5.th *De sentido* are the knowing ones, which having been fought before are not to be deceived and are the most dangerous of all to deal with. 6.th *Abantos* are naturally timid and run away when attacked, and 7.th *Burri-ciegos* are those that, from defective vision, have not their attention attracted at the proper distance, and have to be treated in an exceptional manner.

The bull-fight begins at about 5 o'clock. The circus is crowded with several thousand spectators, and decorated with banners, trophies, evergreens and other devices. The varied costumes of the noisy throng in the gallery and the gay toilets of the ladies in the boxes, lit up by the brilliant rays of the summer sun, with over-head a sky of indigo blue, present a spectacle full of animation and rarely surpassed by any for picturesqueness. In Lisbon deadly weapons are not employed. The *Matador* no longer displays his mortal skill. The only weapon used is a slender wooden dart with an iron barb. These darts called *bandarilhas* or *farpas* are ornamented with bright colors and are about 2 feet long for the fighters on foot, and twice that length for the fighters on horseback. The performers who take part in this contest are the *cavalleiros* or horsemen, the *bandarilheros* or *capinhas*, or fighters on foot, and the *homens de forcado* who are athletic Alemtejanos, whose office is to seize and holdfast the bull by sheer muscular strength. Sometimes, but rarely, Negros are introduced, who offer themselves to be tossed about by the bulls, and whose ludicrous antics cause immense merriment, though they often end by getting seriously hurt and even killed outright. The *cavalleiros* wear an antiquated dress of last century consisting of a broad-tailed coat, breeches, high boots, and a cocked hat. The *bandarilheiros* wear richly embroidered short velvet jackets of various hues, velvet breeches to match, white stockings, thin shoes and a red sash round their waists. The *homens de forcado* in red jackets, strong leather breeches and white stockings, are armed with long poles having a blunt iron prong fixed at the end, called a *forcado*.

Having described its principal elements, let us now give a faint idea of the bull-fight itself. To give anything like a correct description is as impossible as to describe a cricket-match to a person unacquainted with the game and therefore unable to enter into its merits.

The performance opens with the *cortezia* in which all the artists take part, but principally the *cavalleiros*, who put their horses through a variety of evolutions of old Spanish horsemanship, and having made their obeisances to the royal box and to the spectators in general, they retire and the real business of the day begins. The *director da praça* who acts as master of the ceremonies, sits in front of a body of municipal guards under the royal box, and gives his orders by means of a bugler who is at his side.

The bugle sounds and immediately a *bandarilheiro* takes his stand directly in front of one of the small doors, holding in each hand a *farpa* or dart, his object being to fix them in either side of the bull's neck just behind the horns. The wicket is thrown open and the bull rushes in, bewildered and maddened by the shouts of the multitude. On perceiving the *bandarilheiro* he runs at him lowering his head to toss, and at this critical moment the artist fixes the darts in the bull's neck and by a *quebro* or supple movement of the waist avoids being tossed and escapes as best he can, jumping over the barrier into the alley. He is enabled to accomplish this feat because the bull on seeing him, measures the distance at a glance, and closes his eyes before lowering his head to toss, so that he does not notice the altered position of his opponent and tosses the air. The goaded animal now shakes his head with rage, scampers about the ring, and is attacked in turn by the other *bandarilheiros*, while he is further infuriated by the sight of the brilliant colored *capas* or capes which are shaken before his eyes. The behavior of the bull in the ring varies according to his class. He usually selects some spot where he imagines there is some security or chance of escape, and this is technically called his *querença*. To this favorite position he repeatedly returns after chasing his tormentors, and at times obstinately refuses to quit it, till induced to do so by the goads.

There are many ways in which the *bandarilheiro* may await and avoid the attack of the bull, and these are the different *sortes* which are so vociferously cheered or criticised by the *habitué*, tho' their merits are quite lost to the casual looker-on.

After receiving 8 or 10 *farpas*, which hang dangling from his neck, he is now submitted to the operation called *capear* or *passar á capa*, viz. the *bandarilheiros* who are also called *capinhas*, throw aside their darts and play the bull with gaudy capes, deluding him in a most artistic manner and escaping his horns by the agility of their movements.

Master taurus being now partially exhausted is, if he have displeased the spectators by displaying tameness, sentenced to be caught and held fast by the *homens de forcado,* muscular specimens of humanity who risk their lives for a few shillings. One of these reckless individuals awaits the bull and when it lowers its head to toss, throws himself between its horns, and grasping its neck with his arms is dragged about the ring while his companions, six or seven in number, seize the animal by its tail and jump upon its back till it is completely overpowered. It would be well if this part of the entertainment were abolished, for it is certainly most brutal as well as dangerous. The poor foolhardy men are often badly hurt, though after receiving the few coppers which are thrown to them from the gallery, and after smoking a cigarette and drinking a glass of wine, they seem much better than might have been expected. Having thus been punished, the bull is set at liberty, the folding doors are thrown open, and half a dozen trained oxen with bells attached to their necks are driven into the arena, whom he at once recognises as friends and in whose company he is driven out of the ring.

Two or three bulls only out of the 13 are fought by the *cavalleiro,* whose object is to fix a dart about 4 feet long in to the bull's neck and always save his horse from harm. He is assisted by *capinhas* who attract the bull's attention when the horseman is in danger. Many of the wilder bulls jump over the barrier into the trench and some will even leap into the gallery, so that strangers will do well to avoid the front seats.

After the performance, the darts are taken out of the bulls' necks and their wounds, which are mere punctures, rubbed with a mixture of salt and vinagar. The bulls are driven out of Lisbon by night in the same way that they were brought in.

THEATERS.

A few words on the Portuguese theater may not be out of place here. In the early centuries of the monarchy, down to the end of the xv., we find traces of a kind of theatrical representations called *momos,* being a combination of mimicry with dancing, resembling the modern pantomime.

Gil Vicente is the acknowledged father of the Portuguese theater: his first work was represented on the occasion of the birth of D. João III., 7.*th* June 1502, and consisted of a short pastoral monologued. Several of his other plays were performed during the reigns of D. Manuel the Great and of his son D. João III. Gil Vicente was undoubtedly an original writer, his plays exhibiting a complete ignorance of classic models. He wrote 17 *autos* (sacred drama in one act), 4 comedies, 11 farces and various *trovas* (poetic pieces), which were represented in the churches, royal palaces, and other places, on a raised platform or stage, with changeable scenes.

Sá de Miranda, Gil's contemporary, laid the foundation of the Portuguese classic drama, following the example set by Italy, where the classic theater had been already restored. His comedies *Os estrangeiros* and *Vilhalpandos* are in imitation of Terence and Ariosto. Miranda's disciple Antonio Ferreira, though in many respects inferior to his master, wrote the first tragedy entitled *Castro,* after which no other was written for two centuries. Next come the tragi-comedies and magic-comedies, the former invented by the Jesuits and intended for representation in the cloisters of the monasteries with the accompaniment of music. The latter were devised by the comic actor Simão Machado. During the Spanish domination the Portuguese theater fell into decay, being superseded and eclipsed by the superior works of Lope de Vega and Calderon de la Barca. The Italian opera was introduced during the reign of D. João IV., himself an accomplished musician, and was much patronized by the ostentatious D. João V. At the commencement of the XVIII. century the principal theater in Lisbon was in Rua da Rosa, where several Portuguese operas by Antonio José were represented, but towards the end of the century the popular taste had become so vitiated that more attention was paid to the beauties of the actresses than of the plays, which led Dona Maria I. to prohibit the appearance of females on the stage. The only old theater which has survived is that of Rua dos Condes, which was destroyed by the great earthquake, but was soon after rebuilt. Though the senior theater of the capital it is devoted to the lowest comedy. The next theater was built in Rua do Salitre in 1782 and was occasionally used for the Italian opera till 1793, when S. Carlos was built by a company of rich merchants headed by Baron Quintella, the lavish patron of art. Few modern authors of merit appear till Almeida Garrett wrote his *Auto de Gil Vicente* in 1838, whence dates the regeneration of the Portuguese drama, many original plays by talented authors following in quick succession. Through Garrett's influence and exertions the normal theater of Dona Maria II, was established in 1842 and opened in 1846, the first play performed being *Alvaro Gonçalves, o Magriço, e os doze de Inglaterra* by J. H. de Faria Aguiar de Loureiro. Of late years there has been a marked decline on account of the preference given to translations of immoral French comedies, which never fail to draw good houses, the managers thus filling their pockets by pandering to the depraved tastes of the populace.

The Lisbon theaters are open on Sundays as well as week-days. The performances begin from half past seven to eight o'clock and end about midnight. Evening dress is the exception, not the rule. The pit is called *plateia geral*; the stalls, *cadeiras*; the first tier of boxes are called *frisas*; the second tier is the *primeira ordem* or *ordem nobre*, the boxes in this tier being considered the best in the house; the third tier is called *segunda ordem* and so on to the top.

THEATRO DE S. CARLOS.—The Theater of S. Carlos, in the *Rua Nova dos Martyres*, which runs S. out of the Chiado, opposite the hotel Gibraltar.

This theater, devoted to the Italian opera, was built by a company of rich merchants, the chief of whom was the Barão de Quintella, afterwards created Conde de Farrobo. The architect was José da Costa e Silva; the building which is mostly of stone was completed in the short space of six months and was opened on the 29.th of April 1793 to celebrate the birth of Dona Maria Thereza, at that time heir presumptive to the throne and afterwards married to Don Carlos of Spain.

The principal façade is unpretending but neat, having at the entrance an arcade of three arches under which the carriages pass to set down or take up, and are thus protected from the rain. Over the portico are four Doric columns and between these, three windows over which are three tablets, the center one bearing the following inscription:

CARLOTAE
BRASILIAE PRINCIPI
QUOD FELICEM STATUM REI P.
REGIA PROLE CONFIRMARIT
THEAT. AUSPICATO EXSTE
AUD. DED. ING. PIN. MANIQ P. P.
OLYSIPONENSIS CIVES
SOLIC. AMORE ET LONGA FIDE
ERGA DOMUM AUG. PROBATE
IN MON. PUBLICAE LAETITIAE
C.
ANNO MDCCXCIII

The other tablets are ornamented with cornucopia and Mercury's caduceus, the symbols of commerce. The painting on the ceiling of the entrance hall is by Cyrillo Wolkmar Machado and represents the fall of Phaëton. The saloon over the entrance is of noble proportions and neatly decorated; it is often used for concerts and other amusements. The house is elliptical and contains five tiers of 24 boxes. The pit is divided into *geral* and three rows of stalls. The opera season begins on the 29.th of October, the birth day of His Majesty D. Fernando, and lasts until March or April, the number of performances is about 100. On the *dias de grande gala* or great gala days, such as the king's birth day, etc., the royal family appear in state with the high officers of their household, and occupy the *tribuna* or state box. On other occasions the royal family occupy their private box.

The prices of admission are very reasonable compared with London, Paris or St. Petersburg, though the quality of the performances is of a high character, many singers of world wide fame having taken part in them. The first tier of boxes (on a level with the royal box) cost 6$500 réis, the *frisas* 6$000 réis, second tier 4$000 réis, third 2$500 réis, fourth *(torrinhas)* 1$600 réis; stalls *(cadeiras)* 1$200 réis, pit *(geral)* 700 réis. Portuguese ladies do not usually go to the stalls, but foreign ladies often do. Nor is it necessary for gentlemen to wear evening dress, as in some capitals.

THEATRO DE D. MARIA SEGUNDA. (Theater of Mary II).— Situate at the N. end of the praça de D. Pedro commonly called the *Rocio*, architecturally one of the finest in Europe. It was built in 1846 on the site of the palace and prison of the inquisition. The principal façade is adorned with an elegant peristyle supported by six Ionic columns. The center statue represents *Gil Vicente* the father of the Portuguese theater. The side figures represent Melpomene and Thalia, the muses of tragedy and comedy. The tympanum is embellished with a group representing Apollo and the other seven muses. In the attic are four *mezzo-relievos* denoting the natural divisions of the day. The two on the right are dawn and mid-day: the two on the left, evening and night.

The interior decorations are not equal to the magnificent exterior, moreover its acoustic properties are defective. It contains 70 boxes *(camarotes)* in four tiers *(ordens)*, and is constructed with every precaution as to fire, etc., having water cisterns and numerous stone staircases.

This theater is subsidized by government and is a kind of national school for actors, who have the *entrée* gratis. It is devoted principally to tragedy and high comedy.

The best Portuguese actors may be heard here, notwithstanding which, the house is badly attended, low comedy and Offenbach being unfortunately more in vogue with Lisbon audiences.

THEATRO DA TRINDADE, in the Rua nova da Trindade, which runs N. out of the Chiado. This theater, built a few years ago in imitation of the Parisian houses, is handsomely decorated and possesses a large saloon sometimes used for concerts and masked balls.

Comedies and burlesque operas form the staple representations. The prices are as follows:

Lower boxes (frisas)	3$000
Boxes (primeira ordem)	5$500
Boxes, third tier (segunda ordem)	2$500
Boxes, fourth tier (terceira ordem)	1$500
Balcony stalls (balcão)	$600
Stalls (cadeiras)	$500
Pit	$200

THEATRO DO GYMNASIO, in the Rua Nova da Trindade, a little below the Trindade. This theater, recently built, is devoted to comedy and farces, and owes most of its success to Taborda, the celebrated Portuguese comedian, whose appearance on the stage is always the signal for an outburst of merriment. The following are the prices:

Lower boxes (frisas)	2$000
Boxes, second tier (camarotes de primeira ordem)	2$500
Boxes, third tier (camarotes de segunda ordem)	2$000
Boxes, fourth tier (camarotes de terceira ordem)	1$000
Stalls (cadeiras)	$500
Pit (geral)	$200

THEATRO DO PRINCIPE REAL, in the Rua Nova da Palma, a modern theater where comedies and pantomimes are principally given.

Lower boxes (frisas)	2$000
Boxes, second tier (camarotes de primeira ordem)	3$000
Boxes, third tier (camarotes de segunda ordem)	2$000
Boxes, fourth tier (camarotes de terceira ordem)	1$200
Stalls (cadeiras)	$400
Pit (geral)	$200

THEATRO DA RUA DOS CONDES — E. of the Passeio Publico, the oldest theater in Lisbon. The house was destroyed by the great earthquake, after which the present shabby building was erected. Low comedy and burlesques prevail here. Prices:

Lower boxes (frisas)	1$200
Boxes, second tier (camarotes de primeira ordem)	2$400
Boxes, third tier (camarotes de segunda ordem)	1$800
Boxes, fourth tier (camarotes de terceira ordem)	1$500
Stalls (cadeiras)	$400
Pit (geral)	$200

THEATRO DAS VARIEDADES, a small theater to the N. of the Passeio Publico: gives performances of the same class as the Rua dos Condes.

9. LIBRARIES.

BIBLIOTHECA NACIONAL, National Library. In the extinct convent of *S. Francisco,* the entrance being in the *Rua de S. Francisco* which runs out of the *Chiado.*—Open to the public every day, except Sundays and Holidays from, 9 A. M. to sunset. On Saturdays it closes at 2 P. M.

The total number of volumes, arranged in the corridors and cells, exceeds 280,000, the greater part derived from the libraries of the suppressed convents, and it is much to be lamented that many of the most valuable works belonging to the religious houses disappeared during the political tumults attendant on their abolition. A large well ventilated public reading room is provided, with officials in attendance to seek any book which may be asked for. There is no systematic catalogue of the whole.

Of MSS. there are not fewer than 10,000 including 300 of the Cistercian order from the convent of Alcobaça, one of which is the first volume of a Bible taken from the Spaniards at the battle of Aljubarrota in 1385, and said to have belonged to the king of Castile, whose arms it bears.

The following MSS. on vellum deserve particular notice:

The Old Testament in Hebrew with Rabbinic annotations, a splendid MS. bought at a Jew's sale at Amsterdam by the Portuguese ambassador, Conde de Linhares, for 800$000 réis; it has lately been valued at £ 2.000.

Several Latin Bibles and Offices of the B. V., especially an *Horae Beat. Mariae* of the xv. century, beautifully illuminated and having in the Calendar representations of the signs of the zodiac and of the domestic occupations of each month.

Forus Judicum, the first Castilian translation of the Visigothic *Fuero juzgo*, 1 vol. in fol. xiv. century.

Missale fratrum ordinis Beatae Mariae de Monte Carmeli, ill. initials, xv. century.

Another illuminated Missal, 8vo. xiv. century.

St. Ambrose's *Officiorum libri tres*, ill. init. French Gothic.

Diodorus Sierlus, Roman character, ill. init.

Roma triumphans, of Flavius Blondus Forliensis, 1 vol. in fol. xv. century.

Chronica de Fernão Lopez, in Portuguese, 1 vol. in fol. ill.

Commento ó Esposicion á las Chronicas de Eusebeo, 5 vol. in fol. xv. century, in a beautiful state of preservation.

Expositio viginti librorum Titi, written by order of Pope John XXII 2 vol. in fol.

Speculum historiale.

The library contains also numerous specimens of early printing, first and foremost of which is the:

Latin Bible, in 2 vol. fol. printed at Moguncia in 1454 by the inventor of printing the immortal Guttemberg.

Vita Christi, 4 vol. in fol. Lisbon 1495, Gothic. A remarkable edition, printed by order of king D. João II.

Estoria do Muy nobre Vespasiano emperador de Roma, 4to. Gothic with wood engravings, Lisbon, 1490.

List of English works on Portugal in the National Library.

Link, M.', Travels in Portugal and through France and Spain. Translated from the German by Mr. Hinckley. — London, 1801, 8vo.

History (A) of the campaigns of the British forces in Spain and Portugal, from the French usurpation. — London, 1812, 4 vols. 8vo.

History (The) of the revolutions of Portugal from the foundation to the year 1667, with letters from Sir Robert Southwell, during his Embassy there, to the Duke of Ormond. — London, 1740, 8vo.

Murphy (James). Travels in Portugal in the years 1789-1790, illustrated with plates. — London, 1795, 4to.

Murphy (James), A general view of the state of Portugal, containing a topographical description thereof with plates. — London, 1798, 4to.

Landmann (George). Historical, military and picturesque observations on Portugal, illustrated by 75 colored plates. — London, 1821, 2 vol. 4to. (no gabinete).
Annals of the Peninsular campaigns from 1808 to 1814. - Edinburg, 1829, 2 vols.
Badcock (L.), Rough leaves from a journal kept in Spain and Portugal during the years 1832-1833 and 1834. — London, 1835, 8vo.
Baker (R. P.), The history of the Inquisition, illust. with 12 plates. — London, 1736, 4to.
Baretti (J.), A Journey from London to Genoa, through England, Portugal, Spain and France. — London, 1770, 4 vols. 8vo.
Baxter (W. E.), The Tagus and the Tiber, or notes of Travels in Portugal, Spain and Italy in 1850-1851. — London, 1852, 2 vol. 8vo.
Beckford, Recollections of an excursion to the Monasteries of Alcobaça and Batalha by the author of Vathek. London, 1835, 8vo.
Beckford, Italy with sketches of Spain and Portugal. Paris, 1834, 8vo.
Beckford (Mr.), Memoirs. Visit to Portugal, Spain, etc. London, 1859, 2 vol. 8vo.
Brown (general), Portugal in 1820, an historical view of the late revolution of Portugal. — London, 1827, 8vo.
Camões. The Lusiad. Translated by W. G. Mickle. — Dublin, 1791. 2 vol. 8vo.
Camões. The Lusiad. Translated by Mr. Julius Mickle. — London, 1809, 12mo.
Camões. Poems. Translated by Viscount Strangford. — London, 1810, 8vo.
Camões. The Lusiad. Translated by Rich.d Fanshaw. — London, 1655, fol.
Carnarvon (Earl of), Portugal and Galicia, with a review of the social and political state of the Basque Provinces. — London, 1848, 8vo.
Charnock (Dr.), Illustrated hand-book to Spain and Portugal, with maps, plans, and steel engravings. — London, 8vo.
Corner (Miss), The histories of Spain and Portugal. With illustrations. — London, 8vo.
Costigan (A), Sketches of society and manners in Portugal. — London, 2 vol. 8vo.
Dunbar (Lady), A family tour round the coasts of Spain and Portugal during the winter of 1860-1861. — London, 1862, 8vo.
Fanshaw (R.), Original letters during his embassies in Spain and Portugal. — London, 1701, 8vo.
Hervey (C.), Letters from Portugal, Spain, Italy and Germany, in the years 1759-1761. London, 1785, 3 vol. 8vo.
Historic sketches in Spain and Portugal. London, 1835, 12mo.
History of Portugal (A). — London, 12mo.
History of Portugal (The) from B. C. 1000 to A. D. 1814. — London, 1833, 8vo.

Hodges (G. Lloyd), Narrative of the expedition to Portugal in 1832 under the orders of Dom Pedro, Duke of Bragança. — London, 2 vol. 8vo.
Hughes (T. M.) An Overland journey to Lisbon at the close of 1846. With a picture of the actual state of Spain and Portugal. — London, 1847. 2 vol. 8vo.
Journal of a few months, residence in Portugal and glimpses of the south of Spain. — London, 1847, 2 vol. 8vo.
Kingston (W. H. G.), Lusitanian sketches of the pen and pencil, with engravings. — London, 1845, 2 vol. 8vo.
Letters from Portugal on the late and present state of that kingdom. — London, 8vo.
Life of St. Elizabeth, queen of Portugal, by a secular priest. — London, 1859, 12mo.
Lives of the most eminent literary and scientific men of Italy, Spain and Portugal. — London, 1835, 3 vol. 8vo.
Lusitanian scenes and sketches in Portugal. — Porto, 1844, 8vo.
Mathews (Henry), The diary of an invalid, being the journal of a tour in pursuit of health in Portugal, Spain, etc. — London, 1820, 8vo.
Memoirs concerning the Portuguese inquisition. — London, 1761, 8vo.
Mendez Pinto (Fernão) The voyages and adventures of, done into English by H. C. Gent. — London, 1653, fol.
Millingen (Dr.) Stories of Torres Vedras. — London, 8vo.
Mins (Captain). A Narrative of the naval part of the expedition to Portugal under the orders of D. Pedro, Duke of Braganza, etc. with illustrations. — London, 1833, 8vo.
Pardoe (Miss), Traits and Traditions of Portugal. London, 1833.
Porter (Miss Anna Maria), Don Sebastian or the House of Braganza, an historical romance. — Longean, 1809, 4 vol. 8vo.
Scevole and Louis de St. Marthe, A genealogical history of the kings of Portugal, with their arms and emblazons, engraven on copper-plates. — London, 1662, fol.
Sismondi (J. C. L. Simon de de), Historical view of the literature of the south of Europe. Translated by Thomas Roscoe. — London, 1853, 2 vol. 8vo.
Strickland (Agnes), Lives of the Queens of England, vol. 5 contains the life of Catherine of Braganza, wife of Charles the 2nd, etc. with portraits. London, 1857, 8vo.
Thackeray (W. M.), Notes of a journey from Cornhill to Gran Cairo, by way of Lisbon, Athens, etc. London, 1864, 8vo.
Travels through Spain and part of Portugal, with maps. — London, 1808, 2 vol. 12mo.
Vane (C. W.), A steam voyage to Constantinople and to Portugal and Spain, with illustrations. London, 1842, 2 vol. 8vo.
Vertot (Abbot), The history of the revolution in Portugal in the year 1640, translated from the French. — London, 1700, 12mo.
Walton, A letter to the late Marquis of Landsdowne, on the affairs of Portugal and Spain. — London, 1827, 8vo.
Wortley (Lady E. Stuart), A visit to Portugal and Madeira. — London, 1854, 8vo.

The national library possesses a good collection of ancient and modern coins, about 25,000 in number, arranged in a room to the left of the entrance, called *gabinete de medalhas*. The following are the principal series: —Celtiberian coins—Colonies and municipalities of Spain — Cities of ancient Greece — Kings of Macedonia, Syria, Egypt and other eastern states — Consular and Imperial Families from Julius Caesar down to Commenus — Coins and medals of Portugal, Spain, France, Italy, Germany, England and Russia, Moorish coins.

In the numismatic Cabinet are also to be seen a few ancient Roman bronze statues, Roman lamps in bronze and earthenware, Amphoræ, lachrymatory vases and cinerary vases of pot and glass, together with a fine collection of African implements and weapons.

BIBLIOTHECA DA AJUDA, see page 184.

BIBLIOTHECA DO CONVENTO DE JESUS, see page 143.

BIBLIOTHECA DA ACADEMIA DAS SCIENCIAS, see page 144.

10. PICTURE GALLERIES.

GALERIA NACIONAL DE PINTURA, National Picture Gallery, in the *Academia das bellas artes,* Rua de S. Francisco, which runs into the Chiado. Open to the public on week-days till 3 P. M.

The National Gallery is of very recent date being founded in 1836 in connexion with the Academy of fine arts. When the religious orders were abolished in 1833, a decree was issued ordering all the works of art belonging to the extinct monasteries to be collected in a dépôt at Lisbon, and it is from this source that most of the pictures representing the Portuguese school were derived, but as may be imagined, many of the best works taken from the religious houses in those turbulent times, never reached Lisbon.

The gallery contains 366 paintings by Portuguese and foreign artists, hung in 5 rooms. The first is devoted to paintings presented by the artists to the Academy to obtain the title of Academician, and are nearly all by Portuguese. The second room contains but few works by Portuguese artists. The third, called Sala de D. Fernando, contains the pictures bought with the subsidy of £ 5,000 a year generously conceded by his Majesty D. Fernando, who is himself an artist and who has contributed greatly to the elevation of the taste of the people by his example, and by his liberal patronage of the fine arts. In the fourth room are paintings by national and foreign artists, and the fifth is devoted entirely to paintings representing the Portuguese school of the end of the fifteenth and beginning of the sixteenth centuries, and is by far the most interesting part of the collection.

Although foreign artists are represented, amongst others, by the following brilliant names: Michael Angelo (147), Caracci (356), Carlo Dolci (191), Guido (64), Guercino (190 and 350), Murillo (178), Perugino (168), Poussin (140), Rafael (150), Rembrandt (151), Salvator Rosa (80 and 82), Rubens (135 and 136) and Teniers (127 and 128), yet it must be confessed that the works are inferior specimens, and not to be compared with the *chefs d'œuvre* of these renowned masters. England has only one representative, John Gresbant (181 and 182), an Englishman who lived in Lisbon about 1680. Modern native artists are also poorly represented, the principal specimens being those presented by themselves to the Academy.

The whole interest, therefore, of the Gallery centers in the works of the Portuguese painters of the XV. and XVI. centuries.

It appears that a Dutch painter John Van Eyck came to Portugal in 1428 and remained a considerable time in the country surrounded by a group of disciples to whom he taught his art. After Van Eyck quitted Portugal his disciples, left to themselves, began to develop a style of their own, retaining much of the Flemish school but adding new characteristics which may be noted in the surpassing richness of the embroidered vestments studded with precious stones, in the elaborately worked gold ornaments and sacred plate, in the architecture, arms, coins, etc. all of which are undoubtedly Portuguese of the reigns of Manuel and John III.

The chief of this school was one Vasco, commonly called Grão Vasco, there were also Andrea Gonzales,

Campello, Cristoforo Lopes, Fernando Gallegos de Salamanca and some others. All the paintings of these artists are on boards, and are devoted to religious subjects, the church at that time being almost the only patron and supporter of art.

The influence of Italian art and the Castilian usurpation gave the death-blow to this school and from that time to the present day Portugal may be said to have produced no distinctive style; in fact men's minds were so engrossed by wars and political changes that the fine arts were altogether neglected.

Indeed so little attention was given to this subject that it is now very difficult to ascertain with certainty the authorship of the few works which have survived and it is only by comparison and a close examination of their individuality that most of the pictures said to be by Grão Vasco, can be attributed to that master. Those who take an interest in this subject are referred to Raczynsky's «Les arts en Portugal», and Robinson's «Memoir on the Portuguese school of painting».

The library of the Academy, open daily from 9 to 3 not only to students but to the public, contains many valuable books on the fine arts in Portuguese, English, Italian, French and some works of art presented by his Majesty D. Luiz.

At the entrance to the picture gallery a complete catalogue in Portuguese may be purchased: we shall therefore give only a list of the finished works by native artists:

3	St. Peter of Alcantara in ecstacy.	Sequeira (1768–1839).
4	St. Antão and St. Paul.	»
5	St. Onofre.	»
7	St. Bruno prostrated at prayer.	»
9	Egas Moniz and family in presence of Affonso VII. of Leon.	»
11	The Coronation of the Virgin.	»
19	St. Augustine.	Vieira Lusitano (1699–1783).
20	Madonna of the rosary.	»
22	The Infant Jesus adored by saints.	Machado (1749–1823).
23	The Epiphany.	Pedro Alexandrino de Carvalho (1730–1810).
24	Christ with the Doctors.	»

25 Adoration of the Blessed Eucharist.	Pedro Alexandrine de Carvalho (1730–1810).
29 Game.	Monteiro da Cruz (1770–1851).
31 Flowers and Fruit.	Ferreira de Freitas (1770–1857).
33 Mystical marriage of St. Catharine.	Ayalla (1634–1684).
34 St. John the Evangelist writing the Apocalypse.	»
35 The Judgment of Salomon.	Metrass (1824–1861).
44 Village scene.	Marques.
47 The Communion of St. Jerome (copy of Domenichino).	Fonseca.
48 The Transfiguration (copy of Raphael)	»
49 Landscape.	Annunciação.
50 Flowers (on zinc).	»
52 View of the Penha de França.	»
53 Flowers.	»
55 View of Lisboa from Entremuros.	»
56 Fruit and Flowers.	»
58 Cardinal Henrique receiving the news of D. Sebastian's death.	Silva.
59 D. João de Portugal.	Lupi.
60 Morning.	Alfredo de Andrade.
61 Sea piece.	Tomazini.
102 The adoration of the Shepherds.	Reinoso (1641).
175 The Ascension.	Portuguese School.
176 The Annunciation.	»
177 Presentation of Christ in the Temple.	»
193 St. Lucas and St. Jerome.	»
194 St. Matthew and St. John the Evangelist.	»
195 The Martyrdom of a saint.	»
196 Condemnation of a holy Martyr.	»
197 Martyrdom of St. Sebastian.	»
198 Christ with his Apostles.	»
200 Virgin and Child, St. Julia and St. Querito.	»
208 St. Helena finding the Cross.	»
209 The Prophet Daniel and Susannah.	»
211 St. John the Baptist.	»
212 Apparition of Christ to his blessed mother.	»
213 A veronica sustained by two angels.	»
214 The Assumption.	»

215 The Ascension. Portuguese School.
216 Praesepeum. ,,
217 The Virgin and Child with an
   angel. ,,
218 St. Sebastian and another saint. ,,
219 Apparition of Christ to his Apostles. ,,
220 A bishop. ,,
221 Virgin and Child between two
   saints. ,,
223 Marriage of the Blessed Virgin. Grão Vasco.
224 The Annunciation. ,,
225 The Visitation. ,,
226 Praesepeum. ,,
227 The adoration of the Magi. ,,
228 Presentation of Christ in the
   Temple. ,,
229 The Virgin fleeing into Egypt. ,,
230 The death of our Lady. ,,
231 The death of our Lady. Portuguese School.
232 Death of the Blessed Virgin. ,,
233 The Annunciation. ,,
234 Praesepeum. ,,
235 Praesepeum. ,,
236 The Visitation. Grão Vasco.
237 Adoration of the Magi. ,,
238 Presentation in the Temple. ,,
239 Christ with the Doctors. ,,
240 Adoration of the Magi. Portuguese School.
241 The Circumcision. ,,
242 The profession of a Knight. ,,
243 The profession of a Knight. ,,
244 St. John preaching. ,,
245 The manna in the Desert. ,,
246 The Last Supper. ,,
247 A pope celebrating Mass. ,,
248 Abraham offering bread and
   wine to Melchisedech. ,,
249 The Temptation of St. James ,,
250 The corpse of St. James carried
   by two bulls. ,,
251 Christ, St. John and St. James. ,,
252 St. John teaching prince D. João
   to pray. ,,
253 St. Dominic teaching a prayer. ,,
254 Payo Peres Corrêa beseeching
   our Lady. ,,
255 Payo Peres Corrêa vanquishing
   the Moors. ,,
256 St. John writing the Apocalypse. ,,
257 The Holy Trinity. ,,
258 The Eternal Father. ,,

259	The Ascension.	Portuguese School.
260	The Conception of our Lady.	"
261	The Baptism of Christ.	"
262	The Resurrection of our Lord.	"
263	The Descent of the Holy Ghost.	"
264	The Flight into Egypt.	"
265	Christ on his way to Calvary.	"
266	An Infanta of Portugal and a Cardinal.	Grão Vasco.
267	Virgin and Child with two Angels.	Portuguese School.
268	Virgin and Child with Angels.	"
269	St. John in the desert.	"
271	St. Vincent and St. John.	"
270	The adoration of the Magi.	"
272	St. Nicholas and St. James.	"
273	St. Margarite and St. Magdalen.	Grão Vasco.
274	St. Lucy and St. Agatha.	"
275	The profession of a nun.	Portuguese School.
276	The carmelites giving their rule to the nuns.	"
277	St. Thomas of Aquino.	"
278	St. Anthony at prayer.	"
279	Deposition of Christ in the sepulcher.	"
280	The Descent from the cross.	"
281	A bishop.	"
282	A bishop.	"
283	The Last Judgment.	"
284	Jesus praying in the garden.	"
285	Christ on his way to Calvary.	"
289	Burning of a country house.	Rocha (1730-1786).
290	Burning of a house in the city.	"
291	Still nature.	"
292	Flowers and Fruit.	Ayalla.
293	Flowers and Fruit.	"
325	A Fisherman playing the guitar.	Rezende.
326	The Kiss of Judas.	"
328	A halberdier.	Metrass.
333	Flowers.	Chaves.
334	St. Michael.	Portuguese School.
335	Apollo.	"
341	A scene from one of Herculano's romances the Monge of Cister.	Bordallo Pinheiro.

In connexion with the Academy, is a museum of works of art in silver and gold, consisting principally of sacred plate, chalices, crosses, remonstrances etc., taken from the suppressed monasteries. Many of them are exquisitely chased and studded with precious stones: they correspond exactly with those represented in the paintings of Grão Vasco. – Permission to visit the museum may be obtained by applying to the director of the Academy.

Galeria de quadros no Palacio da Ajuda. — Picture gallery at the Ajuda palace, see page 172.

11. MUSEUMS.

Museu Nacional de Lisboa, in the Polytechnic school, a little to the N. of the Praça do Principe Real.

This museum is divided into two sections viz. zoology, and mineralogy, the latter occupying a suit of rooms on the ground floor, running the whole length of the E. side of the building, while the former is installed in a similar position on the second floor.

The mineralogical department is open to the public on Thursdays from 11 to 3 and consists of 5 distinct collections as follows:

1. General collection classified according to Dufrenoy, but with some modification of nomenclature. It comprises 7,114 specimens, representing 50 genus and 352 species.
2. Collection to demonstrate the physical characteristics of the minerals and intended for the use of the students of mineralogy. It was purchased of Louis Sœmann at Paris in 1865 and consists of 405 specimens arranged so as to demonstrate the following properties — Crystaline form — Pseudomorphosis — Imitative form — Splinter — Fracture — Refraction of light — Transparency — Phosphorescence — Glitter — Color — Powder — Magnetism — Electricity — Cohesion — Hardness — Touch — Taste — Fusibility — and Smell.
3. Collection of Crystals; comprising 176 specimens arranged to illustrate the science of crystallography.
4. Collection of minerals of Portugal, classified after Dufrenoy. It is very incomplete.

5. Collection of minerals of Russia, Vesuvius, Canary Isles, and Brazil, which formerly formed part of the Royal museum of Ajuda, including an immense block of native copper weighing 2,666 lbs. and found at Caxoeira in the Brazils: it has stamped on it the royal arms and the following Latin legend:

MARIA I ET PETRO III
IMPERANTIBUS
CUPRUM NATIVUM
MINERAE FERRI MIXTUM
PONDERIS LIB. MMDCLXVI
IN
BAHIENSI PRAEFECTURA
PROPE
CAXOEIRAE OPPIDUM
DETECTUM
ET IN
BRASILIENSIS PRINCIPIS
MUSEO
P.
MDCCLXXXII

Notice also the flexible stone flags from the Brazils.

FOSSILS.

The paleontological section comprises the following collections:

1,722 Specimens of animal fossils presented by M. Alcide d'Orbigny to D. Pedro V. in 1855. They all belong to the sub-kingdoms of mollusca and radiata.

140 Specimens of mollusca presented to D. Pedro V. by Senhor Carlos Ribeiro.

Fossils of Sicily and fossil trunks of trees. The above collections are the gift of his Majesty D. Luiz, in addition to which are four others acquired by the museum, viz:

1. A collection of 2,406 specimens arranged according to the strata in which they were found, and comprising mollusca, radiata, insects, annellata, crustacea, fish, reptiles and mammalia.

2. A collection of 475 specimens (principally mollusca) of the tertiary period.
3. 29 Specimens of vegetable fossils.
4. Collection of Portuguese fossils, very imperfect.

There are also several collections of rocks and marbles, both native and foreign.

The Zoological department up stairs, is open to the public on thursdays from 12 to 3.30. It is on a small scale, and contains but few specimens except of birds and shells. Among the former is a very rare one of the *Pinguinus, alca impennis,* an extinct species of the Arctic regions. It was presented by king Victor Emmanuel of Italy, and is valued at 5 contos (£ 1,111). The only other specimen extant is in the museum at Florence. The last six compartments in the same room contain a fair collection of the birds of Portugal.

In the center of the room is a beautiful collection of shells, some of them very rare; for instance, a *Gloria maris* cost £ 80. *Ovulo volva* £ 100, three specimens of *Conus ledonulli* £ 150. *Hermitis Angolensis* £ 500 and *Spondylus regius* £ 100.

In the S. room are also shells and birds, together with some fine specimens of the *Crocodilus niger* from the Brazils and an immense *Sphargis Coriacea* taken on the coast of Portugal near Peniche.

MUSEU COLONIAL, see page 225.
MUSEU DO INSTITUTO INDUSTRIAL, see page 232.
MUSEU ARCHEOLOGICO, see page 146.

12. ROMAN ANTIQUITIES.

Considering the long period Lisbon was occupied by the Romans, it is surprising so few Roman remains are to be found. Before the earthquake of 1755 there were many tablets bearing Latin inscriptions which had been found in digging the foundations, and were built into the walls of the houses and churches, and it is greatly to be regretted that these interesting relics, instead of being preserved, have been concealed in the foundations of the new buildings.

Four inscriptions which have escaped this Vandalism, may be seen built into the wall of a house in the *Travessa do Almada*, a small street near the church of St. Magdalen. They are in good preservation and may be easily read. The larger one runs as follows:

L. CAECILIO. L. F. CELERI RECTO
QUAEST. PROVINC. BOET.
TRIB. PLEB. PRAETORI.
FEL. JUL. OLISIPO.

« Lucio Caecilio Lucii Filio Celeri Rectissimo Quaestori Provinciae Baeticae Tribuno Plebis Praetori Felicitas Julia Olisipo. »

The city of Lisbon, now called Felicitas Julia, erects this tablet to Lucius Caecilius son of Lucius Celer, most upright Quaestor of the province of Boetica, Tribune of the people and Pretor.

The inscription on the stone to the right of the larger one, runs thus:

MATRI. DE
UM. MAG. ID
AE PHRYG. T. L.
LYCH. CERNO.
P. H. R. PERN. IIVI
CASS. ET. CASS. STA.
M. AT. ET. AP. COSS. GAI

which is explained thus:

«Matri Deum Magnae, Idae Phrygiae Titus Licinius Lychaoniae Cerno Provinciae Hispaniae Rector Pernobilis Duumviri Cassius et Cassianus Statuti Mario Attilio et Apronio Nobilissimis Consulibus. Gaio.»

Titus Licinius Cerno of Lychaonia dedicated this tablet to the mother of the gods, the great Idae of Phrygia: Cassius and Cassianus being duumviri; Attilius and Apronius consuls; and Gaius governor of Spain.

Several interpretations have been given, but what appears beyond doubt is that the tablet is dedicated to Cybeles, wife of Saturn, worshiped as the mother of the gods under the title of *magna mater*.

On the left of the larger stone is a small quadrangle resting on the shaft of a column which has been cut plain with the surface of the wall into which it is embedded, containing the following inscription:

```
DEUM MATR.
T. LICINIUS
AMARANTIUS
V. S. L. M.
```

« Deum Matri Titus Licinius Amarantius votum suo libens merito. »

Titus Licinus Amarantius, willingly makes this votive offering to the mother of the gods for the benefits he has received.

The fourth stone, about a yard in height has been broken longitudinally and the inscription thereby truncated. The letters which remain are:

```
MERCUR. . .
CAESA. . .
AUGUST. . .
C. JULIUS F. JU. . .
PERMISSU DEC. . .
DEDIT F. . .
```

which may be reconstructed thus:

« Mercurio Caesare Augusto, Caius Julius Felicitas Julia permissu Decurionum dedit fieri. »

Caius Julius, a native of Felicitas Julia (Lisbon) dedicated this tablet by permission of the Decurions, to Mercury and to Augustus Caesar.

These stones were found in 1749 when digging the foundation of the house in which they are placed: many others were found with Latin inscriptions, together with sculptured fragments evidently forming part of an important building: also many broken columns and a capital of the Ionic order beautifully executed, all of which have been lost. It was plain that these buried ruins extended far beyond the area excavated, but no further efforts at discovery were made, on the contrary several highly interesting remains were covered up again because it was found difficult to extract them!

In the small village of Chellas, about a league to the east of Lisbon, are some Roman antiquities which may be interesting to the antiquary. A temple of Vesta is said to have existed there. Also near Setubal there are the highly interesting ruins of the ancient Roman town of Caetobriga, which now goes by the name of Troy. Setubal is on the Southern railway, and can easily be visited from Lisbon in one day.

13. AQUEDUCT AND FOUNTAINS.

AQUEDUCTO DAS AGUAS LIVRES E CHAFARIZES.—This stupendous work was constructed during the reign of D. João V., having been commenced in 1719 and completed in 1738. It was designed by Manuel da Maia, and does great credit to the engineering skill of its constructors. The entire length of the aqueduct is some 9 miles, and it conveys the waters called *Aguas livres* from near Bellas to the immense reservoir, or *Mãe d'agua,* at the NW. of Lisbon, whence they are distributed to the various fountains which supply the city. During its course the channel alternately dips below the surface of the earth and is carried at varying heights above the level of the ground by means of series of stone arches, in all 127 in number. But by far the most wonderful part of this undertaking is the *Arco grande* or great arch which with its 34 lesser companions, carries the duct over the deep valley of Alcantara, just before entering Lisbon. Though this aqueduct cannot be compared, in point of extent, with the miles of arches of the ancient Romans, yet in the colossal proportions of the larger arches it is perhaps unrivaled by any other in Europe. The total height of the principal arch is 263 feet, with a span of 110 feet. The 14 larger arches are pointed, and the rest semi-circular, which somewhat detracts from the harmony of the view. Some idea of their solidity and correct equilibration may be formed from the fact that they were able to withstand the terrific earthquake of 1755, though its shocks were so violent as to shake down 3 of the 16 ventilators on the summit of the aqueduct. A broad stone causeway, protected by a low parapet, runs on each side of the duct over the valley of Alcantara, and was formerly used by the inhabitants of the villages in the neighborhood, but for some years this road has been closed on account of the many suicides committed by persons jumping off and being dashed to pieces by the fall. It was also a favorite place for robbers to lay in wait for their victims, many of whom were precipitated from the arch after being robbed.

A plain Doric arch carries the aqueduct over the road, just before entering the reservoir. It was erected by the city of Lisbon to commemorate the happy completion of the work, and bears the following inscription on the south side:

JOANNES V
REGUM MAXIMUS
BONO PUBLICO LUSITANIAM
MODERANTE
SOLIDISSIMIS AQUAE DUCTIBUS
ET
AETERNUM MANSURIS
PER CIRCUITUM NOVEM MILLE PASSUUM
AQUAE SALUBERRIMAE IN URBEM
INTRODUCTAE
AERE PUBLICO SED TOLERABILE
ET
COMMUNI OMNIUM
PLAUSU
ANNO DOMINI MDCCXXXVIII

On the N. face:

JOANNES V
LUSITANORUM REX
JUSTUS, PIUS, AUG. FELIX P. P.
LUSITANIA IN PACE STABILITA
VIRIBUS, GLORIIS, OPIBUS FIRMATA
PROFLIGATIS DIFFICULTATIBUS
IMO PROPE VICTA NATURA
PERENNES AQUAS IN URBEM INVEXIT

ET
BREVE UNDEVIGINTI ANNORUM SPATIO
MINIMO PUBLICO
IMMENSUM OPUS CONFECIT
GRATITUDINIS ERGO
OPTIMO PRINCIPE
ET
PUBLICO UTILITATIS AUCTORI
HOC MONUMENTUM POS. S. P. Q. O.
ANNO D. MDCCXXXVIII.

Not far from this arch, the aqueduct terminates in a covered massive stone reservoir which is styled «Ornament of the city» and «Miracle of the world» in the inscription over the entrance, which in fulsomeness is not inferior to the two preceding ones and runs thus:

JOANNES V
LUSITANORUM REX MAGNIFICUS
LIBERALIS
CIVITATE PROPITIUS
EXCIPIENDIS AQUIS POPULO
MANANTIBUS
HANC MOLEM STRUENDAM
CURAVIT
URBIS ORNAMENTUM
ORBIS MIRACULUM
TANTI NOMINIS
AETERNITATI. S

This structure called vulgarly the *Mãe d'agua* (mother of water) was not finished till the reign of D. Pedro IV., and is said to be able to store sufficient water to supply Lisbon for a month, when economically used.

On entering the reservoir the visitor finds himself in a large quadrangular chamber with a vaulted roof resting on 4 square pillars springing from the bottom of an immense basin which occupies the central space and is surrounded by a stone parapet, and has a walk all round. The water flows from the mouth of a dolphin at the top of a mass of rough stones which form a cascade at the summit of which is a statue of Neptune whose jurisdiction is not confined to the briny ocean, but extends also to rivers and fountains. The object of the cascade is to purify the water as it falls by bringing it into contact with the air and light. The ancient Romans used also to interrupt the course of the water in their aqueducts for this purpose, by low cascades called *piscina limaria*. From the reservoir the visitor can enter the aqueduct which is a vaulted corridor some 5 feet wide and nine feet high. In the center is a flag causeway, and at each side a semicircular channel 13 in. wide, by which the water is conducted, one of them being used while the other is being cleaned or repaired.

The cost of this work is said to have exceeded 13.000,000 cruzados or £ 1.130,000. To see the interior of the *Mãe d'agua* and aqueduct a ticket is necessary, which is to be obtained from the *camara municipal*. The cool atmosphere and continued murmur of the falling waters, render this place a delightful retreat in hot weather, and the extensive view of Lisbon and surrounding country, to be had from the terrace on the roof, is of itself sufficient to repay a visit.

THE FOUNTAINS. (CHAFARIZES.)

Though the fountains of Lisbon cannot with justice be called monuments of art like those of Rome, yet they never fail to present a lively and picturesque appearance, surrounded by throngs of noisy *Gallegos* or water carriers with gaily painted barrels awaiting their turn to fill. With the exception of three or four near the hill on which is the castle of St. George, all the fountains are supplied with the *aguas livres*, brought by the aqueduct. In the dry season the water becomes very scarce and it is not uncommon to see hundreds of barrels in a row waiting to be filled.

Before the great earthquake there were three famous fountains viz: in Black Horse Square, in the Rocio, and near the church of S. Julião, which were entirely destroyed by that catastrophe. Those at present in existence are 31 in number, all with more or less artistic pretensions. The finest one is the Chafariz das Necessidades, opposite the palace of the same name. It was constructed by order of D. João V. in 1747. In the center of a marble basin, approached by three steps, rises a square pedestal on which is placed an obelisk of pink marble surmounted by a spiked globe and a cross of bronze. The following inscription is cut on the pedestal:

> B. V. MARIAE DEI. GEN.
> JOANNES V IUS. REX
> OBSE. SERVATUM POSUIT
> DIE NATALIS SUO
> AN. DOM. MDCCXLVII

The water issues from the mouths of four colossal grotesque faces, each placed between two dolphins, and encircled by marine plants.

The chafarizes *do Carmo, S. Paulo, Janellas Verdes,* and *Praça d'armas* also deserve attention.

In point of antiquity and historic interest the *Chafariz do Rei* claims the first place. Down to the reign of D. Manuel, this was the only fountain to supply the whole of the city. The water, which flows abundantly both winter and summer, is not from the *aguas livres* brought by the aqueduct, but is from an independent spring, and possesses the valuable property of keeping a long time without becoming unfit to drink. This water was in such great request during the reign of D. Manuel for the numerous ships which made long voyages to India and to the Brazils, that the inhabitants often had to fight for it and many deaths resulted from these tumults, till the municipal senate made stringent regulations, sanctioned by fine and imprisonment, to prevent the monopolization of the precious element and insure its equitable distribution to the different classes.

List of the fountains with their respective numbers.

At Lisbon.

N.º 1. Chafariz do Thesouro Velho.
N.º 2. Chafariz do Carmo.
N.º 3. Chafariz de S. Pedro de Alcantara.

N.º 4. Chafariz do Rato.
N.º 5. Chafariz da Rua Formosa.
N.º 6. Chafariz do Campo de Sant'Anna.
N.º 7. Chafariz da Esperança.
N.º 8. Chafariz de S. Paulo.
N.º 9. Chafariz das Janellas Verdes.
N.º 10. Chafariz da Praça das Armas.
N.º 11. Chafariz da Praça das Flores.
N.º 12. Chafariz do Arco.
N.º 13. Chafariz das Amoreiras.
N.º 14. Chafariz da Estrella.
N.º 15. Chafariz das Terras.
N.º 16. Chafariz de Santa Rita.
N.º 17. Chafariz da Cruz do Taboado.
N.º 18. Chafariz do Rei.
N.º 19. Chafariz de Dentro.
N.º 20. Chafariz da Praia.
N.º 21. Chafariz da Bica do Sapato.
N.º 22. Chafariz da Alegria.
N.º 23. Chafariz do Largo do Intendente.
N.º 24. Chafariz da Graça.
N.º 25. Chafariz da Samaritana.
N.º 26. Chafariz do Soccorro.

At Belem.

N.º 1. Chafariz de Belem.
N.º 2. Chafariz de Pedrouços.
N.º 3. Chafariz da Junqueira.
N.º 4. Chafariz da Memoria.
N.º 5. Chafariz do Largo da Paz.

14. OBSERVATORIES.

OBSERVATORIO ASTRONOMICO, situate in the Royal park called Tapada da Ajuda, on the high ground to the east of the Palace of the same name.

The observatory had its origin in 1857 when the lamented D. Pedro V., ever anxious for the advancement of science, made a donation of 30 contos as a nucleus for the establishment of an astronomical observatory. The next year, government sent out Lieut. Frederico Augusto Oom, R. N., to the famous Pulkova observatory near St. Petersburg, with the object of studying sidereal astronomy and acquiring every information necessary to carry out the project.

The building was commenced in 1861 and is, with slight modifications, an imitation of the Pulkova observatory. It consists of a central octagonal body with four wings radiating from it, corresponding with the cardinal points of the compass. The principal entrance is in the S. wing, which is ornamented by a neat peristyle opening into a vestibule which communicates with the upper and lower stories of the central octagon and with the subterranean apartment destined for the normal pendulum.

The N. wing is occupied by a Vertical instrument, by Repsold of Hamburg, according to the design of Professor Struve of St. Petersburg. Its aperture is 6.3 inches and its focal distance 7 feet 7 in. In this apartment is also a Zygonometer, for the graduation of the spirit levels.

In the E. room is a portable Transit instrument constructed by Repsold on the plan devised by Mr. Oom. The aperture is 2.3 in., and the focal distance 30.7 in.

The W. room contains a Meridian circle, also by Repsold. The graduated circles are 3 feet in diameter. The aperture, 5.9 in. and the focal distance 6 feet 7 in.

The great Equatorial refractor in the cupola, is on the Hansen system; its aperture is 15 in. and its focal distance 23 feet. The lenses of all these instruments are by Merz of Munich.

The Tapada da Ajuda is open to the public and affords a pleasant walk: a foot-path runs through it, one entrance is at Alcantara and the other near the palace of Ajuda.

OBSERVATORIO METEOROLOGICO DO INFANTE D. LUIZ, at the Polytechnic School is supplied with instruments for making meteorological observations which are published every year.

There is also a small observatory at the Naval arsenal, which contains nothing demanding notice.

15. HOSPITALS.

HOSPITAL REAL DE S. JOSÉ, St. Joseph's Royal Hospital, situated on the rising ground to the W. of *Rua Nova da Palma*.

The building was erected by the Jesuits in 1593, for their celebrated college of Santo Antão, and it was here that the famous Portuguese divine, Padre Antonio Vieyra, preached his memorable sermons, which are considered models of sacred eloquence.

On the expulsion of the Jesuits from Portugal by Pombal, their college was converted into a hospital, and its name changed, out of compliment to the then reigning monarch, to S. José. The patients from the old hospital of *Todos os Santos* were removed thither on the 3.rd of April 1755. Over the entrance arch improvised out of the materials taken from the church, are the arms of Portugal supported by two genii; above the columns are two marble figures, one of them holding an escutcheon on which is inscribed:

MONUMENTUM HOC AD PERPETUAM MEMORIAM
RESTAURATIONIS PORTUGALIAE IN HAC DIE COMMEMORATAE,
ERECTUM FUIT ANNO DOMINI DIE DECIMA QUINTA
SEPTEMBRIS MDCCCXI.

The statues of the apostles, ranged against the wall were at the same time marched out of the demolished church. On St. Joseph's day (19.th of March) the hospital is thrown open to the public, and is thronged by great numbers who go to see the king and queen distribute food to the sick. Though not constructed for a hospital it answers the purpose very well, the spacious well ventilated galleries being used as wards. There are beds for about 900 patients. There are also private rooms for persons who do not need gratuitous treatment and who, on payment of a few tostoons a day, have the benefit of the best medical advice, together with every advantage that science and careful attention can afford.

In connection with this institution is a medico-surgical school with dissecting rooms and an anatomical museum.

HOSPITAL DA MARINHA INGLEZA, supported by the British government for the treatment of members of the navy. It is under the direction of Dr. Lloyd.

HOSPITAL DA MARINHA, in the *Campo de Santa Clara*, to the east of the church of St. Vincent.

This naval hospital was erected by government in 1797 on the site of the Jesuit College of St. Francis Xavier. It consists of ten wards with accommodation for 400 patients. In the entrance hall, called *sala do Principe*, is a statue of king D. João VI. by Fabre. The situation is good, having a beautiful sea view, which is a great advantage for a hospital destined for the seafaring class.

HOSPITAL DA ESTRELLINHA, near the public garden of Estrella: it is exclusively for the army.

HOSPITAL DO DESTERRO, and *Hospital de S. Lazaro,* the former for women of the unfortunate class and the latter for persons suffering from cutaneous diseases, are worked in conjunction with the Royal Hospital of S. José.

There is also a veterinary hospital attached to the agricultural Institute.

16. LAW COURTS.

BOA HORA, half way down the *Rua Nova do Almada* which runs S. from the bottom of the *Chiado*.

This site was formerly occupied by a theater belonging to the Lords of Barbacena, who ceded it to the Irish Dominicans in 1633. The good friars made the boxes into cells, in which they lived, and converted the stage into a chapel. When the Irish Dominicans removed to Corpo Santo in 1659, the house passed into the hands of the Oratorians who continued in it till 1674 when it became the property of the *Padres Agostinhos descalços* who demolished the old theater and built in its place a church and convent called *Nossa Senhora da Boa Hora*. The great earthquake of 1755 almost entirely destroyed the fabric and the decree of 1833 extinguished the order itself. It is now used as a court-house tho' it is not in the least adapted for the purpose and the government is about building a *Palais de Justice* worthy of the capital. At present the various tribunals are located and constituted as follows:

SUPREMO TRIBUNAL DE JUSTIÇA, on the N. side of Black Horse Square. This is the highest tribunal of justice in the kingdom and is composed of eleven judges called *conselheiros*, who hear appeals from the courts of *segunda instancia*.

SUPREMO TRIBUNAL DE JUSTIÇA MILITAR, in the naval arsenal at the S. side of the *Largo do Pelourinho*. It is divided into two sections, one for naval and the other for military offences. Each is composed of six General officers and a registrar.

RELAÇÃO DE SEGUNDA INSTANCIA DE LISBOA, over the principal entrance of the naval arsenal. It has 15 Judges, who hear appeals from the courts of *primeira instancia*.

TRIBUNAES DE PRIMEIRA INSTANCIA, six in number, corresponding with the six *varas* or judicial districts into which Lisbon is divided. They hold their sittings in the extinct convent of Boa Hora. Each is presided over by a judge called *juiz de direito de primeira instancia*.

TRIBUNAL DO COMMERCIO, exclusively for commercial causes and Bankruptcy cases, holds its sittings in a handsome room over the Exchange in the Pavilion at the SE. corner of Black Horse Square.

RELAÇÃO ECCLESIASTICA, at the Patriarch's residence in S. Vicente de Fóra.

17. ARSENALS.

ARSENAL DA MARINHA, the Naval Arsenal, situate at the river side, the principal entrance being from the *Largo do Pelourinho*.— This site was formerly occupied by a royal palace called Paços da Ribeira which was destroyed by the great earthquake of 1755 and the present arsenal was soon afterwards built under the auspices of the marquez de Pombal. In the yard are the usual workshops necessary for shipbuilding, but since the introduction of iron vessels, only small ships are built here. There is also a graving dock and small observatory where a ball falls at one P. M. for the adjustment of the ships' chronometers.

The naval school is in a large room termed *Sala do Risco*, 250 feet long by 65 broad and 50 high. At one end is an immense model ship fully rigged, where the students are taught their exercise. It has also some marble busts of D. Pedro, Dona Maria II. and D. Fernando. The arsenal possesses also a pair of huge sheers worked by steam for elevating the masts of ships and also for unloading very heavy weights, up to 50 tons. Its services are available to the public on payment of a moderate charge for coal and attendance, which is a great convenience, as the Custom-House cranes cannot lift weights exceeding 3 tons.

Near the sheers and rising out of the bed of the Tagus is a spring of sulphuretted fresh water which is supposed to be useful in rheumatic and other diseases: it is now conveyed in pipes to a bathing establishment near St. Paul's church. (See page 6.)

On the third floor is an interesting museum of colonial products especially from the Portuguese Possessions of Angola, Moçambique and Goa. It is open to the public every day from 11 to 3 P. M. The entrance is by a door in the Rua do Arsenal, a little to the W. of the chief entrance.

ARSENAL DO EXERCITO. — Military arsenal, close to the river, three quarters of a mile to the E. of Black Horse Square. This building, vulgarly called *Fundição* to distinguish it from the other arsenal, is of irregular architecture. The façade is elaborately ornamented with Corinthian columns, military trophies, etc., but the effect produced is not pleasing. It dates from 1760 and was constructed by direction of the energetic Marquez de Pombal, the architect being M. Larre.

The establishment is divided into several departments, including a foundry for artillery and a small-arms manufactory. In the yard is a curious old bronze cannon called *Tiro de Diu* taken from the king of Cambaia by Nuno da Cunha at the siege of Diu in 1533. It is 19.^{ft} 8.^{in} in length. This monster gun was formerly kept at fort St. Julian, and was brought to the arsenal in the reign of D. José for the purpose of being melted down to form part of the equestrian statue of that monarch.

It was however rescued from the furnace by the intervention of the Tunis ambassador, who, accidentally reading the Arabic inscription on the breech explained its meaning to the authorities who determined on preserving so memorable a trophy. The following is a translation of the inscription:

«Of our sovereign Mahey, king of the kings of the age, son of the noble lady Rahân, Defender of the Mahometan law, Conqueror of the Taneous, Exterminator and Vanquisher of the Ebaditas (on the day of the memorable battle with king Salib) Heir of king Suliman, Confider in God, Father of his country and of the sciences, king of Madercha. This cannon was cast on the fifth day of the month of Til-Kâde in the year 939 of the hegira.»

This date corresponds with the 16.th of January 1526.

In the interior are some specimens of ancient armor and also several good paintings on the ceilings by Pedro Alexandrino, Bruno and Berardo, together with a full-lenght likeness of Dona Maria II. by Joaquim Raphael.

Permission to see the arsenal is readily granted to tourists on application to the inspector or officer on duty (official de dia).

18. PRISONS. (PRISÕES.)

LIMOEIRO, a little above the cathedral, is the chief prison of Lisbon. The building, which is not at all adapted for its present purpose, was originally a Royal palace called *Palacio dos Infantes*. King Fernando «the Handsome» resided here in the XIV. century and it was here also that the Mestre d'Aviz, afterwards king John I., assassinated the infamous Andeiro, conde de Ourem, before the eyes of his mistress queen Leonor Telles de Menezes.

The inmates of the prison are allowed to remain in a wretched state of filth, nor is their moral, superior to their physical condition since criminals encarcerated for light offenses generally become confirmed felons.

Government is at present erecting a spacious penitenciary on the principle of Pentonville which will be one of the greatest boons conferred on the present generation of thieves and vagabonds.

ALJUBE.— Formerly a place of detention for ecclesiastics who were entitled to clerical privileges, but now used as a prison for female criminals.

CASTELLO DE S. JORGE, military prison.

TORRE DE BELEM and S. JULIÃO DA BARRA are also used as prisons for military and political offenders, the latter containing some horrid dungeons partially under water, which call to mind the shocking cruelties of Naples.

19. MARKETS.

PRAÇA DA FIGUEIRA, a few paces to the E. of the *Rocio* or Praça de Dom Pedro. This large square, paved in the center and planted with trees, is the Covent Garden of Lisbon. Here are displayed every kind of fish, flesh, fowl, fruit and vegetable, and the picture presented by this market, early in the morning, is extremely animated and picturesque. The vendors spread their wares under huge white umbrellas which contrast agreeably with the verdure of the foliage, and the richly tinted fruits interspersed with bouquets of camelias and a thousand other flowers of brilliant hues. A bell rings at 2 P. M. when every thing must be cleared out of the square. Should the visitor happen to be in Lisbon on the of eve the feast of St. Anthony (13.th of June), of St. John (24.th of June) or St. Peter (29.th of June) he should not fail to pay a visit to this square, which is on those nights illuminated and decked with the choicest fruits and flowers of the season, together with cakes and wine and a variety of articles not usually to be seen here.

The concourse of country people is very great and the market continues crowded the whole night till 8 o'clock next morning. Countless pots of *mangericão*, an aromatic herb called Basil Royal or Basil gentle, are exposed for sale, as well as innumerable *alcachofras* or wild artichokes, both of which it is the popular custom to buy on these nights. The former is a favorite present which the swain makes to his sweetheart, and the latter is bought by the damsel to ascertain whether her lover be true. This difficult problem is solved by charring the upper part of the *alcachofra* in the fire and laying it by till next morning: if it be found to have bloomed during the night the answer is favorable and the damsel's heart at ease.

RIBEIRA NOVA, a little to the W. of the *Caes do Sodré*. — This is the fish market, though fruit and vegetables are also sold in the surrounding sheds. Few capitals in Europe are so well supplied with fish as Lisbon, both as regards variety and freshness, the latter quality being a *sine qua non* in this article of food. The following are the names of the several kinds of fish most generally to be met with:

Savel, shad.
Enguia, eel.
Camarão, prawn.
Lagosta, lobster.
Peixe Rei.
Arenque, herring.
Ostras, oysters.
Lampreia, lamprey.
Carala, mackarel.
Pescada.
Eirós, sea eel.
Chicharro.
Mexilhão, mussels.
Goraz, rochet.
Sardinha, sardine.
Linguado, sole.
Atum, tunny.
Rodovalho, turbot.
Pargo, rochet.

Peixe espada, sword fish.
Carapau.
Tainha.
Enchovas, anchovy.
Salmonete, barbel.
Barbudo.
Sargo, a kind of mullet.
Dourada, St. Peter's fish.
Sólho, a kind of sturgeon.
Cadoz, dudgeon.
Arraia, skate.
Peixe Gallo, John Dory.
Dragão marinho.
Corvina.
Ameijoa, cockle.
Chôco.
Lula, cuttle fish.
Sarda, small mackarel.
Safio, a kind of conger.

RIBEIRA VELHA, to the E. of the custom-house. A market for pork, cheese, and the dried fruits of the *Alemtejo:* also cartloads of melons and water-melons, the latter of which attain to an immense size and are very refreshing in hot weather.

FEIRA DA LADRA, literally translated, «The thief's fair», held every Tuesday afternoon in the *Campo de Sant'Anna* near the Bull circus.

Every article capable of being sold second hand is here to be seen, clothing and furniture forming the staple. Many persons make a point of attending this market in quest of rare books or articles of *vertu* which occasionally appear and may be bought for an old song. The *auri sacra fames* is so plainly depicted on the bronzed countenances of the wily vendors, that it is needless to caution the stranger against falling into the mistake of paying more than about a quarter of the price first demanded.

20. PUBLIC WALKS AND GARDENS.

PASSEIO PUBLICO or PASSEIO DO ROCIO, a short distance N. of the Praça de D. Pedro, or Rocio.

This is the principal public promenade: its form is that of a parallelogram a quarter of a mile long and 100 yards wide, enclosed by lofty iron railings with massive entrance gates at each end. A broad gravel walk passes up the center between two rows of trees and benches. Near the S. entrance is a fountain with large marble basin and at the other extremity a cascade, and midway, on either side of the walk, two recumbent figures of marble surrounded by a small lake, representing the rivers Tagus and Douro.

This promenade is much frequented on Sundays and Holidays, when a military band performs a selection of music. In addition to the ordinary seats, chairs are let for 10 réis by pensioners of the Mendicity asylum, the proceeds reverting to that institution. During the day and on Sundays and Holidays the public are admitted free, but on the summer evenings when the *passeio* is illuminated and a band of music performing till midnight, the price of admission is 50 réis. On these occasions it is one of the fashionable rendez-vous of the capital. There is also a pavilion where coffee, wine, beer, and ices may be had. Concerts and displays of fireworks also occasionally take place here.

PASSEIO DA ESTRELLA, near the church of the same name, a mile and a half N. W. of Black Horse Square.

This public garden, laid out in 1853, is now one of the prettiest in Lisbon, and contains many rare plants and shrubs. Winding gravel walks shaded from the sun by the foliage of luxuriant trees under which are numerous seats, afford a most agreeable retreat in hot weather. A military band performs on Sunday and Holiday afternoons.

From an artificial mound, a good view of Lisbon and the Tagus is obtained. There are also artificial grottos and lakes with swans; a hot-house, *estufa*; and a magnificent lion in a cage.

PASSEIO DE S. PEDRO DE ALCANTARA, situated N. of the church of S. Roque, consists of a promenade planted with rows of trees. On a lower level is a terrace laid out with flowers and shrubs. From its elevated position S. Pedro de Alcantara is a favorite place of resort on summer evenings, to enjoy the cool refreshing breeze and the splendid panorama of the eastern part of the city. The upper promenade is open at all hours, but the terrace garden is closed after sun set.

JARDIM BOTANICO. — Botanical garden, near the Palace of Ajuda at Belem. Established by Dona Maria I. at the end of last century. Within the entrance gate are two rude military figures of stone dug up near Portalegre in 1735 and declared by some archaeologists to be of Phoenician workmanship. The plants are mostly arranged in the Linnean system. The finest specimen in the garden is a dense *Dracœna Draco*, or Gum Dragon tree, upwards of 21.^{ft} in diameter. There is also a collection of wretched specimens in pots headed «Systema de Lindley:Familias naturaes» which tho' not very successful, is a step in the right direction. The garden is open to the public on Thursdays.

There are also small botanical gardens connected with the Polytechnic and with the hospital of S. José which may be visited every day.

21. PUBLIC EDUCATIONAL ESTABLISHMENTS.

ESCOLA POLYTECHNICA, one of the handsomest buildings in Lisbon, a little to the N. of the Praça do Principe Real. The site was originally occupied by a college of the Jesuits and after their expulsion it was converted by Pombal into the *Collegio dos Nobres* for the education of young noblemen. In 1836 it was changed into the Polytechnic school and destroyed by fire in 1843, when the present noble edifice was built in its place.

The Polytechnic school is a government establishment. There are 12 professors and the number of students is great. In the same building is the National Museum, (see p. 210) and Meteorological observatory (see p. 221).

ESCOLA MEDICO-CIRURGICA, adjoining the Hospital of S. José. The school has been reformed three times, viz. in 1825, 1836 and 1844 and is now one of the best in Europe. There are 11 professorships for the following subjects 1.st Anatomy, 2.nd Physiology, 3.rd Materia medica, 4.th External Pathology, 5.th Medicine, 6.th Midwifery, 7.th Internal Pathology, 8.th Clinical medicine, 9.th Clinical surgery, 10.th Legal medicine, 11.th Pathological anatomy. The school possesses an anatomical amphitheater, medical library, and pathological museum.

ESCOLA DE PHARMACIA or Pharmaceutical school is in the same edifice as the above.

INSTITUTO AGRICOLA E ESCOLA VETERINARIA.—The agricultural institute, situate at the N.

of the city near the *Matadouro*, is maintained by the state: there are eleven professors who lecture on agriculture, chemistry, and the veterinary art. The lectures are gratis.

ESCOLA NAVAL E AULA DE CONSTRUCÇÃO NAVAL.—The naval school, and school of naval architecture are both in the Naval Arsenal, Largo do Pelourinho.

ESCOLA DO EXERCITO, for preparing young men for the army, in the Palacio da Rainha, Bemposta. There are 6 professors.

AULA DO COMMERCIO, in the Instituto Industrial, Rua da Boa Vista.

CONSERVATORIO REAL DE LISBOA.—The Royal conservatory is in the extinct convent of the Caetanos near the English college. There are 10 professors of music, and 3 of the dramatic art; there are also classes for mimicry, dancing, fencing, elocution, history, declamation, Latin, Italian and French.

CURSO SUPERIOR DE LETRAS, in the extinct convent of Jesus. This course of lectures on literature was established by the late king D. Pedro V., and is frequented by students of the highest class of society. There are 5 professors.

INSTITUTO INDUSTRIAL E COMMERCIAL, in the Rua da Bella Vista, a little to the W. of the Gas Works. This institution, established in 1852 by the Minister of Public Works, affords gratuitous technical education to a large number of pupils. There are 11 professors who deliver lectures in the evening, and in connection with the institution is a workshop where practical mechanical engineering is taught.

The technological Museum belonging to this establishment contains models of engines, machines, tools, castings, etc., and is open to the public on Mondays. In a shed near the workshop is a collection of products principally from Belgium.

COLLEGIO DOS APRENDIZES DO ARSENAL.—Consists of 60 pupils, 20 being sons of soldiers, 20 sons of operatives in the arsenal, and 20 from the charitable institutions of the *Misericordia* and *Casa Pia*. They are taught reading, writing, arithmetic, grammar, geometry and applied mechanics, and are allowed to make choice of any trade that can be learned in the military arsenal.

LYCEU DE LISBOA.—This examining body consists of 17 professors who give certificates of proficiency in the following subjects. Philosophy, Literature, Geography, Greek, Latin, English, German, Natural Philosophy, Portuguese, Elocution, Drawing, Mathematics French and Arithmetic.

In addition to the above, there are many elementary schools in Lisbon supported by the state and by private charity.

22. BARRACKS.

Artillery, 1.st reg., Calçada da Ajuda, Belem.
Engineers, Cruz dos Quatro Caminhos.
Cavalry, 2.nd Lancers, Calçada da Ajuda, Belem.
Cavalry, 4.th Reg., Campolide.
Infantry, 1.st Reg., Calçada da Ajuda, Belem.
Infantry, 2.nd Reg., S. João de Deus.
Infantry, 7.th Reg., Torre da Polvora.
Infantry, 10.th Reg., Convento da Graça.
Infantry, 16.th Reg., Campo de Ourique.
Infantry, 2.nd Bat. Caçadores, Valle de Pereiro.
Infantry, 5.th Bat. Caçadores, Castello de S. Jorge.
Marines, Praça de Alcantara.
Guarda Municipal, Convento do Carmo.

23. CEMETERIES.

CEMITERIO E IGREJA DOS INGLEZES or *Os Cyprestes*.—English protestant cemetery and church, situate near the public garden called *Estrella* in the neighborhood of Buenos Ayres.

At the lower entrance stands the parsonage, a building originally erected by Gerard Vimes, Esq., and made over by him to the British factory at Lisbon as a hospital for poor British subjects. The cemetery is intersected by rectilinear walks shaded by lofty cypress trees. Among the numerous tombs may be noticed that of Henry Fielding, the celebrated novelist. His grave was suffered for a long period to remain without memorial till by the exertions of the late Rev.[d] C. Nevill, British Chaplain, the present large plain monument was placed over it. The inscription, heavy and inelegant as the tomb itself, runs thus:

<pre>
            HENRICI FIELDING
         A SUMERSETENSIBUS APUD
            GLASTONIAM ORIUNDI,
            VIRI SUMMO INGENIO,
              EN QUAE RESTANT
         STYLO QUO NON ALIUS UNQUAM,
  INTIMA QUI POTUIT CORDIS RESERVARE, MORES HOMINUM
              EXOLENDOS SUSCEPIT.
      VIRTUTE DECOREM, VITIO FAEDITATEM ASSERUIT,
              SUUM CUIQUE TRIBUENS,
       NON QUIN IPSE SUBINDE IRRETIRETUR EVITANDIS.
    ARDENS IN AMICITIA, IN MISERIA SUBLEVANDA EFFUSUS,
      HILARIS URBANUS ET CONJUX ET PATER ADAMATUS,
                ALIIS, NON SIBI VIXIT.
          VIXIT: SED MORTEM VICTRICEM VINCIT
        DUM NATURA DURAT DUM SAECULA CURRUNT
         NATURA PROLEM SCRIPTIS PRAE SE FERENS
        SUAM ET SUAE GENTIS EXTENDET FAMAM.
</pre>

Fielding came to Lisbon for the good of his health, and after a few months sojourn expired in October 1754, at the age of 47.

The church is situated at the upper end and is a neat tho' plain building. The present British Chaplain is the Rev.[d] Godfrey Pope.

CEMITERIO DOS PRAZERES, literally translated the «Cemetery of pleasures» rather an odd name for a place of this kind. It derives its festive appellation from having been formerly the site of a chapel dedicated to Our Lady under the title of *Nossa Senhora dos Prazeres*. This cemetery being situated at the extreme W. of the city is also called *Cemiterio occidental*. It is laid out in walks and planted with cypress trees and contains many magnificent mausoleums, amongst which are most notable, those belonging to the families of the Duke of Palmella and Conde das Antas.

The funerals at Lisbon are not conducted as in England. Near relatives do not accompany the corpse to its last resting place, but remain secluded at home in a darkened room for eight days, which is called *estar de nojo*, and receive the condolence of their friends. An amusing story is told of a certain English ambassador, who went to pay a visit of condolence to a distinguished Portuguese family of his acquaintance, and on entering the gloomy apartment out of the glaring sunshine, being unable to distinguish the objects around him, made a profound obeisance and presented his *pezames*, or condolence, to a large China vase standing in a corner, and seated himself with his back to the assembled mourners. After remaining a few minutes in silence, as etiquette required, he made another profound bow to the China vase and left the room, having done more to dispel the mournful thoughts of his friends by his ludicrous mistake than he could have done by the most eloquent discourse. The coffins resemble huge trunks, having a convex lid fixed on hinges and fitted with a lock and key. On reaching the cemetery the lid is raised, a little quick-lime thrown on the face, after which the coffin is locked and the key given to the chief mourner. The coaches in which the priests accompany the *cortège* are called *berlindas*, and are interesting specimens of the Portuguese vehicles of last century.

CEMITERIO DO ALTO DE S. JOÀO, at the east of the city, is called also *Cemiterio oriental*. It contains some fine monuments though not equal to those in the *Prazeres*. The mortuary chapel is a modern building and contains some splendid marble.

Besides the above cemeteries there are the following:

De S. Luiz, for the French, near the church of the same name;

Da Ajuda, at Belem;

Dos Allemães, for the Germans, rua do Patrocinio, á Boa-Morte;

Dos Judeus, for the Jews;

Val Escuro, for animals.

24. OTHER PUBLIC BUILDINGS.

COCHES REAES, Royal Coaches. To be seen in the coach-house, a little way up the *Calçada da Ajuda,* on the left, near the palace of Belem.

Coaches were introduced into Portugal by Philip II. of Spain, when in 1581 he came to Lisbon to take possession of the usurped throne. Prior to that period the kings, princes, and nobles traveled on horseback. The ladies, invalids, and infirm in a kind of Sedan chair called *liteira,* and the other classes of society made use almost exclusively of mules. On the introduction of coaches and other vehicles, they were confined entirely to Lisbon and afterwards reached Oporto and Coimbra. It is only very recently that carriages are to be found in any other towns, in fact 20 years ago there were no roads in the provinces on which a carriage could run.

This collection comprises many curious specimens of the coach-builder's art, especially during the reign of D. John V. who was extremely fond of ostentatious displays. The extent to which this monarch indulged his taste for brilliant pageants may be judged from the composition of the royal *cortège* on the occasion of the double marriage of his son, prince of the Brazils, with an infanta of Spain and of the prince of Asturias with an infanta of Portugal. The Portuguese royal family went in procession from Elvas to the frontier to meet the Spanish court and exchange the brides. This *cortège* consisted of 49 royal coaches drawn by 354 horses, 150 royal carriages drawn by 468 horses and mules, 673 saddle-horses with velvet saddle-cloths embroidered with gold, and 316 mules, besides an immense number of carriages and horses belonging to the retinues of the nobles and other persons who accompanied their Majesties.

The number of coaches possessed by the crown has been greatly reduced; the earthquake of 1755 destroyed many; upwards of 50 were taken to the Brazils by the royal family; and many in a dilapidated condition were sold during the reign of D. Maria II.; nevertheless 39 still remain in the royal coach-house. Amongst this number may be mentioned as most notable:

A coach brought by queen Maria Francisca from France, being a present from Luis XIV. Richly carved and gilded, with a painting at the back representing her Majesty seated on the throne, and which is said to be a very good portrait.

Three chariots which served at the marriage of D. John V. with D. Maria Anna of Austria in 1708. Also one presented to this lady by the emperor of Austria Francis Joseph I.

A coach presented to king John V. by his Holiness Clement XI.

Three coaches used at the marriage of the prince of the Brazils, son of king John V., with the infanta of Spain D. Marianna Victoria, one of which was a present from the bride's father king Philip V.

An immense unwieldly cumbersome octagonal traveling carriage, with a table in the center, used by D. John V.

Several coaches brought by the Philips from Spain, and some which belonged to John IV., Affonso VI. and Pedro II.

Two modern traveling carriages made in England for queen Maria II.

CASTELLO DE S. JORGE, St. George's Castle. — The history of this fortress goes back to the time of the Arabs, by whom it was founded, and for more than four centuries it was alternately in the hands of the Castilians and Leoneses, and abandoned to Islamism, till the Portuguese finally expelled the Moors in 1147. In early times it was a place of great strenght, defending the city which was enclosed by two lines of walls of small circumference. Later on, it became the residence of the Portuguese Monarchs who had a palace in it called Alcaçova, by which appellation the castle was at first known, till John I. gave it the name of St. George and declared that saint patron of the fort and of the kingdom. Devotion to St. George in Portugal dates from the arrival of John of Gant, and was increased after the marriage of John I. with Philippa of Lancaster.

When Lisbon had grown out of its ancient walls, and the adjoining hills and valleys were covered with houses, the castle became worthless as a military defence and of late has only served to threaten the city during civil wars and political commotions, or for the more genial purpose of firing salutes on festive occasions, from a dozen nine pounders planted on the platform.

The enclosure of the castle comprised within the walls and fortified turrets, denominated from tradition the towers of Ulysses, forms the independent parish of *Santa Cruz*, consisting of about 320 hearths.

The principal entrance, called St. George's gate, is on the south west side. It has a statue of the patron saint in a niche on the left. On the north is another gateway through which the valiant D. Martim Moniz forced a passage in the famous assault, when the city was taken from the Moors. The prowess of this warrior, who perished on the occasion, was rewarded by Affonso Henriques who ordered his bust in marble to be placed over the gate. Underneath it is the following inscription:

> El Rei Dõ Afonfo Henriques mandou aqui collocar efta eftatua e cabeça de pedra em memoria da gloriofa morte que Dõ Marti Moniz progenitor da familia dos Vafconcellos recebeu n'efta porta quando atraveffando-fe n'ella franqueou aos feus a entrada com que fe ganhou aos Mouros efta cidade no anno 1147.
>
> João Rõis de Vafconcellos e Soufa Conde de Caftel Melhor feu decimo quarto neto por varonia fez aqui pôr efta infcripção no anno de 1646.

«The king, D. Affonso Henriques, ordered this statue and head of stone to be placed here in memory of the glorious death which D. Martim Moniz, progenitor of the family of Vasconcellos, met at this gate, when, throwing himself across it he obtained for his men an entrance by means of which this city was taken from the Moors in the year 1147.»

«John Roderic de Vasconcellos e Sousa, Count of Castel Melhor his fourteenth male heir, caused this inscription to be placed here in the year 1646.»

A little below this gate there was formerly a village known by the denomination of *Villa Quente*, which was totally swallowed up by an earthquake, on the 26.th Jan. 1531.

From a turret to the right of the entrance of Martim Moniz, is obtained a magnificent view of the north east part of the city.

TORRE DE BELEM.—Belem Tower is situated at the extreme W. of Lisbon, if we consider the suburb of Belem as forming part of the city. Its prominent position and picturesque appearance render it the first object that claims the visitor's attention on his entering the Tagus. Vessels entering the port stop in front of this tower to receive the customs and sanitary visits, and the passenger cannot fail to be struck with admiration by this graceful specimen of the military architecture prevailing at the end of the XV. century.

The original design was made by Garcia de Rezende, brother of the celebrated André de Rezende, in the reign of D. João II., and was intended to defend the port from the sudden attacks of pirates, at that time by no means uncommon. It was not, however, till 1495, in the reign of his successor D. Manuel surnamed the Great, that the project was put into execution, though doubtless with many modifications of the original design, as is abundantly obvious from the repeated introduction of the cross of the order of Christ and the armillary sphere, both emblems adopted by the latter monarch. At the time of its erection it was completely surrounded by water, being built on a rock far removed from the shore, so that ships could sail between the tower and the land, and even down to the latter half of last century, small craft still made use of the northern channel. The tendency of the river to deposit sand on the N. bank, increased by the obstruction which the tower itself offered to the flowing waters, gradually caused an accumulation of sand which in the course of three centuries has united it with the land, forming a kind of promontory jutting into the river.

The building consists of two parts, the fortress and the tower. The former has a casemate with embrasures for 15 guns, now without artillery, and over it a platform with an embattled parapet, on which are seven cannon of ancient and elaborate workmanship. In a military point of view the fort is of little or no value, being armed with old fashioned guns, whose projectiles would make no impression whatever on the armor plated vessels of the present day, and whose walls, though ten feet thick, would be instantly shattered by modern artillery.

The tower is three stories high: on the first is the royal saloon called *sala regia* opening on to a balcony looking towards the river. This saloon possesses peculiar acoustic properties. Its roof is ellipsoidal and two persons placed at the foci at the opposite sides can converse with each other without their words being audible to those who may be in the middle of the room and consequently between the interlocutors. Above this are two other chambers and at the top a terrace from which a delightful prospect may be enjoyed. The tower is often styled *Torre de S. Vicente* having been dedicated to St. Vincent in remembrance of the martyr's entry into the Tagus, when his remains were brough from the *Promontorio Sacro* to Lisbon in 1173. The tower is now used for firing salutes and as an occasional prison for military or political criminals. In an architectural point of view it is a most interesting exemplification of the *Manueline* style of Portuguese Gothic, as may be at once perceived on comparing it with its neighbor, the famous convent of St. Jerome, built also by king Emmanuel.

To the poet as well as to the archaeologist the tower of Belem is an object of enchantment and he must be indeed devoid of soul who can gaze unmoved on this venerable monument of by-gone glories, with its massive walls pitted by the finger of time, its crenellated terrace, the watch towers hanging in the air, and the flowered crosses of the order of Christ so delicately carved on the battlements; while he listens to the sound of the waves as they beat against its foundation, and to the whistling of the wind as it sweeps over its summit, reminding him that it was on this identical spot that the immortal Vasco da Gama set his foot, on returning from the discovery of a new empire.

LAZARETO.— On the S. bank of the Tagus, immediately opposite the tower of Belem. This establishment, built by government within the last few years, consists of a large stone edifice divided into seven separate pavilions, each capable of lodging 150 passengers. The situation is elevated and airy, and the view from the terrace charming. Each pavilion is fitted up to accommodate three classes of passengers. The charge for the 1.st class is 1,5095 por diem, 2.nd class 595 réis, and 3.rd 299 réis. Luggage is now examined by the customs authorities at the lazaretto, so that travelers can proceed on their journey direct, without having to go to the custom-house as heretofore.

The revenue derived by government from the lazaretto exceeds £10,000 per annum.

CORDOARIA, Rope walk. At Junqueira a little to the E. of Belem.

This building about a quarter of a mile in length, was erected in the reign of D. Maria I., and is one of the conspicuous objects that strike the eye on entering the port of Lisbon. It is occupied as a rope and sail factory by the government and formerly gave employment to a large number of operatives. Now, however, it is almost abandoned, most of the machinery having become obsolete.

ALFANDEGA GRANDE. The Custom-House forms the E. side of the Praça do Commercio or Black Horse Square.

An immense fire-proof building erected by the Marquez de Pombal after the great earthquake. It is constructed with the greatest solidity, all the warehouses having vaulted roofs. The *sala grande* upstairs is a room of noble dimensions. To clear anything through the Custom-House is a business requiring great patience. No less than sixteen signatures are required before the operation is complete. Some improvements have been introduced of late, such as a steam crane, hydraulic elevator, and tramways. No further description is necessary for if the visitor arrive at Lisbon by sea, he will have ample time to make himself familiar with every nook and corner of this vast edifice before his luggage be examined.

The amount of the duties collected at the Lisbon Custom-House exceeds £1.150,000 per annum. Tobacco is the chief item producing £400,000.

The following is a list of the vessels which entered the port of Lisbon in 1870:

Nationality.	Sailing.	Steamers.
American	22	–
Austrian	3	–
Belgian	6	–
Brazilian	3	–
German	30	5
Danish	34	–
French	32	59
Spanish	13	12
Dutch	24	21
English	432	490
Italian	7	–
Portuguese	251	67
Portuguese Coasters	761	49
Russian	29	–
Swedish and Norwegian	109	2
Entered the port thro'stress of weather	78	–
	1,834	705
Total number of vessels...	2,539	

The annexed statistics of the Imports and Exports of Portugal during the year 1870 will give the reader a fair idea of its present trade with foreign nations:

ALFANDEGA GRANDE.

	Imports.		Exports.	
	Réis.	£.	Réis.	£.
England............	12.511:824$600	2,780,405	12.468:668$000	2,770,815
Brazil............	3.178:255$700	706,275	3.207:793$000	712,843
France............	2.390:701$600	653,126	397:591$000	88,353
Spain............	1.821:229$200	404,717	1.815:969$000	410,215
United States......	1.690:817$400	375,737	185:610$000	41,247
Russia............	1.199:875$200	266,639	220:991$000	49,108
Africa (Portuguese possessions)...	926:555$200	205,901	756:344$000	168,077
Sweden and Norway......	478:263$900	106,280	152:364$000	33,857
Germany............	399:658$400	88,813	174:270$000	38,726
Holland............	398:707$200	88,609	209:755$000	46,612
Italy............	133:174$100	29,594	115:179$000	25,595
Asia (Portuguese possessions)...	69:236$300	15,386	49:994$000	11,110
Morocco............	47:393$600	10,532	3:683$000	818
South American Republics......	28:085$400	6,241	107:244$000	23,832
Turkey............	22:025$000	4,894	140$000	31
Belgium............	1:880$000	418	91:390$000	20,309
Austria............	948$000	211	–5–	–
Denmark............	18$000	4	110:871$000	24,638
Other countries......	42:595$500	9,465	195:601$000	43,469
Total......	25.341:244$300	5,631,387	20.263:457$000	4,508,655

Imports from Great-Britain in 1870
as classified by the Portuguese custom-house,
with the chief items in each class.

Classes	Réis	£	Chief items	£
I – Live animals............	4:184$000	930		
II – Animal substances...	581:216$000	129,159	Butter............	105,550
			Tallow............	5,334
			Cheese...........	1,777
III – Fish.................	1.065:421$000	236,760	Salt cod..........	234,222
			Cloth.............	140,890
IV – Wool and hair.......	785:068$000	174,460	Carpets..........	4,890
			Shawls...........	4,690
V – Silk.................	213:929$000	47,540	Unmanufactured.	38,444
			Cloth, raw......	449,000
			Cloth, bleached..	175,660
			Cloth, printed..	131,330
VI – Cotton...............	4.004:080$000	889,791	Kerchiefs........	51,550
			Thread..........	27,110
			Muslin...........	8,440
			Canvas..........	32,220
			Hemp............	15,560
VII – Linen................	385:247$000	85,610	Cloth............	11,100
			Thread..........	5,560
VIII – Wood..............	91:973$000	20,438		
			Rice.............	91,560
			Wheat...........	14,670
IX – Farinacea............	574:996$000	127,777	Flour............	14,000
			Biscuits..........	4,220
			Sugar...........	74,220
X – Colonial produce.....	853:171$000	189,594	Tea	72,670
			Tobacco.........	20,450
XI – Vegetable matter....	151:950$000	33,766	Linseed oil......	12,670
			Dye woods......	5,330
			Gold coin........	240,450
			Iron, wrought...	70,450
			Iron, plates.....	26,670
			Iron, pig........	5,780
XII – Metals...............	1.934:943$000	429,987	Tin and tin plate	20,000
			Brass............	10,800
			Copper-plates...	7,560
			Cutlery..........	9,310
			Coal.............	212,220
XIII – Minerals............	1.055:164$000	234,480	Flower of sulphur	13,330
XIV – Beverages..........	63:231$000	14,051	Spirits...........	6,670
			Beer.............	4,450
			Glass............	5,560
XV – Glass and crystal....	70:065$000	15,580	Delf..............	5,340
			Crystal	2,450
XVI – Paper................	27:083$000	6,018		
			Carbonate of soda	13,780
			Saltpeter........	8,000
XVII – Chemicals...........	220:619$000	49,026	White lead......	5,110
			Red lead.........	2,450
XVIII – Various products.....	165:893$000	36,865	Indigo...........	25,780
			Machinery......	29,780
XIX – Various manufactures	263:594$000	58,570	India rubber....	5,340
			Ships............	4,560
	12.511:824$000	2.780,405		

Exports to Great-Britain in 1870 as classified by the Portuguese custom-house with the chief items in each class.

Classes	Réis	£	Chief items	£
I — Live animals	1.752:844$000	389,521	Bullocks	389,330
II — Animal products	209:307$000	46,513	Bee's wax	12,000
			Ivory	10,000
			Eggs	8,450
			Hides	13,560
III — Fish	12:499$000	2,777		
IV — Wool and hair	224:175$000	49,817	Sheep's wool	49,550
V — Silk	4:202$000	934		
VI — Cotton	67:255$000	14,945	Embroidered	5,110
VII — Linen	1:726$000	383		
VIII — Wood	292:629$000	65,029	Cork	64,670
IX — Farinacea	96:811$000	21,513	New potatoes	16,890
X — Colonial produce	54:949$000	12,211	Coffee	6,890
			Sweets	4,000
XI — Vegetable products	1.292:876$000	287,306	Oranges	159,560
			Onions	25,110
			Locust bean	17,330
			Figs	12,440
			Olive oil	10,000
			Purgueira oil	8,450
			Palm oil	4,890
			Grapes	15,780
			Other fruits	2,670
			Gum copal	5,560
			Almonds	6,060
			Orchella weed	5,330
XII — Metals	36:018$000	8,004		
XIII — Minerals	1.829:083$000	406,462	Copper ore	367,110
			Manganese	22,220
			Lead ore	9,110
			Other ores	5,330
XIV — Beverages	6.337:105$000	1.408,245	Port wine	1.347,330
			Madeira	52,890
			Other wines	5,110
XV — Glass and crystal	1:293$000	287		
XVI — Paper	3:953$000	878		
XVII — Chemicals	40:512$000	9,003	Salt	5,550
			Bitartarate of potash	3,330
XVIII — Various products	199:727$000	44,386		
XIX — Various manufactures	11:704$000	2,601		
	12:468:668$000	2.770,815		

MOEDA, The Mint. In the Rua da Boa Vista, a little to the W. of the church and square of St. Paul.

This establishment is well fitted up on a small scale with steam machinery for coining gold, silver, and copper. Postage and inland revenue stamps are also printed here.

In a room adjoining the archives, is an interesting collection of Portuguese coins from the earliest period down to the present day. The influence of the discovery of gold mines in the Brazils is plainly visible in the size and number of gold coins struck during the reign of D. João V. The intrinsic value of the largest is £30 and the number of coinages in gold 96. The silver coins were formerly so heavy in proportion to their nominal value that immense quantities were exported to England to be melted. Recent governments however have gone to the opposite extreme and the present silver currency is about 20 per cent less in intrinsic, than in nominal value.

Many valuable works of art in gold and silver which used to be exhibited in this collection, have been disporsed, the principal part having gone to the Museum of the Academy of fine arts or to the Palace of Ajuda.

Permission to go over the Mint is readily granted on application to the director or his substitute who is usually on the spot. Visitors are admitted on week-days from 11 to 3.

XABREGAS.—This edifice was formerly a convent belonging to the Franciscans and usually contained upwards of one hundred friars. It possessed a handsome church, and in a side chapel a representation of Calvary beautifully executed with figures, life size. On the suppression of the monks the building and ground were sold by the government, and converted into a Tobacco manufactory. In Lisbon, the male section of society are almost without exception Tobacco consumers, and the duty levied on this article, is the chief source of revenue to the government. Little boys of 5 years are often to be seen puffing their cigarettes with the complacent air of *connaisseurs*. Indeed Lisbon was one of the first cities to adopt this habit. Tobacco was discovered in

1520 in the province of Yucatan in America. The first portions, however, came to the peninsula from the island of Tabago, where the plant abounds, and whence its name was derived. Jean Nicot, French ambassador at the court of his Most Faithful Majesty in 1560, took a quantity of prepared tobacco from Lisbon to Paris, and the French botanists gave it the name of Nicotiana Tabacum. Catherine de Medicis, to whom Nicot had presented a portion, at once became addicted to its use, which becoming fashionable, rapidly spread throughout Europe.

STATUE OF ST. JOHN NEPOMUCENE. — On the bridge of Alcantara, just outside the most westerly gates of the city.

The martyr St. John, called Nepomucene from the place of his birth, was a native of Nepomuk, a small village in the kingdom of Bohemia, 15 leagues distant from the famous city of Prague. He suffered martyrdom in 1383, being thrown from the bridge of Prague into the waters of the Moldaw, by order of the cruel Wenceslau IV. king of Bohemia, for refusing to violate the secrecy of confession. From the circumstance of his death St. John Nepomucene was selected to be the patron of bridges, and the present statue was erected by D. Maria Anna of Austria, being solemnly-inaugurated in 1744. It is the work of the sculptor Padua and is considered a fair specimen of his skill. On the pedestal is the following inscription:

> S. Joanni Nepomuceno, novo orbis thaumaturgo terrae, aquis, igni, aerique imperanti, atque cum alias tum praesertim in itinere maritimo lucelento fofpitatori fuo, grati animi erga hanc statuam cliens devotiss. An reparat falut. MDCCXLIII.
> João Antonio de Padua a fez.

TERREIRO DO TRIGO.—Corn Exchange. This capacious public granary and corn market was built in the reign of Joseph I. and intended, according to the ideas of political economy at that time prevailing, to secure an abundance of bread for the citizens of Lisbon and prevent monopolies, as may be gathered from the following inscription over the principal entrance:

OTHER PUBLIC BUILDINGS.

AUGUSTO INVICTO PIO
REI E PAE CLEMENTISSIMO
DOS SEUS VASSALLOS
PARA SEGURAR A ABUNDANCIA DE PÃO
AOS MORADORES DA SUA NOBRE E LEAL CIDADE DE LISBOA
E DESTERRAR D'ELLA A IMPIEDADE DOS MONOPOLIOS
DEBAIXO DA INSPECÇÃO DO SENADO DA CAMARA
SENDO PRESIDENTE D'ELLE PAULO DE CARVALHO
DE MENDONÇA
MANDOU EDIFICAR DESDE OS FUNDAMENTOS
ESTE CELLEIRO PUBLICO
ANNO MDCCLXVI

Part of this building is at present used as the municipal custom-house.

A wide passage, open at the top, runs longitudinally through the middle of the *Terreiro* to insure thorough ventilation. In it are ranged the merchants' stalls on which are displayed a variety of kinds of grain, such as wheat, barley, oats, indian corn, etc.

The east end of the ground floor is devoted to wine, principally the common quality called *vinho de pasto*, which pays duty here before going into consumption.

During business hours a great number of mules are to be seen tied to the row of rings extending the whole length of the front of the edifice. They are waiting for the corn which they have to convey to the innumerable windmills in the vicinity of Lisbon.

MATADOURO.—Slaughter-house at the *Cruz do Taboado* at the extreme N. of the city.

This establishment belongs to the municipality, and is fitted up with every requisite demanded by sanitary science. All the cattle destined for the consumption of the capital must be slaughtered here, being first examined by a veterinary surgeon to see that they be in a sound state.

The price charged, including food, is 1$200 réis for oxen, 700 réis for calves and 140 réis for sheep. Upwards of 22,000 oxen, 2,000 calves and 16,000 sheep are annually slaughtered, leaving a net profit to the municipality of £ 2,000.

IMPRENSA NACIONAL. — National printing-office, a short distance to the NW. of the *Escola Polytechnica*.

This establishment belongs to the state, and was founded by the Marquez de Pombal in 1768. It is well worth a visit; every process of the typographic and lithographic arts can here be witnessed. The work turned out bears comparison with the first establishments of Europe. The touching episode of Ignes de Castro from Camões' great poem, has lately been printed in fourteen languages by the *Imprensa* for the Vienna Exhibition, and is a good specimen of its capabilities. It is under the direction of the Conselheiro Firmo Augusto Pereira Marécos, who has occupied that position since 1844, and to whom are due many of the improvements introduced of late years.

CASA DOS BICOS, in the rua dos Bacalhoeiros, near the custom-house.

This curious old house, has for centuries been an object of wonder to the inhabitants of Lisbon, and many are the popular stories related with reference to it. Some say that it was commenced by a modern Crœsus, who intended to place a diamond in the apex of each of the pyramids which project from the front, but when it was half finished, the king became jealous of there being in his capital a house which would eclipse his own palace in splendor, and an embargo was put on the further progress of the work, which thus remained in its present unfinished state. Others say that in the reign of D. Manuel, it was the residence of a colored queen who possessed an enormous amount of brilliants. Be it as it may the house has always been associated in the popular mind with the idea of immense wealth, so that in common parlance it is synonymous with riches and is applied to denominate anything of great value: *Ora não se perca a casa dos Bicos*, is a saying which still survives and has got incorporated into Portuguese phraseology.

The true history, however, does not bear out the popular version. The house was built in 1523 by Affonso de Albuquerque, natural son of the renowned Vice Roy of India, and when completed was three stories high, the principal façade being towards the rua do Almargem. The great earthquake reduced it to a ruin, and what is now left is the back part. As to whether it really ever was studded with diamonds, is a *vexata quaestio*. It certainly was called *Casa dos diamantes*, during the reign of the Philips, but this appellation probably had its origin in the shape of the pyramids with which the house is covered.

25. THE ENVIRONS OF LISBON.

Nothing can be more delightful than an occasional excursion into the country, and the tourist who has sufficient time at his disposal, should not fail to visit some of the villages in the neighborhood, where he will meet with many things to excite his curiosity. In summer time especially, these *villeggiature* are in great favor with the Lisbonites, and all who have the means, contrive to spend a few months in the country during the hot season. The country immediately around Lisbon, is more productive than picturesque, lacking wood and water. The principal trees to be seen are the olive, orange, and lemon. The vine flourishes in full luxuriance, and nothing can exceed the wondrous beauties of nature as exhibited in this plant: how it embraces with its tendrils, as with hands, whatever it meets, and climbing aloft, spreads out its broad leaves to protect the ripening grape from the too ardent rays of the sun. As Cicero says:

«Vitis quidem quae natura caduca est et nisi fulta sit fertur ad terram, eadem ut se erigat claviculis suis quasi manibus quidquid est nacta complectitur; quam serpentem multiplici lapsu et erratico ferro amputans coercet ars agricolarum, ne silvescat sarmentis et in omnes partes nimia fundatur. Itaque ineunte vere in iis quae relicta sunt exsistit tamquam ad articulos sarmentorum ea quae gemma dicitur, a qua oriens uva sese ostendit; quae et succo terrae et calore solis augescens primo est peracerba gustatu, deinde maturata dulcescit, vestitaque pampinis nec modico tempore caret et nimios solis defendit ardores. Qua quid potest esse, tum fructu laetius tum adspectu pulchrius?»

De Senectute, cap. xv.

How immutable are the laws of nature! And how true is Cicero's description to-day, thought it was written 2,000 years ago!

The *alfacinha* (nickname given to the inhabitants of Lisbon on account of their supposed fondness for *alface,* lettuce) passionately loves a garden, and it is his greatest ambition to be the possessor of a *quinta,* or country-house surrounded by a garden, in which he may spend at least his Sundays and Holidays, if not a greater part of the year. The grounds are usually divided into a *pomar,* orchard; *jardim,* flower-garden; and *horta,* vegetable-garden. The environs of Lisbon are thickly studded with these delightful *quintas,* and their proprietors are most liberal in admitting strangers and even throwing them open to the public, thus converting them, not only into a source of gratification to the many, but also into a means of elevating and refining the tastes of the people. As Lord Bacon says:

«God Almighty first planted a garden and indeed it is the purest of human pleasures; it is the greatest refreshment to the spirits of man; without which buildings and palaces are but gross handy works; and a man shall ever see, that, when age grows to civility and elegancy men come to build stately sooner than to garden finely; as if gardening were the greater perfection.»

During summer and autumn, *arraiaes* are held at some of the *quintas.* An *arraial* is a kind of rural religious feast attended by the peasantry of the surrounding district. It is on these occasions that the visitor has the best opportunity of observing the dress, customs, and manners of the *saloios,* as the peasants in the neighborhood of Lisbon are styled.

The Portuguese as a nation are noted for politeness. Cervantes, speaking of the people of Lisbon, says:

«Aqui el amor y la honestedad se dan las manos y se pasean juntos; la cortesia no deja que se llegue la arrogancia, y la braveza no consiente que se le acerque la cobardía: todos sus moradores son agradables, son corteses, son liberales y son enamorados porque son discretos.»

To the testimony of the illustrious author of Don Quixote may be added that of the noble Earl of Carnarvon:

«If I could divest myself of every national partiality, and suppose myself an inhabitant of the other hemisphere traveling solely for my amusement, noting men and manners, and were asked in what country society had attained its most polished form, I should say Portugal: Portuguese politeness is deligthful, because it is by no means purely artificial, but flows in a great measure from a natural kindliness of feeling.

«As I am here alluding to the manners of the country I will just state that in Portugal a gentleman never quits an apartment in which there are ladies without turning round on arriving at the door although he has already taken leave, to renew his parting salutation to his friends, who gracefully return it; and so invariable is this practice, that a man disregarding it would be considered as positively deficient in the courtesies of good society, and a lady would feel somewhat disconcerted by the omission of such a customary mark of attention. Habit is so completely second nature, that on returning to England, after a considerable residence in Portugal, I could hardly refrain from this practice; and till British customs had again in some degree effaced my foreign impressions, I felt on seeing our Englishmen quit the drawing-room without this salutation, that kind of uncomfortable sensation which is involuntarily excited in the mind by witnessing a rather course neglect of any of the recognised *convenances* of society.

«I remember a striking instance of the great extent to which mere ceremony is carried by Portuguese of the old school, and it may not be amiss to relate it while I am touching on the subject. I called one morning on a high dignitary of the church, and ascending a magnificent staircase, passed through a long suit of rooms to the apartment in which the reverend Ecclesiastic was seated. Having concluded my visit, I bowed and departed, but turned, according to the invariable custom of the country, when I reached the door, and made another salutation: my host was slowly following me, and returned my inclination by one equally profound; when I arrived at the door of the second apartment, he was standing on the threshold of the first, and the same ceremony again passed between us; when I had gained the third apartment, he was occupying the place I had just left in the second; the same civilities were then renewed, and these polite reciprocations were continued till I had traversed the whole suit of apartments. At the banisters I made a low and, as I supposed, a final salutation: but no: when I had reached the first landing-place, he was at the top of the stairs, when I stood on the second landing-place, he had descended to the first; and upon each and all of these occasions our heads wagged with increasing humility. Our journey to the foot of the stairs was at length completed. I had now to pass through a long hall divided by columns, to the front door, at which my carriage was standing. Whenever I reached one of these pillars, I turned and found his Eminence waiting for the expected bow, which he immediately returned, continually progressing, and managing his paces so as to go through his share of the ceremony on the precise spot which had witnessed my last inclination. As I approached the hall door, our mutual salutations were no longer occasional but absolutely perpetual; and ever and anon they still continued, after I had entered my carriage, as the Bishop stood with uncovered head till it was driven away.

It has often been said that if civility were civilization, Portugal would be the most civilized country on the face of the earth. Civility, however, is certainly not one of the concomitants of *modern civilization*, for the nearer we approach the great centers of civilization the less civility do we meet with among the people.

Here the tourist will also have many occasions of noting the primitive methods of agriculture. The plough is often little else than a curved piece of wood, tipped with iron, and drawn by a yoke of oxen. Horses are rarely used in agricultural labors: for the lighter kinds of work, mules are employed. The breed of horses has been allowed to degenerate, but of late, efforts have been made to effect an improvement in this respect, by the establishment of races, prizes, etc. The Lusitanian horses of ancient times were famed for swiftness, and this quality gave rise to the belief that the mares near Lisbon and on the banks of the Tagus, conceived of the wind. Pliny, states this as a fact, in his Natural History:

« Constat in Lusitania, circa Olysiponem et Tagum amnem, equas Favonio flante obsersas, animalem concipere spiritum idque partum fieri. »

The mules are found capable of enduring greater hardships and are more economically fed. Some of them are very vicious and the stranger will do well to beware of their heels and mouths, though they generally give notice of their hostile intentions by throwing back their ears and giving a kind of squeak. This is alluded to in the following proverb, which as it contains a reflection on learned ladies, we will not translate:

> Do macho que diz *im*,
> E da mulher que sabe latim,
> Libera nos Domine.

The corn harvest begins in June, and all its operations are carried on in the open air. The threshing-floor, called *eira*, is formed in the field, by leveling a circular piece of land, and having thoroughly saturated it with water, driving over it a flock of sheep who patter it with their feet until it dries, when it becomes hard and smooth. On this *eira* the wheat is spread and threshed by the feet of oxen and mules which are driven round and round, first in one direction and then in another, accompanied by harvest songs and music. The winnowing is accomplished by the winds of heaven, which seem to spring up on purpose at this season.

During the hottest part of the day, is heard the shrill chirping of the tree-cricket (cicada) which by certain organs in the interior of its abdomen, is enabled to produce a remarkably loud sound:

> Et cantu querulae rumpent arbusta cicadae.
> (Virg, *Geor.* III.)

The feathered songsters, join also in the harvest concert, and as evening draws on, the sweet tones of the nightingale, add enchantment to the scene:

> As aves velozmente discorrendo,
> O ar de varias penas esmaltando,
> Em reciprocos cantos respondendo
> E em suaves coros alternando,
> Em confusa harmonia suspendendo,
> Aos que alegres deixavam duvidando
> Se era mais grato ouvi-las, se mais vel-as
> Cantando doces, ou voando bellas.
>
> O melro[1] canta da intrincada rama,
> Entre cuja verdura o ninho esconde;
> A tutinegra[2] está dizendo que ama
> A quem ingratamente corresponde;
> A chamariz[3] incauta a prisão chama,
> O pintasirgo[4] vario lhe responde:
> De uma parte a calandria[5] forma hum coro,
> O pintarouxo[6] de outra mais sonoro.
>
> Mas sobre todos suave na harmonia
> Saudava em canções a tarde amena
> E mestre do coro alado parecia
> A Siréa do bosque, a Filomena[7],
> Tam docemente as queixas repetia,
> Que fez alhea gloria a propria pena,
> E em requebros de voz, fugas e accentos
> Movia os montes, quando atava os ventos.
>
> Com estilo tam vario modulava
> Articulada voz, que juntamente
> Harpa, laúde, e citara imitava
> Com alma, em um só corpo, differente.

1. Melro, blackbird.
2. Tutinegra, kind of duck.
3. Chamariz, golden oriole, a kind of thrush.
4. Pintasirgo or pintasilgo, linnet.
5. Calandria or calhandra, lark.
6. Pintarouxo, robin-red-breast.
7. Filomena or rouxinol, nightingale.

> Que digo corpo? quando a voz formava
> Espirito de corpo independente
> Hum canto vivo na aura só fundado,
> Hum atomo sonante; hum flato alado.
>
> *(Ulyssipo,* cant. III.)

The choir of Angels seems also to take part in the general harmony of nature when the sound of the Angelus bell bids every one join in the solemn memento of the great mystery of the Redemption:

> Ave Maria! Blessed be the hour!
> The time; the clime; the spot; where I so oft
> Have felt that moment in its fullest power
> Sink o'er the earth so beautiful and soft,
> While swung the deep bell in the distant tower,
> Or the faint dying day-hymn stole aloft,
> And not a breath crept thro' the rosy air,
> And yet the forest leaves seemed stirr'd with prayer.
>
> (BYRON.)

Even after dark the air is filled with a multitude of sounds: the monotonous creaking of the *noras* or wooden engines for drawing water; the hoarse croaking of the frogs, the metallic ring of the toads, the hooting of the owls, the squeaking of the bats, and the flitting lights of the *luzcuz* or fire-fly, all testify to the superabundance of life with which nature has endowed this fertile country.

26. CINTRA.

To go to Lisbon and not visit Cintra, is like going to Rome and not seeing the Pope. There are several ways of reaching this far famed spot; on horseback; by the steam tramway; by omnibus; or in a carriage, the latter being by far the most comfortable method. A carriage-and-pair may be hired at the *Companhia de Carruagens Lisbonense;* the fare to Cintra and back in one day (from sunrise to midnight) is 6$600 or about 30ˢ. A *char-à-bancs* for 9 persons, for the same service costs 10$200 or £ 2. 5ˢ. An omnibus starts at 6 A.M. from the *Rua do Ouro,* and returns in the evening. Fare there and back 1$000.

The oldest and best hotel is the Victor, where the traveler will find comfortable accommodation, as he may

also at the Hotel Europa, or Mrs. Lawrence's Hotel.
One day is hardly sufficient to see the principal lions
of Cintra, and to explore it thoroughly at least a week
is required. Cintra is about 16 miles W. of Lisbon. The
first village after leaving the city is the long straggling
one of Bemfica. The objects most likely to engage the
traveler's attention, as he passes along, are the windmills
playing on the neighboring heights, an occasional grove
of orange trees, the turreted line of the aqueduct, and
the hedge-rows of aloe and Indian fig. Bemfica is the
residence of Dona Izabel Maria, great-aunt of the king,
and formerly regent, before the return of her brother
D. Miguel from banishment. Her palace and *quinta*
lie on the left at a short distance from the high road,
and contain a collection of natural curiosities and rare
botanical specimens. In the neighborhood stands the
extinct Dominican convent and church, containing the
chapel and mausoleum of the celebrated Vice Roy of
India D. João de Castro, and the tombs of the Portuguese classic writer Frei Luiz de Sousa and of João das
Regras, the famous lawyer whose eloquence procured
the election of D. João I. at the Cortes of Coimbra (see
page 164). After passing Queluz (see page 188), the road
lies over an extensive heath, in which there is nothing
to divert the traveler's attention from the magnificent
scene which expands itself before him. The elevated
mass of rocks which seen in the distance presents only
a smooth undulating outline, displays as he approaches:

> Horrid crags by topling convent crowned,
> The cork trees hoar that clothe the shaggy steep.
> The mountain's top by scorching skies embrowned,
> The sunken glen whose sunless shrubs must weep.

Not unfrequently a zone of clouds is seen hanging
about the middle of the mountain, while its loftiest peaks
are glittering in brilliant sunshine; and at nightfall the
rays of the sun linger on these summits long after it
has set for the plain below.

RAMALHÃO.—The termination of the heath brings
us to the palace and *quinta* of Ramalhão. This estate
was the private property of Dona Carlotta, wife of

D. João VI. and great-grandmother of his present Majesty. It was the residence of the pretender D. Carlos of Spain in 1832, and it was from this place that he dated his protest against the recognition of his niece queen Isabel II. It was brought to the hammer in 1851 and purchased by a rich merchant of Lisbon.

QUINTA DO MARQUEZ DE VIANNA.—The village at the foot of the rock, which we next reach is called S. Pedro and is remarkable for a beautiful *quinta* belonging to the Marquis of Vianna. It is here that the tourist, as he turns the edge of the mountain and descends towards the town of Cintra, which lies N. of the rock, is gratified with the first magnificent burst of scenery.

> Lo! Cintra's glorious Eden intervenes
> In variegated maze of mount and glen.
> Ah me! What hand can pencil guide or pen
> To follow half on which the eye dilates,
> Through views more dazzling unto mortal ken,
> Than those whereof such things the bard relates,
> Who to the awe-struck world unlocked Elysium's gates.

Cintra has something peculiar in the position and appearance of its buildings, raised one above another, and here and there perched like birds' nests in the rock, and displaying, in striking contrast with the mountain on which they stand, the littleness of the works of man compared with those of the Creator.

PALACIO REAL.—It is a common remark that there is but one step from the sublime to the ridiculous, and this the reader will believe to be verified when after all the magnificent descriptions he has heard and read of this romantic spot, he learns that the most striking objects that the town presents when seen at a distance, are two large kitchen chimneys. Every one who has visited the place will immediately know that we allude to the large conical chimneys of the royal palace, which rise conspicuous in every view of the town. To this palace, called the *palacio real* we will, if he please, conduct the tourist. Permission to see it in the absence of the royal family, may be obtained from the *almoxarife*, or resident superintendent.

The building is a strange compound of Moorish and Christian architecture. The ornaments of the windows are Arabesque and represent interlaced branches of trees, without leaves. In each window there are slender columns of granite supporting arches composed of a single piece of stone. Every thing within the palace corresponds with the anachronisms of the exterior. Historical reminiscences of widely distant events meet the eye in almost every apartment. The numerous fountains, reservoirs, and *jets d'eau* in every part of the building, the prevailing style of the architecture, and the very names by which many of the apartments are still known, prove it to have been of Moorish origin, probably the Alhambra of a king. D. João 1. repaired and adapted it for his own residence. The saloon of magpies, *sala das pegas*, was painted by his orders. It is a large room painted all over with magpies, each bird holding in its beak the legend *por bem*, literally «for good» but used in sense of «no harm». *Por bem* was the motto of D. João 1., and the expression and incident that gave rise to it strongly remind one of the *Honi soit qui mal y pense* of Edward III. On a certain occasion D. João was detected by his queen Philippa of Lancaster, in the act of bestowing some very questionable mark of attention on one of her maids of honor. When his eye met the dagger looks of his English consort, he felt the full extent of his indiscretion, yet unconscious of any evil intention, he condescended to apologize by the memorable words *Por bem*. Certain gossiping tongues of the palace having given publicity to the affair he determined to chastize their malevolent loquacity by representing them as chattering magpies.

The *sala das armas* is the work of D. Manuel. This apartment has a circular roof. In the center of the ceiling are the royal arms of Portugal and immediately around them are the escutcheons of the five sons and two daughters of the king. The rest of the ceiling is covered with the coats of arms of the Portuguese nobility, each shield hanging from a stag's head. The escutcheons, 74 in number, are painted in two concentric circles, so that precedence is given to none. Two of the shields have been erased, those of the families of Tavora and Aveiro, who were implicated in the pseudo-conspiracy against the life of Joseph I. Under the cornice the following words are inscribed in gold letters:

> Pois com esforços e leaes
> Serviços forão ganhados,
> Com estes e outros taes
> Devem de ser conservados.

In another part of the palace is pointed out the room in which the unfortunate D. Sebastião held his last audience before he undertook his ill-fated African expedition, and the chair of state is still shewn on which the youthful monarch sate on that occasion when the crown is said to have fallen from his head.

Near the chapel may be seen the apartment in which Affonso VI. was confined during the last nine years of his life. That unhappy prince whiled away the dreary hours of his captivity in pacing up and down one side of his cell, whence he could see the rocky steep that overhangs the town, where it is said that one who still remained faithful to the monarch in his misfortunes, daily made him a sign of recognition. By thus continually walking to and fro the bricks forming the floor are worn away on that side. Such was the rigor with which the royal prisoner was guarded, that in order to prevent recognition on his attending Mass, a small aperture was made over the choir, where without being seen he could assist at the holy sacrifice. He died on the 12.th of September 1683.

PALACIO DA PENA or de D. FERNANDO.— On the summit of one of the highest peaks and being the most conspicuous object at Cintra. The convent of Pena formerly belonged to the monks of the Jeronymite convent of Belem and was built by D. Manuel on the rock, which he so often ascended to see if he could descry the returning fleet of Vasco da Gama, and from which in fact he was the first to discover it. When the monastery was secularized and sold, it became the property of a private gentleman from whom it was purchased in a ruinous state by his Majesty D. Fernando., who has changed it into a fairy-like palace.

The style of its architecture is the Norman Gothic that flourished at the end of the XII. century.

A broad road in the rock partly walled and partly open, conducts after many windings to a draw-bridge, leading to the principal entrance of the palace, over which are sculptured the arms of Portugal and Saxony. A large tower, several lateral turrets, walls crowned with niched battlements and an open court, surround the two principal buildings. The whole stands between lofty peaks of the rock, and colossal masses of granite. The monastic character of the interior has been in a great measure preserved. The cloister and chapel exist nearly in the same state as in the time of the monks, so that the building may be said to be a combination of Palace, Castle, and Convent.

In the chapel is a rich altar-piece of transparent jasper inlaid with alabaster. It is carved in relief exhibiting some of the stages of the Passion, and is surmounted by niches in which are groups representing various passages in the life of our Lord; over these are festoons of flowers supported by columns of black jasper. A lighted taper held behind the tabernacle will shew its transparency. The work was executed by an Italian artist by order of D. João III., early in the XVI. century.

The Pena is certainly a marvelous structure, both as regards its situation and construction.

The view descried from its summit is magnificent beyond description. The deep azure of the vast Atlantic spreading far to the west; the scenery south of the Tagus, with its regular succession of undulating hills, backed by forests of pines and these again by the dim peaks of the Arrabida mountains; the noble river itself « which poets vainly pave with sands of gold » the distant hills of Monsanto in the direction of Lisbon; and to the north as far as the eye can reach, an extensive plain variegated with heath and cultivated tracts dotted with *quintas* and villages, and the solitary pile of Mafra, form altogether a panorama which it would be hard to parallel.

The grounds surrounding the palace are laid out in shrubberies, with ornamental water and beds of flowers. The softness of the rock, which it was often necessary to cut through for the purpose of forming walks, facilitated these improvements which however cost a large sum of money.

CASTELLO DOS MOUROS.—From these gardens a path conducts to the Moorish castle. The ruins so termed crown the peak to the W. of that on which the Pena stands and immediately overhang the town of Cintra. They consist of the remains of ancient walls, constructed over the cavities and along the ridges of the rock. About half way up the steep are ruins said to be the remains of a Moorish mosque. Part of the vaulted roof has resisted the ravages of time, and on it vestiges of stars painted on an azure ground may still be discerned. Here and there Arabic characters are seen on the wall. In another part of the same inclosure is a quadrangular cistern supposed to have been a Moorish bath. It is 50 feet long by 17 broad and is built of stone with a vaulted roof.

CONVENTO DA CORTIÇA or de SANTA CRUZ.—From the Pena a road over a wild and rugged tract conducts to the Cork convent. This poor monastery standing in dreary solitude in a recess of the *serra* is worthy of its projector D. João de Castro, the pious and pennyless hero of a hundred battles, of whom, in his dying moments St. Francis Xavier, his intimate friend, is reported to have said « the Viceroy of India is dying so poor, that he has not wherewith to buy a fowl ».

This convent or hermitage consists of a church, sacristy, chapter-house, refectory, and about 20 cells. These various apartments are partly formed of holes in the rock and are partly built on its surface. They are lined with cork as a means of counteracting the damp; and from this circumstance the convent derives its name. Each cell is about 5 feet square, and the doors are so low that they cannot be entered without stooping, and are proportionately narrow.

Every thing about the place is in perfect keeping with the above description. In the time of the monks, who were Reformed Franciscans, the luxury of a comfortable bed was never known within the precincts of the cork convent. The bell at the entrance was rung by the aid of a vine-stem instead of a rope. The seats of the dining-room, if the cavern used as such may be so called, as well as the dining-table are cut out of the solid rock. At a little distance from the building is shewn a hole, partly covered by an enormous stone, in which a hermit of the name of Honorius dwelt for the last sixteen years of his life. This holy man, after the labors of the day, and after spending a good part of the night with the rest of his brethren in singing the praises of God in the church, would retire to this incommodious recess, where he had only a few leaves for his couch and a stone for his pillow, and where from the smallness of the cave it was impossible for him to stretch himself out at full length. Yet notwithstanding the severity of these and other acts of penance, which the annals of his order recount of him, he lived to the age of ninety five. A simple stone was placed by his brethren in front of the cave with the following inscription:

HIC HONORIUS VITAM FINIVIT,
ET IDEO CUM DEO IN COELO REVIVIT.
OBIIT ANNO DOMINI 1596.

To those whose notions rise no higher than the matter which surrounds them, and who know no higher pleasure than the gratification of those senses which they have in common with the brute, the conduct of such men as Honorius must seem little better than insanity or driveling enthusiasm.

Such seems to have been the opinion of the sensualist Lord Byron, when he wrote:

Deep in yon cave Honorius long did dwell
In hope to merit Heaven by making earth a Hell.

COLLARES. — Descending the mountain, we descry lying at some distance to the N. W. the village of Collares, which gives its name to the well known wine so called. This rich valley, covered as it is with orange groves and orchards, offers a most delightful object for the eye to dwell upon, and contrasts most beautifully with the bare and arid mountain along the foot of which it extends. The village itself is small and straggling. Several Roman inscriptions have been found in the neighborhood, and are described in a work by Viscount Jerumenha. At the extremity of the valley is an artificial lake or pond called the *Varsea*, on which is a pleasure-boat. Here parties from Cintra often meet for purposes of amusement.

A small rivulet winds its way from this spot to the ocean. Formerly when it was a navigable river, the fruit from the trees overhanging its banks were carried down its stream and gave to the beach the name by which it is still known, *Praia das Maçãs,* apple beach.

PEDRA D'ALVIDRAR. — Above the beach, about a league from Collares, there is a rock or headland rising to a perpendicular height of about 200 feet and is known by the name of *Pedra d'Alvidrar*.

At certain points the waves of the Atlantic dash against its base and have undermined it to a great extent, as may be seen at some distance from the edge of the precipice where there is a circular hole or chasm, at the bottom of which the sea is visible and by its incessant chafing strikes terror into the stoutest heart when viewed from above. At the highest point of the rock, immediately over the ocean, a horrifying feat is performed by persons who inhabit the neighborhood. Without any assistance or support but their hands and feet they descend the perpendicular rock, from the summit to the water's edge and return in the same manner. The least slip or the giving way of a piece of rock must inevitably plunge them to certain destruction, and yet they are eager to venture down the steep in the hope of receiving a few *vintens* from the visitor. Sometimes fishermen, laden with baskets of fish will ascend the dangerous steep merely for their own convenience.

MONSERRATE. — Returning in the direction of Cintra we come to the beautiful *quinta* of Monserrate, now the property of Mr. Cook, who has lately received from the Portuguese sovereign the title of Visconde de Monserrate. Situated on an eminence branching from the *serra* it presents one of the most charming prospects that even Cintra can present. The site was selected by the celebrated Mr. Beckford, whose refined taste for the beautiful no one will dispute. He built a chateau and laid out the grounds in a most tasteful manner, but after a few years the place was abandoned and allowed to fall into utter ruin and thus it remained till purchased by its present possessor who has spared no expense to render it a paradise on earth. All the most beautiful and valuable trees and shrubs that can grow in this climate are here to be seen, and the Palace, besides containing many curiosities, has in its interior some wonderfully fine carving in marble of the Moorish style. The Viscount resides here during the months of May–July, when permission to see the quinta may be obtained from him on the spot. At other times a ticket of admission must be obtained from his agent at Lisbon.

PENHA VERDE.— Near the above is the *quinta* of Penha Verde, once the property of the renowned D. João de Castro. This distinguished hero, one of the greatest men Portugal has produced, chose this spot as his favorite retreat after his many victories in two quarters of the globe. After the memorable defence of Diu, the only reward he asked from his sovereign was that a rock on which stood six trees might be annexed to his *quinta*, and it is still known as the *Monte das Alviçaras*. Here also is a chapel built by him in honor of Our Lady. At the bottom of the steps which conduct to it, are two stones which he brought from the east as trophies and on which are carved various emblematic figures and below these a long inscription in sanscrit dedicated to the god Seva. Over the chapel door is the following:

> Joannes Castrensis cum viginti annos in durissimis
> bellis in utraque Mauritania pro Christi religione
> consumpsisset et illa clarissima Tunetis expugnatio-
> nem interfuisset atque tandem sinus Arabici littora
> et omnes Indiae oras non modo lustrasset sed lit-
> terarum monumentis mandavisset Christi numini
> salvus domum rediens Virgini Matri fanum ex voto
> dicavit anno 1542.

The great hero bequeathed this property to his descendants with the express condition of their not deriving pecuniary advantages from its cultivation, saying that even from the earth he would accept no reward for his labors.

SETIAES.— Before reaching Cintra after leaving Penha Verde, we come to the palace belonging to the Duke of Loulé and which derives some celebrity from the disgraceful convention between Sir H. Dalrymple and Junot which is said to have been signed here:

> And ever since that martial synod met,
> Britannia sickens, Cintra! at thy name;
> And folks in office at the mention fret
> And fain would blush, if blush they could, for shame.

This place, known by the name of *Setiaes*, is the fashionable promenade for the visitors on summer evenings.

QUINTAS.— Besides the foregoing there are many delightful *quintas*, generously thrown open to visitors by their owners.

The principal ones are those of the Duke of Saldanha, Barão da Regaleira, Marquis of Pombal and Mr. Smith. In the *quinta de D. Caetano*, between Cintra and the new quarter called Villa Estephania, is a douche bath of crystaline water, which is much frequented.

27. MAFRA.

Seven leagues NW. of Lisbon and three leagues N. of Cintra. Tourists generally take Mafra on their return from Cintra. A carriage-and-pair may be hired at the *Companhia de carruagens lisbonenses*, to go to Mafra and back in two days for 9$000 or £2. A *char-à-bancs* for the same service, with nine places, costs £4.

The hotel near the palace offers good accommodation.

The village itself is of no importance, the whole interest centers in the Palace, Convent, and Basilica, a building of stupendous magnitude.

D. João V. anxious to have issue to succeed him on the throne, made a vow that on the birth of a son he would erect a magnificent monastery on the site of the poorest priory in his kingdom. On the birth of Prince José, Mafra was selected for the fulfilment of the vow, for on this spot stood a hut in which dwelt twelve Arrabidos, the poorest order in Portugal. The plan was drawn and having met with the monarch's approval, was executed by the German architect Frederic Ludovici. The foundation stone was laid on the 17.th November 1717 and this ceremony alone cost 200,000 crowns. Thirteen years were spent in the erection of the building. According to documents still existing the average number of workmen daily employed during that period was 14,700. The bills from June to October of 1730 shew that no fewer than 45,000 persons were employed in this interval, of whom 7,000 were soldiers who received 150 réis per diem, in addition to their ordinary pay. The king ordered a temporary hospital to be erected for the sick workmen, containing eight wards capable of holding 5,350 sick, in addition to two others for 240 convalescents.

In the five years 1729–1734, the hospital received 17,007 patients and the expense is set down at 92 million réis. The total cost of this immense fabric has never been exactly stated, but it is calculated at 19,000,000 crowns.

The basilica was consecrated on the 22.nd Oct. 1730, the king's birthday, with the greatest possible pomp. The festivities lasted eight days. The king ordered refreshments to be given from his kitchen, to all who applied and 9,000 persons partook of his hospitality on the single day of the consecration.

The entire edifice forms an immense parallelogram, the longest sides of which extend N. and S. 1,150 ft.

The building comprises a basilica, a monastery, and two royal palaces.

It contains 866 rooms, two lofty towers each 350 feet high, one very large court, two of more moderate size and six small ones. The front of this imposing pile which faces the W. is formed by the church and palaces, the former being in the center, approached by a noble flight of steps.

The palace on the N. was the king's residence and that on the S. the queen's; both are four stories high and terminate in large turrets, at the extreme angles. The masonry has been well executed: the walls widen gradually to their base where they are twenty palms thick, and are surmounted by a parapet 16 palms high. The roof of the whole building forms a vast platform elevated 90 feet above the ground, on which 10,000 soldiers might be reviewed.

The two palaces so closely resemble each other in their architectural details, that a description of one will serve for both. On entering, the visitor will be struck with the number and magnificence of the apartments through which he is conducted. Allegorical or mythological subjects are painted in fresco on the ceilings and walls. The floors are of marble of various hues, and many of the rooms are adorned with handsome pillars of the same material.

It has been remarked, and perhaps not unjustly, that in this long suit of apartments, there is not one room whose size corresponds with the vast proportions of the whole. The audience chamber is still preserved in the same state in which it was when D. João VI. inhabited the palace previous to the invasion of the French, as well as after his return from Brazil.

It is hung with curtains of blue velvet and damask, and is the only apartment by which we are enabled to judge of the *tapesserie*, when Mafra was actually the residence of a wealthy and gorgeous court. All the wood of the doors and windows is the best that the Brazils could furnish, but it is to be lamented that its beauty has been concealed under a coating of paint.

The convent, dedicated to St. Anthony, was held by the Reformed Franciscans. They were for some time superseded by the canons regular of S. Vicente, but were again restored and continued in possession till the suppression of monastic orders in 1834. This part of the building is square, with an open cloister in the interior in which is a noble fountain.

The various entrances into the convent, as well those from without as those from the church or palaces, lead to a spacious corridor which runs E. and W. the whole lenght of the building. Entering it from the cloister we pass the chapel *do Campo Santo*, destined for the interment and obsequies of the brethren. It is very richly and appropriately decorated: its altar is of white marble, supported by black and white columns of the same material. The chapel is 120 palms by 40.

Another apartment worthy of attention is the *Casa dos actos*. It is 110 palms by 40. Here were held the scholastic theses: at one end is a pulpit, below a large table of white marble bearing a Latin inscription. There are also two tribunes where the king and court occasionally attended to hear the discussions of the learned disputants.

Near this is the lavatory, an octagonal apartment with vaulted roof, supported by arches and fitted up with marble fountains and basins of chaste and elegant finish. From this we pass through another room equally spacious, to the refectory, which is deservedly celebrated for its noble proportions, its light airy character and the simplicity of its decorations. Above the head table is a large painting of the Last Supper framed in light blue marble. The tables are 36, each 20 palms in length and 3 in breadth; the seats are of Brazilwood with backs of polished yellow marble.

The convent contains about 300 cells. The infirmary is divided into separate partitions, each containing a porcelain figure of Our Lady and the divine Babe, or the representation of some mystery of faith. At one end is a handsome chapel with galleries corresponding to the different floors, so that invalids from each could attend without inconvenience or exposure. The chapter room is a noble oval-shaped apartment, having a remarkable echo. The library is a magnificent room 300 ft. in length, and broad and high in proportion. The pavement is of red and white marble, and the arched roof beautifully stuccoed. A light gallery runs round the interior at an elevation of 16 palms. The book-cases are made of Brazilwood and contain about 50,000 volumes.

Annexed to the convent is a walled inclosure, containing an ample tank, a ball court, kitchen garden, orchard, and shrubberies ornamented with statues and artificial lakes. Beyond this extends the royal park which is 10 miles in circumference and is inclosed by a 12 feet wall. The park is stocked with deer and various kinds of game.

Returning to the roof of the building and ascending one of the turrets, we come to the belfry. The machinery of the clocks fills a good sized room, and the complicated works remind one more of an engineering establishment than of a religious house. There are two immense cylinders covered with spikes which act upon levers connected with the bells and produce from them, the beautiful chimes for which they are famed. The bells were cast in Belgium and their weight of metal and richness of tone, are perhaps unrivaled. The entire weight of metal in each tower is 207 tons. These chimes cost upwards of 2.000,000 crowns. Orders were first given for a single set of chimes, and before the work was commenced one of the ministers said to D. João V. that perhaps his Majesty was not aware of the immense expense to be incurred. «How much», asked D. João. «More than a million crowns», replied the minister». «Is that all», said the monarch, «in that case order two sets». In the S. tower the hands of the clock mark the time in the common way: those in the N. in the Roman method, that is, with only six divisions in the circumference of the face. Before the clock strikes, the bells ring a pleasing chime, and they can be made to play any of the tunes at pleasure.

We now descend to the church, which, in splendor and magnificence far surpasses all that we have hitherto described. The façade and portico are adorned with colossal statues of saints, finely executed in white marble. The exterior, as well as the interior, is encrusted with polished marble, and carved into an endless variety of tasteful and appropriate designs. The first coup d'œil on entering is very imposing. The high altar adorned with two majestic columns of red variegated marble, each a single block about 50 feet in height, immediately fixes the attention. Trevisani painted the altar-piece, which represents St. Anthony in ecstasy, beholding the infant Jesus descending into his cell amid an effulgence of glory. «Never did I behold», says the autor of *Vashek*, who visited Mafra in 1789, «an assemblage of such beautiful marble as gleamed above, below, and around us. The collateral chapels, six in number, are each enriched with finely finished *bassi relievi* and stately portals of black and yellow marble, richly veined, and so highly polished, as to reflect objects like a mirror. The pavement, the vaulted ceiling, the dome, and even the topmost lantern, is encrusted with the same costly and durable material. Roses of white marble and wreaths of palm branches, most exquisitely sculptured, enrich every part of the edifice. I never saw Corinthian capitals better modeled, or executed with more precision and sharpness than those of the columns which support the nave. Having satisfied our curiosity by examining the ornaments of the altar, we pass through a long covered gallery to the sacristy, a magnificent vaulted hall, paneled with some beautiful varieties of alabaster and porphyry, and carpeted, as well as the chapel adjoining it, in a style of the utmost magnificence. We traversed several more halls and chapels, adorned with equal splendor, till we were fatigued and bewildered like knights errant in the mazes of an enchanted palace». Such is Mr. Beckford's account of the impression produced on him by the inspection of the church, seen at the time when it was at the zenith of its splendor.

The length of the church from the entrance to the sanctuary is 283 palms. Its total breadth including the lateral chapels 142 palms. The dome over the transept is 300 palms in height and is infinitely superior in point of design to the rest of the edifice and may certainly be reckoned among the lightest and best proportioned in Europe. The visitor may if he please mount to its summit, and from the balustrade survey the wide prospect below. The arch of the dome is closed by a single stone, hollowed out and pierced by eight circular windows.

The circumference of this stone is 33 feet, its height 10 feet: it was drawn from the quarry by 172 oxen, and during its transit, forty masons were hammering away without any embarrassment upon it. It was raised to its present position by four cranes, worked by 160 men in the space of two hours.

In conclusion Mafra may be characterized as being at once rich and simple. Its design was grand and its execution uniformly successful.

As an architectural production it has been declared by an able critic to be faultless, neither vitiated by a mixture of styles, nor blemished by absurd anachronisms.

PART III.

SUPPLEMENTARY.

1. THE ROYAL FAMILY.

The king. — Sua Magestade Fidelissima El-Rei o Senhor D. Luiz Filippe Maria Fernando Pedro de Alcantara Miguel Rafael Gabriel Gonzaga Xavier Francisco de Assis João Augusto Julio de Bragança e Bourbon, Rei de Portugal e dos Algarves, d'aquem e d'alem mar, em Africa Senhor de Guiné, e da Conquista, Navegação e Commercio da Ethiopia, Arabia, Persia e da India, etc. The reigning Sovereign, under the title of His Most Faithful Majesty D. Luiz I.; born Oct. 31, 1838, son of queen Dona Maria II. and of prince Ferdinand of Saxe-Coburg; succeeded his brother D. Pedro V., Nov. 11.th, 1861; married by proxy at Turin 27.th Sept. 1862 and personnally at Lisbon 6.th Oct. of the same year to,

Queen. — *Dona Maria Pia,* born Oct. 16.th, 1847, the youngest daughter of king Victor Emmanuel of Italy. Issue of the union are two sons:

Sons of the king. — Sua Alteza Serenissima o Principe Real o Senhor *D. Carlos Fernando,* heir to the throne, born Sept. 28.th, 1863.

Sua Alteza o Senhor Infante *D. Affonso Henrique,* born July 31.st, 1865.

Father of the king. — *Prince Ferdinand* of Saxe-Coburg, titular king of Portugal, born 29.th Oct. 1816, eldest son of the late prince Ferdinand of Saxe-Coburg; married 9.th April 1836 to Dona Maria II, queen of Portugal; received the title of king, 16.th Sept. 1837; widower Nov. 15.th 1853; regent of Portugal during the minority of his son D. Pedro V. from 15.th Nov. 1853 to 16.th Sept. 1855; married a second time 10.th June 1869 to Madame Hensler, condessa d'Edla.

BROTHER AND SISTERS OF THE KING.—O Senhor Infante *D. Augusto,* born 4.th Nov. 1847.

A Senhora Infanta *Dona Maria Anna,* born 21.st July 1843, married 11.th May 1859 to prince George, second son of the king of Saxony.

A Senhora Infanta *Dona Antonia,* born 17.th Feb. 1845, married 12.th Sept. 1861 to prince Leopold of Hohenzollern-Sigmaringen.

GREAT AUNT OF THE KING.—A Senhora Infanta *Dona Izabel Maria,* born 4.th July 1801, Regent of Portugal from 10.th March 1826 to 26.th Feb. 1828.

The reigning dynasty belongs to the House of Bragança which dates from the beginning of the fifteenth century, and the first monarch of this line was D. João IV., the Fortunate, who was proclaimed in 1640 on the expulsion of the Spaniards.

The average duration of the reign of the Portuguese sovereigns is 22 years.

The royal arms are, argent, five escutcheons, azure, placed crosswise, each charged with as many besants as the first placed falterwise and sable for Portugal. The shield bordered, gules, charged with seven towers or three in chief and two in each flank. The supporters are two winged dragons, and the crest a dragon, or under the two flanches, and the base of the shield appears at the end of it, and two crosses, the first flower-deluce vert, which is for the order of Aviz, and the second patee, gules, for the order of Christ; the motto is changeable, but it is frequently Pro Rege et Grege « For the king and People ».

The following is the civil list paid by the government to the members of the royal family:

The king............	365:000$000 réis = £	81,030
The queen...........	60:000$000 réis = £	13,320
D. Carlos Fernando..	20:000$000 réis = £	4,440
D. Affonso Henriques.	10:000$000 réis = £	2,220
D. Fernando........	100:000$000 réis = £	22,200
D. Augusto.........	16:000$000 réis = £	3,552
Dona Izabel Maria...	20:000$000 réis = £	4,440
	591:000$000 réis = £	131,202

2. TITLES OF NOBILITY.

After the conquest of the Peninsula by the Arabs at the beginning of the eight century, the christians were reduced to the abject condition of slaves, their former distinctions ceased and they were all made equals in misfortune and driven to take refuge in the mountains of Asturias.

After several centuries of suffering the Christians succeeded in shaking off the hated Mussulman yoke, and established the monarchy of Asturias, and the first distinctions which appear are *escudeiros,* applied to those who fought with sword and shield (escudo) *cavalleiros,* those who possessed a horse (cavallo) and *ricos-homens* (literally rich men) who had acquired fortunes at the expense of the enemy. Subsequently, when the kingdom of Asturias merged into the more extensive monarchy of Leon, titles of nobility were for the first time introduced at court, and they consisted of *ricos-homens, infanções* and *vassallos.* Affonso Henriques, when he founded the Portuguese monarchy, followed the example of Spain and introduced the same titles. At that time there was no regular pay for the army. The chiefs were rewarded by the spoils of the enemy. The king, however, was obliged to provide food for the soldiers, and as this obligation at times weighed heavily on his shoulders he devised the plan of conceding the title of *ricos-homens,* with certain privileges, to such as maintained a given number of soldiers at their own expense. This title is now obsolete yet nevertheless the *homens ricos* (rich men) of the present day receive quite as much consideration as their ancient prototypes, there being no place in the world where the Golden calf is more worshiped than at Lisbon. The titles of *infanção* and *vassallo* are also extinct.

In the reign of Affonso III. the term *fidalgo* was introduced. This word is an abbreviation of *filho d'algo* (son of somebody) to distinguish those nobles who had derived their titles from their ancestors, from those who were ennobled by royal favor. This addition combined with former titles produced *escudeiro fidalgo, cavalleiro fidalgo* and *moço fidalgo*, the two latter being still recognized at the Portuguese Court.

The first king of Portugal, being merely a *conde* (count) at the time of his acclamation, did not possess sufficient authority and prestige to confer this title on others, and it was not till the reign of D. Diniz that the kings of Portugal assumed this prerogative, and created the County of Barcellos in 1298.

Next in order of antiquity comes the title of Duque (Duke). King John I. of Portugal, having routed the Spaniards in the famous battle of Aljubarrota, the more firmly to establish his throne, made proposals of alliance to John of Gant, duke of Lancaster, offering him ships and every assistance in order to prosecute the claims of his (the duke's) wife to the throne of Castille and avenge the murder of her father D. Pedro I. This alliance having been cemented the duke of Lancaster accompanied by his wife and daughter and many noblemen embarked in a fleet of English and Portuguese ships, and landed with an army on the Spanish coast. John I. hastened to meet his new ally and a close friendship sprang up between the two. John I. married John of Gant's eldest daughter Philippa. The matrimonial and political alliance, together with the familiar intimacy which existed between the two Johns, caused many English customs to be introduced into Portugal, and there can be no doubt that it was owing to these influences that, on his return from the conquest of Ceuta in 1415, king John, wishing to reward his two sons Pedro and Henrique, for their services during the siege, created them respectively duque de Coimbra and duque de Vizeu. The title of duke has generally been reserved for members of the royal family and very rarely conceded to members of the aristocracy for distinguished services.

The title of marquez (marquis) was first given by Affonso V., who in 1451, on the occasion of his sister's marriage with Frederic III., emperor of Germany, conferred the dignity of marquez de Valença on the count d'Ourem who escorted the bride to Germany and represented the person of his royal master.

The titles of *visconde* (viscount) and *barão* (baron) were also introduced by Affonso V., the former in 1476 and the latter in 1475. Since the establishment of constitutional monarchy in Portugal, successive governments have advised great liberality in the concession of titles, especially of the two latter, mostly for one life only.

The term *fidalgo* is only applied to those who are descendants of ancient families: the new men are simply *titulares* (titled).

The visitor will observe that many persons prefix the title of *Dom* to their christian names. Dom or D. is an abbreviation of the latin *Dominus* and was formerly conceded very sparingly by Portuguese monarchs, being at first confined, to the legitimate descendants of royal blood. D. João I. was the first natural son of the king who was permitted to make use of this distinction. In later times it was given in exchange for signal services and was held in great estimation, so much so that Emmanuel the Great, thought he had fully requited the services of Vasco da Gama for the discovery of a new empire, when he bestowed upon the distinguished navigator the title of Dom, and a pension of 1,000 cruzados (£ 40) per annum!

At present, however, it has become much vulgarized though not quite so much as in Spain, where every one without exception arrogates to himself the title of Don. In Portugal it is confined principally to the descendents of noble families, but is often assumed by those who have no right to it: as Garcia de Rezende says:

"Os reis por acrescentar
As pessoas em valia
Por lh's serviços pagar
Vimos a uns o Dom dar,
E a outros fidalguia.
Já os reis não hão mister
Pois toma o Dom quem quer,
E armas nobres tambem
Toma quem armas não tem
E dá o Dom á mulher."

The title of Dona is given by courtesy to all ladies.

3. THE MUNICIPALITY.

The **CAMARA MUNICIPAL**, or municipal chamber, holds its sittings temporarily in a small building called *Sete casas*, E. of the Custom-house, until such time as their new hall, in the Pelourinho, be completed. The *camara* consists of 12 members or *vereadores* elected in November every two years, by burgesses who pay 5$000 property tax or 1$000 income tax or *decima*. The *camara* is assisted by a council, *Conselho municipal*, composed of 13 of the greatest tax-payers in the city, who deliberate conjointly with the municipal chamber on questions relating to finance. The *administrador do concelho*, an official appointed by government, has also the right of being present and voting at the meetings of the chamber. Its duties are divided into departments or *pelouros*, as follows: 1, Litigation; 2, Police, markets, squares; 3, Paving, draining and other works; 4, Adjustments and stamping of weights; 5, Slaughter-house; 6 Cemeteries; 7, Quays and shores; 8, Public walks and gardens; 9, Fires; 10, Lighting; 11, Scavenging; and 12, Water supply.

Each *pelouro* is taken charge of by one of the *vereadores* who is elected for that purpose by his colleagues:

The total revenue amounts to about 340:000$000 réis or £ 74,500, and its principal sources are:

Government grant........	150:000$000	£	33,300
Slaughter-house	44:000$000	»	9,768
Rents and interest........	36:000$000	»	8,000
Granting of licenses.......	27:000$000	»	6,000
Cemeteries	11:000$000	»	2,442
Markets.................	8:000$000	»	1,776

The expenditure is about balanced by the receipts and its chief items are:

Lighting	61:000$000	£	13,555
Scavenging..............	60:000$000	»	13,333
Paving..................	30:000$000	»	6,666
Slaughter-house..........	30:000$000	»	6,666

Public gardens and works..	40:000$000	£	8,888
Cemeteries...............	5:000$000	»	1,111
Water..................	6:000$000	»	1,333

An *octroi* duty is levied on the following articles of consumption on entering the city, the proceeds being taken by the government, out of which they pay *réis* 150:000$000 to the municipal chamber for lighting, scavenging and paving, and retain the rest for national purposes.

Octroi duties collected in the financial year 1872–1873:

Meat................	357:283$649	£	79,317
Corn................	241:856$072	»	53,692
Vegetables...........	23:416$261	»	5,199
Wine................	429:675$095	»	95,388
Brandy..............	1:558$660	»	346
Olive oil............	60:176$644	»	13,360
Vinegar.............	2:423$675	»	538
Liqueurs............	8$700	»	2
Gin.................	7$590	»	2
Beer................	767$870	»	170
Oils (not olive)......	1:716$900	»	381
Fuel................	28:924$228	»	6,421
Fruit................	81:419$977	»	18,075
Rs........	1.229:235$321	»	272,891

The *guarda municipal* and *policia civil* are both paid by government.

4. FIRE SIGNAL.

As the tourist who remains some time in Lisbon will probably be startled from his sleep by the hurried tolling of the church bells as a signal of fire, it may be convenient to have at hand a means of ascertaining whether the danger be near or remote. On counting the number of strokes, and referring to the following table the locality of the fire will be discovered (see page 87).

WITHIN THE CITY WALLS.

Name of Church	Number of strokes	Name of Church	Number of strokes
Santa Engracia	11	Penha de França	20
Beato Antonio	11	S. Sebastião	21
S. Vicente	12	Coração de Jesus	21
Santo Estevão	12	Monserrate	22
Graça	13	S. Mamede	22
S. Thiago	14	Santa Izabel	23
Sé (Cathedral)	14	Estrella	24
S. Christovão	14	Lapa	24
Carmo	15	Necessidades	25
Conceição Nova	15	S. Francisco de Paula	26
S. Nicolau	16	Santos o Velho	27
Soccorro	17	Paulistas	28
S. José	18	Chagas	29
Pena	19	S. Roque	30
Bemposta	20	Martyres	31
Anjos	20	S. Paulo	32

OUTSIDE THE CITY WALLS.

Name of Church	Number of strokes	Name of Church	Number of strokes
Carnide	6	Alcantara	8
Odivellas	6	Erm. das Dores, Belem	9
Benfica	7	S. Jeronymo, Belem	9
Porcalhota	7	Torre da Ajuda	10
S. Domingos	7	Boa Hora	10

4. COMMUNICATIONS.

TELEGRAPH. (TELEGRAPHO.)

The principal telegraph station *(estação telegraphica)* is under the arcade at the N. W. corner of Black Horse Square.

In telegraphing to England care should be taken to state *by the submarine cable* (pelo cabo submarino): a message sent overland is subject to many delays, and when it arrives is so mutilated and changed by repeated transfers in different countries, as to be scarcely readable.

Besides the principal station, there are branches at Belem, Bom Successo, Carnide, S. Bento, Ajuda, and in other quarters of the city, between which telegrams may be exchanged for 50 réis (20 words).

Telegrams of not more than 20 words (including name and address of receiver and name of sender) between any two stations in Portugal, cost 200 réis, and for each succeeding series of 10 words, 100 réis.

Prices of telegrams not exceeding 20 words (including receiver's name and address, and sender's name) from Portugal to other European countries.

Destination.	By cable via Falmouth.	Overland.
Austria	3$350	1$950
Belgium	2$650	1$400
Denmark	3$000	1$850
France	2$850	$950
Germany	3$200	1$750
Gibraltar (direct)	–	$750
Great Britain and Ireland	1$950	1$950
Holland	2$850	1$550
Greece	–	2$450
Italy	3$300	1$500
Norway	3$000	2$200
Russia (European)	4$100	2$650
Spain	–	$400
Sweden	3$450	2$100
Switzerland	3$200	1$400
Turkey (European)	5$100	2$400

POST-OFFICE AND POSTAGES

(CORREIO E PORTES)

The General Post-office (correio geral) occupies a ruined palace in the *Calçada do Combro*, a short distance to the W. of the *Praça de Luiz de Camões*. Here lists are kept, of letters addressed to foreign countries and detained for want of sufficient stamps: also of letters whose owners cannot be found. Letters may be registered here to England or other countries for 100 réis.

There is a branch post-office at the S. W. corner of the *Praça do Commercio* where a list is hung up at the door, of steamers about to sail for foreign ports, with the hour when the mail is made up for each. Letters to go by any of the above steamers can be posted here up to the latest moment.

The postage for inland letters, i. e. between any two places in Portugal, is 25 réis for every *10 grammes* (about $1/3$ oz.) or fraction thereof; letters unstamped are charged double on delivery.

Letters to any place in Great-Britain or Ireland, sent by the daily overland mail, 120 réis for every $7\frac{1}{2}$ gram. (about $1/4$ oz.) or fraction thereof. Letters for the same destination sent by steamer, 120 réis for every 15 grams (about $1/2$ oz.). Newspapers by the former route 30 réis for every 40 gr., and by the latter 20 réis for the same weight. Books, samples, photographs, etc., can be sent only by sea, and must not weigh more than 480 gram. (a little over 1 lb.), postage 20 réis for each 40 gram.

It is expressly prohibited to enclose money or valuables in unregistered letters. Any such letters are intercepted, opened, and whatever they contain confiscated to the public treasury.

Registered letters may contain money or valuables, but in case of miscarriage the post-office will only indemnify the sender to the extent of 55000 réis. Letters presented for registry must be sealed with wax.

Postages from Portugal to other countries

Destination	Letters Weigth in grammas	Letters Postage in réis	News papers Weigth in grammas	News papers Postage in réis
Austria	15	70	50	20
Belgium	10	120	40	20
Brazil, per subsidized steamer	7 1/2	150	30	20
Brazil, per private steamer	10	80	40	10
Denmark	15	95	50	35
France	10	80	40	20
Germany	15	70	50	20
Gibraltar	10	60	40	20
Great Britain and Ireland per str	15	120	40	20
Great Britain and Ireland overland mail	7 1/2	120	40	30
Holland	15	90	50	30
Greece	15	140	50	40
Italy, overland	10	120	40	20
Italy, by steamer	15	100	40	20
India, China, Australia, via Gibraltar	7 1/2	150	30	20
Norway	15	105	50	35
Russia	15	105	50	30
Spain	10	25	40	10
Sweden	15	110	50	35
Switzerland	10	140	40	15
United States, per str. via England	15	160	40	30
United States, via Spain	7 1/2	160	40	45

RAILWAYS. (CAMINHOS DE FERRO.)

Portuguese railway-companies might appropriately adopt as their motto the Italian proverb: «*Chi va piano va lontano e sano*», the quickest trains running only 16 miles an hour, (including stoppages) and fatal accidents to passengers being things unknown.

There are two companies having termini in Lisbon, the «*Caminho de ferro do Norte e Leste*», which connects the capital with Oporto and Badajoz, and the «*Caminho de ferro do sul e sueste*», which connects it with Setubal, Evora, and Beja. The following tables shew the names of the intermediate stations, their distance in *kilometros* (5 kilometros = 3 miles) and fares. Passengers should be at the station at least half an hour before the time for starting in order to book their luggage, the weighing of which occupies a considerable time:

COMPANHIA DO NORTE E LESTE.

The terminus in Lisbon is at Santa Apolonia, at the extreme E. of the city.

From Lisbon to the Junction. (Entroncamento.)

Name of stations.	Distance from Lisbon. Kilom.	Fares from Lisbon.		
		1.st class Réis	2.nd class Réis	3.rd class Réis
Poço do Bispo	4	$120	$099	$070
Olivaes	7	$140	$110	$080
Sacavem	10	$190	$150	$110
Povoa	18	$350	$270	$190
Alverca	22	$420	$330	$240
Alhandra	26	$500	$390	$280
Villa Franca	31	$590	$460	$330
Carregado	37	$700	$550	$390
Azambuja	47	$890	$700	$500
Ponte de Reguengo	55	1$040	$810	$580
Sant'Anna	61	1$160	$900	$650
Santarem	75	1$420	1$110	$790
Valle de Figueira	84	1$590	1$240	$890
Matto de Miranda	94	1$780	1$390	$990
Torres Novas	103	1$950	1$520	1$090
Entroncamento (Junction)	107	2$030	1$580	1$130

RAILWAYS.

From the Junction to Oporto.

Names of stations.	Distance from Lisbon. Kilom.	1.st class Réis	2.nd class Réis	3.rd class Réis
Thomar (Payalvo)	121	2$290	1$780	1$280
Chão de Maçãs	130	2$460	1$920	1$370
Caxarias	140	2$650	2$060	1$470
Albergaria	150	2$840	2$210	1$580
Vermoil	162	3$070	2$390	1$710
Pombal	170	3$220	2$500	1$790
Soure	186	3$520	2$740	1$960
Formoselha	202	3$820	2$970	2$130
Taveiro	212	4$010	3$120	2$230
Coimbra	218	4$130	3$210	2$290
Souzella	225	4$260	3$310	2$370
Mealhada	237	4$480	3$490	2$490
Mogofores	245	4$640	3$610	2$580
Oliveira do Bairro	253	4$790	3$720	2$660
Aveiro	273	5$160	4$020	2$870
Estarreja	288	5$450	4$240	3$030
Ovar	301	5$690	4$430	3$170
Esmoriz	312	5$900	4$590	3$280
Espinho	318	6$020	4$680	3$340
Granja	321	6$070	4$720	3$380
Valladares	328	6$200	4$830	3$450
Oporto (V. N. de Gaia)	333	6$300	4$900	3$500

From the junction to Badajoz.

Names of stations.	Distance from Lisbon. Kilom.	1.st class. Réis.	2.nd class. Réis.	3.rd class. Réis.
Barquinha	111	2$100	1$640	1$170
Praia	119	2$250	1$750	1$250
Tramagal	130	2$460	1$920	1$370
Abrantes	135	2$560	1$990	1$420
Bemposta	147	2$780	2$170	1$550
Ponte de Sor	164	3$100	2$420	1$730
Chança	184	3$480	2$710	1$940
Crato	200	3$780	2$940	2$100
Portalegre	217	4$110	3$190	2$280
Assumar	227	4$300	3$340	2$390
Santa Eulalia	246	4$650	3$620	2$590
Elvas	265	5$010	3$900	2$790
Badajoz	282	5$350	4$160	

COMPANHIA DO SUL E SUESTE.

The terminus is at Barreiro on the S. bank of the Tagus, whither passengers are conveyed by steamers which start from the jetty at the SW. corner of the *Praça do Commercio* or Black Horse Square, where tickets may also be bought.

Lisbon to Setubal and Beja.

Name of stations.	Distance from Lisbon. Kilom.	Fares from Lisbon.		
		1.st class. Réis.	2.nd class. Réis.	3.rd class. Réis.
Barreiro............	7	$150	$150	$100
Lavradio............	9	$320	$290	$210
Alhos Vedros........	12	$320	$290	$210
Moita...............	15	$400	$350	$240
Pinhal Novo.........	23	$600	$500	$350
Branch to Setubal				
Palmella.........	30	$770	$630	$430
Setubal..........	35	$900	$720	$500
Poceirão............	38	$980	$780	$530
Pegões..............	49	1$250	$990	$670
Vendas Novas........	64	1$630	1$270	$860
Montemór............	82	2$080	1$610	1$090
Casa Branca (junction).	97	2$460	1$900	1$280
Alcaçovas...........	109	2$760	2$120	1$430
Vianna..............	117	2$970	2$270	1$530
Villa Nova..........	124	3$140	2$410	1$620
Alvito..............	132	3$340	2$560	1$720
Cuba................	144	3$650	2$780	1$870
Beja................	161	4$070	3$100	2$080
Baleisão............	173	4$380	3$330	2$240
Quintos.............	180	4$550	3$465	2$320

Lisbon to Evora and Extremoz.

Names of stations.	Distance from Lisbon. Kilom.	1.st class. Réis.	2.nd class. Réis.	3.rd class. Réis.
Lisbon to Casa Branca, junction, as above ...	97	2$080	1$610	1$090
Evora..................	123	3$120	2$390	1$610
Azaruja................	143	3$620	2$780	1$860
Valle de Pereiro......	148	3$750	2$860	1$920
Venda do Duque......	156	3$950	3$010	2$020
Extremoz..............	175	4$430	3$370	2$260

Fares and distances from Lisbon by rail to the principal cities of Europe.

	Distance		Fares.	
	Kilom.	Miles.	1.st class. Réis	2.nd class. Réis
Amsterdam..........	2,861	1,777	58$650	44$340
Berlin...............	3,467	2,153	73$050	56$980
Bordeaux...........	1,748	1,084	36$210	27$370
Brussels............	2,643	1,642	54$120	40$810
Copenhagen	3,300	2,050	70$770	56$080
Dresden	3,559	2,210	75$000	57$670
Edinburgh..........	3,358	2,085	77$240	57$830
Florence	3,609	2,241	76$600	58$320
Frankfort	3,014	1,892	62$100	46$640
Geneva.............	2,958	1,836	60$600	45$670
Hague..............	2,801	1,740	57$470	43$000
London, via Dieppe..	2,624	1,630 ·	54$870	41$320
London, via Boulogne	2,718	1,688 ·	60$390	45$150
London, via Calais...	2,881	1,858 ·	61$490	46$350
Madrid.............	881	547	18$000	13$790
Milan...............	3,290	2,044	65$280	49$050
Moscow.............	5,595	3,475	120$880	91$590
Naples..............	4,261	2,646	89$490	68$210
Paris	2,333	1,449	48$000	36$220
Rome...............	4,000	2,485	83$770	63$820
St. Petersburg......	5,126	3,185	106$740	82$020
Turin...............	3,142	1,952	67$170	47$510
Vienna..............	3,748	2,328	78$780	58$760

* Exclusive of Channel passage.

HACKNEY CARRIAGES. (TRENS DE PRAÇA.)

Fares for 1 or 2 persons.

	By day-light. Réis.	By night.	
		Up to 1 A. M. Réis.	After 1 A. M. till day-break. Réis.
Within the city walls.			
From any one point to any other, viz. a course (*uma corrida*)....	$300	$320	$620
By time (*ás horas*):			
For the first hour............	$400	$420	$820
For every additional quarter of an hour or fraction thereof...	$100	$105	$205
Outside the city walls.			
(But within a radius of 10 kilometros, 6 miles)			
By time:			
For every quarter of an hour in going.....................	$150	$155	$305
For every quarter of an hour, waiting....................	$100	$100	$100
For returning, two thirds of the fare due for going.			

If more than 2 persons, the fare is *half as much again* for each additional passenger. Thus for a single course by day for one or two persons the fare is 300 réis; for three persons 450 réis; for four, 600 réis; and for five 750 réis.

Children over one year, can be legally charged as passengers. To avoid disputes or overcharge it is advisable to agree with the cabman beforehand.

LISBON CARRIAGE COMPANY.

(COMPANHIA DE CARRUAGENS LISBONENSES.)

This Company formed for supplying the capital with respectable looking vehicles of all descriptions, is highly useful. The coachmen, dressed in decent livery, contrast favorably with their brethren of the whip who ply in the public streets and who never fail to impose upon their fares, except when they have not the opportunity of doing so.

The head office of the Company is in the *Largo de S. Roque,* a little above the Trindade theater. There is a branch at *n.º 50 Rua direita de Alcantara:* also telegraphic stations at *n.º 85 Travessa de Santa Justa* and *n.º 25 Rua de S. Bento,* at any of which places carriages may be ordered. They do not ply in the street for hire.

Prices of the Lisbon Carriage Company.

	Carriage and pair	
	For 2 persons (coupé)	For 4 persons (caleche)
	Réis	Réis
Within the demarkation[1].		
By time (ás horas):		
For 2 hours (not less) between sunrise and midnight............	1$200	1$300
Third and each succeeding hour....	$300	$400
Half an hour (after first two)	$200	$200
By the day (por dia):		
A whole day, from sunrise to midnight	3$500	4$000
Half day (from sunrise to noon)....	1$800	2$000
Half day (from noon to midnight)...	2$500	3$000
For each hour before or after the times above specified............	$300	$400
Outside the demarkation[1].		
In addition to the above prices, an extra charge for each league beyond the boundry.............	$300	$400
For half league.................	$200	$200

1. The demarkation extends to *Dafundo, Largo d'Ajuda, Largo do Calhariz, Benfica* church, *Largo de Carnide, Calçada de Carriche* (Nova Cintra), *Ameixoeira, Largo da Charneca, Alto da Portella* and *Largo dos Olivaes.*

	Carriage and pair.	
	For 2 persons (coupé) Réis	For 4 persons (caleche) Réis
Special fares		
Cintra. A whole day, from sunrise to midnight there and back......	5$200	6$600
Cintra, a single journey there or back........................	4$000	4$800
Collares. A whole day, there and back........................	6$600	8$600
Collares, single journey either way..	5$000	6$200
Mafra, two days, there and back...	9$000	12$000
Mafra single journey either way...	6$400	8$000
Ericeira, two days, there and back	11$000	14$200
Ericeira, single journey either way	8$400	10$200
Mafra and *Cintra,* three days. 1.st to Mafra, 2.nd Mafra to Cintra, 3.rd home	13$000	16$800
Estoril and *Cascaes,* whole day, there and back....................	5$000	6$000
Estoril and *Cascaes,* single journey.	4$000	4$500
Queluz or *Bellas,* at the same rate as within the demarkation	–$–	–$–
Railway station, to fetch or take...	1$000	1$200
Theater, taking to, and fetching....	1$200	1$500
Ball, taking to, and fetching	2$400	3$000
Bath, taking to, and fetching	1$500	1$800
By the month (aos mezes)		
Each month of 30 days............	70$000	78$000

The Company have also *char-à-bancs* for 10 persons, the price of which is double that for a *caleche.*

Besides the Company there are many other hackney carriage proprietors in different quarters of the city, whose prices are much the same as above.

VAPORES LISBONENSES.

Start from the jetty opposite the hotel Central, *Caes do Sodré.*

To Alcantara, every half hour—fare 30 réis.
To Belem, every half hour—fare 50 réis.
To Cacilhas, every 40 minutes—fare 50 réis.

BOATS. (BOTES.)

There is no fixed tariff for the boatmen (catraieiros), the visitor must therefore take care to agree beforehand as to the fare, otherwise he will have to pay three times the proper amount.

OMNIBUSES.

(COMPANHIA DE CARRUAGENS OMNIBUS.)

Central station, n.° 16 *Largo do Pelourinho*. Opposite the new town-hall, whence omnibuses start for the following places:

To Belem, every half hour, 60 réis by daylight, and 100 réis by night. As far as Alcantara 40 réis.

To Bemfica, five times a day in summer and three in winter, 120 réis by day, 160 réis by night. To any place on the route, within the city walls, 60 réis by day and 30 réis by night.

To Lumiar, the same as to Bemfica.

To Poço do Bispo, four times a day in summer and three in winter 80 réis, as far as Xabregas 60 réis.

To Oeiras, every day at $3\frac{3}{4}$ P. M., returning at $6\frac{1}{4}$ A. M. 240 réis. As far as Pedrouços 120 réis. As far as Cruz Quebrada 160 réis.

To Cintra, during the summer months 600 réis, return ticket 1$000 réis.

The omnibuses belonging to the above Company have «Companhia» printed on a cross board to distinguish them from the others.

TRAMWAY.

To Alcantara, Belem, Pedrouços, and Santa Appolonia. *Carris de ferro de Lisboa*, vulgarly called *O Americano*.

This tramway runs the entire length of the city, extending to the W. as far as Pedrouços, a favorite sea bathing place 4 1/2 miles from Black Horse Square. The carriages run every ten minutes and the fare is 50 réis for any distance within the walls, and an additional 30 réis from Alcantara to Belem or intermediate distance.

STEAM TRAMWAY.

TO CINTRA AND TORRES VEDRAS.

(Vulgarly called *O Larmanjat.*)

The terminus is at the *Portas do Rego,* outside the walls 2 miles due N. of Black Horse Square. Passengers are conveyed gratis to the station by omnibuses which start from the *Portas de Santo Antão*, near the NE. corner of the *Rocio*. The trains run three or four times a day.

Fares from Lisbon to Torres Vedras and intermediate stations.

	Fares from Lisbon	
	1.st Class Réis	3.rd Class Réis
Campo Pequeno	120	100
Campo Grande	120	100
Lumiar	160	120
Nova Cintra	180	140
Povoa de Santo Adrião	200	160
Loures	280	200
Pinheiro de Loures	360	260
Lousa	400	320
Venda do Pinheiro	500	400
Malveira	520	420
Villa Franca do Rosario	680	540
Barras	740	580
Freixofeira	820	640
Tureifal	840	660
Carvalhal	880	680
Torres Vedras	900	700

Each passenger is allowed to take 22 lbs. of luggage. Children under 3 years gratis, over 3 half price.

Fares from Lisbon to Cintra and intermediate stations.

	1.st Class Réis	3.rd Class Réis
Sete Rios	140	100
Bemfica	160	140
Porcalhota	200	160
Ponte de Carenque	260	200
Queluz	260	200
Cacem	340	260
Rio de Mouro	420	300
Ranholas	500	360
Cintra	550	400
Return tickets to Cintra	950	700

Each passenger is allowed to take 22 lbs. of luggage. Childen under 3 years gratis, over 3 half price.

STEAMERS. (VAPORES.)

Alphabetical list of ports with which there is regular steam communication from Lisbon.

Destination.	Line of steamer.	Fare. 1st class.	Fare. 2nd class.	Date of sailing.	Lisbon agent's name and address.
		£ s.	£ s.		
Ambriz......	Empreza Lusitana......	33 7	24 10	5th each mo..	E. George, 4, rua do Ferregial de Cima.
Amsterdam....	Companhia Neerlandeza...	8	—	Fortnightly...	E. George, 4, rua do Ferregial de Cima.
Antwerp......	Spanish line........	8	—	Fortnightly...	J. M. Alcobia, 7, calçada do Ferregial.
	Ryde line..........	9	5	Monthly......	Piombino & Filhos, 7, beco dos Apostolos.
Arica........	Pacific Steam Navigation Cº	67	42	Fortnightly...	E. Pinto Basto & Cº, 64, caes do Sodré.
	Royal Mail Steam Packet Cº	24	15	13th each mo.	R. Knowles & Cº, 31, rua dos Capellistas.
	Pacific Steam Navigation Cº	26	20	Twice a mo...	E. Pinto Basto & Cº, 64, caes do Sodré.
	Liverpool and River Plate..	15	—	Twice a mo...	Garland, Laidley & Cº, 10, rua do Alecrim.
	Messageries maritimes.....	24	18	Monthly	Torlades & Cº, 1, travessa do Sequeiro das Chagas.
Bahia........	Chargeurs réunis..........	20	18	6th and 20th each mo.	Pereiras & La Rocque, 120, rua dos Capellistas.
	Hamburg line............	20	—	12th and 26th each mo.	E. George, 4, rua do Ferregial de Cima.
	German line..............	—	—	—	E. George, 4, rua do Ferregial de Cima.
Benguella....	Empreza Lusitana........	35 10	26 13	5th each mo..	E. George, 4, rua do Ferregial de Cima.

Destination	Line				Frequency	Agent
Bordeaux	Pacific Steam Navigation C.º	8		5	Fortnightly..	E. Pinto Basto & C.º, 64, caes do Sodré.
	Messageries maritimes	8		6 4	Monthly	Torlades & C.º, 1, travessa do Sequeiro das Chagas.
	Royal Mail Steam Packet C.º	32		20	13.th and 29.th each mo.	R. Knowles & C.º, 31, rua dos Capellistas.
	Pacific Steam Navigation C.º	35		20	Fortnightly..	E. Pinto Basto & C.º, 64, caes do Sodré.
	Liverpool and River Plate	25		—	Fortnightly..	Garland, Laidley & C.º, 10, rua do Alecrim.
Buenos Ayres	Messageries maritimes	36		26	Monthly	Torlades & C.º, 1, travessa do Sequeiro das Chagas.
	Hamburg line	25		—	16.th and 26.th each mo.	E. George, 4, rua do Ferregial de Cima.
	Chargeurs réunis	30		20	6.th and 20.th each mo.	Pereiras & La Rocque, 120, rua dos Capellistas.
	Ryde line	35		—	Monthly	Piombino & Filhos, 7, beco dos Apostolos.
	Clyde line	26		20	Monthly	Joseph Mellicott, 23, travessa dos Remolares.
Cadiz	Spanish line	3	6	—	Weekly	J. M. Alcobia, 7, calçada do Ferregial.
	Ligne Péninsulaire	3	4	—	Monthly	H. Juhel, 19, largo do Pelourinho.
Callao	Pacific Steam Navigation C.º	67		42	Fortnightly..	E. Pinto Basto & C.º, 64, caes do Sodré.
Ceará	North Brazilian Navigation C.º	22		—	Monthly	Garland, Laidley & C.º, 10, rua do Alecrim.
	Red Cross line	20		—	20.th each mo.	Pereiras & La Rocque, 120, rua dos Capellistas.
Civitta Vecchia	Spanish line	8		—	Irregular	J. M. Alcobia, 7, calçada do Ferregial.
Dakar	Messageries maritimes	21	12	16 4	Monthly	Torlades & C.º, 1, travessa do Sequeiro das Chagas.
Fayal	Empreza Insulana	7	2	5	15.th each mo.	G. S. Arnaud, 84, caes do Sodré.

COMMUNICATIONS.

Destination.	Line of steamer.	Fare. 1st class. £ s.	Fare. 2nd class. £ s.	Date of sailing.	Lisbon agent's name and address.
Genoa	Companhia Neerlandeza	8 —	—	Fortnightly	E. George, 4, rua do Ferregial de Cima.
	Spanish line	8 —	—	Irregular	J. M. Alcobia, 7, calçada do Ferregial.
Gibraltar	Spanish and Port. Steam Navigation Cº	3 —	—	Weekly	E. Pinto Basto & Cº. 64, caes do Sodré.
Glasgow	Spanish line	3 —	—	Weekly	J. M. Alcobia, 7, calçada do Ferregial.
	Clyde line	8 —	—	Monthly	Joseph Medlicott, 23, travessa dos Remolares.
Graciosa	Empreza Insulana	7 2	5 —	15.th each mo.	G. S. Arnaud, 84, caes do Sodré.
Hamburg	Hamburg and Med. Cº	8 —	—	Thrice a mo.	E. George, 4, rua do Ferregial de Cima.
	Ligne Péninsulaire	6 13	—	Fortnightly	H. Juhel, 19, largo do Pelourinho.
Havre	Spanish line	6 —	—	Weekly	J. M. Alcobia, 7, calçada do Ferregial.
	Thetis line	5 —	—	Fortnightly	Henry Burnay, 10, rua dos Fanqueiros.
Hull	Empreza Lusitana	8 —	—	Irregular	E. George, 4, rua do Ferregial de Cima.
Islay	Pacific Steam Navigation Cº	67 —	42 —	Fortnightly	E. Pinto Basto & Cº. 64, caes do Sodré.
Leghorn	Companhia Neerlandeza	8 —	—	Fortnightly	E. George, 4, rua do Ferregial de Cima.
	Spanish line	8 —	—	Irregular	J. M. Alcobia, 7, calçada do Ferregial.
	Pacific Steam Navigation Cº	10 —	7 —	Fortnightly	E. Pinto Basto & Cº. 64, caes do Sodré.
Liverpool	Spanish line	6 —	—	Fortnightly	J. M. Alcobia, 7, calçada do Ferregial.
	Bibby's boats	8 —	—	Weekly	Mascarenhas & Cº. 8, travessa do Corpo Santo.
	North Brazilian Navigation Cº	6 —	—	Monthly	Garland, Laidley & Cº, 10, rua do Alecrim.

STEAMERS. 297

	Line			Frequency	Agent
Liverpool (con)	Red Cross line	6	—	Monthly	Pereiras & La Roeque, 120, rua dos Capellistas.
	Liverpool and Maranhan Steam Ship C.º	6	—	20.th each mo.	R. Knowles & C.º, 31, rua dos Capellistas.
Loanda	Spanish line	—	—	—	—
	Empreza Lusitana	33	7	5.th each mo.	F. Martin & Filhos, 103, rua do Alecrim.
	Spanish and Port. Screw Steam Shipping C.º	8	—	Weekly	E. George, 4, rua do Ferregial de Cima.
London					E. Pinto Basto & C.º, o4, caes do Sodré.
	Spanish line	8	—	Weekly	J. M. Alcobia, 7, calçada do Ferregial.
	Empreza Lusitana	6	—	5.th each mo.	E. George, 4, rua do Ferregial de Cima.
Madeira	Maria Pia	6	4	Monthly	G. S. Arnaud, 84, caes do Sodré.
	Ligne Péninsulaire	4	5	Weekly	H. Juhel, 19, largo do Pelourinho.
Malaga	Spanish line	3	—	Weekly	J. M. Alcobia, 7, calçada do Ferregial.
Manáos	Liverpool and Amazon River Steam line	31	6	Every 2 mo.	José J. das Neves & Filhos, 4, praça de D. Luiz.
Maranhan	North Brazilian Navigation C.º	22	—	Monthly	Garland, Laidley & C.º, 10, rua do Alecrim.
	Liverpool and Maranhan S. S. C.º	—	—	8.th each mo.	R. Knowles & C.º, 31, rua dos Capellistas.
	Red Cross line	22	—	20.th each mo.	Pereiras & La Roeque, 120, rua dos Capellistas.
Messina	Spanish line	8	—	Irregular	J. M. Alcobia, 7, calçada do Ferregial.
	Royal Mail Steam Packet C.º	32	20	13.th and 29.th each mo.	R. Knowles & C.º, 31, rua dos Capellistas.
Montevideo	Pacific Steam Navigation C.º	35	20	Fortnightly	E. Pinto Basto & C.º, 64, caes do Sodré.
	Liverpool and River Plate	25	—	Fortnightly	Garland, Laidley & C.º, 10, rua do Alecrim.
	Messageries maritimes	36	26	Monthly	Torlades & C.º, 1, travessa do Sequeiro das Chagas.

Destination.	Line of steamer.	Fare. 1st class.	Fare. 2nd class.	Date of sailing.	Lisbon agent's name and address.
Montevideo...	Clyde line........	£ 26 s. —	£ 20 s. —	Monthly.....	Joseph Mellicott, 23, travessa dos Romulares.
	Chargeurs réunis...	30 —	20 —	6.th and 20.th each mo.	Pereiras & La Rocque, 120, rua dos Capellistas.
	Hamburg line.....	25 —	—	12.th and 26.th each mo.	E. George, 4, rua do Ferregial de Cima.
	Ryde line.........	35 —	—	20.th each mo.	Piombino & Filhos, 7, beco dos Apostolos.
Mossamedes...	Empreza Lusitana...	37 16	29 —	5.th each mo.	E. George, 4, rua do Ferregial de Cima.
	Companhia Neerlandeza...	8 —	—	Fortnightly...	E. George, 4, rua do Ferregial de Cima.
Naples.......	Spanish line.......	8 —	—	Irregular.....	J. M. Alcobia, 7, calçada do Ferregial.
Obidos.......	Liverpool and Amazon Steam line.	27 10	—	Every 2 mo...	José J. das Neves & Filhos, 4, praça de D. Luiz.
	Portuguese Brazilian line...	1 2	0 18	Monthly.....	José J. das Neves & Filhos, 4, praça de D. Luiz.
Oporto.......	Thetis line........	0 136	—	Fortnightly...	Henry Burnay, 10, rua dos Fanqueiros.
Palermo......	Spanish line.......	8 —	—	Irregular.....	J. M. Alcobia, 7, calçada do Ferregial.
	North Brazilian Navigation C.º	22 —	—	Monthly.....	Garland, Laidley, & C.º, 10, rua do Alecrim.
	Red Cross line.....	22 —	—	20.th each mo.	Pereiras & La Rocque, 120, rua dos Capellistas.
Pará.........	Liverpool and Amazon River Steam line.	22 —	—	Every 2 mo...	José J. das Neves & Filhos, 4, praça de D. Luiz.

STEAMERS.

Pernambuco...	Royal Mail Steam Packet C.º	22	15	13.th each mo.	R. Knowles & C.º, 31, rua dos Capellistas.
	Pacific Steam Navigation C.º	24	18	Fortnightly..	E. Pinto Basto & C.º, 64, caes do Sodré.
	Messageries maritimes.....	22	16 12	Monthly	Torlades & C.º, 1, travessa do Sequeiro das Chagas.
	Chargeurs réunis............	18	15 10	6.th and 20.th each mo.	Pereiras & La Rocque, 120, rua dos Capellistas.
	Pernambuco line.............	15	—	Every 20 days	Garland, Laidley & C.º, 10, rua do Alecrim.
Principe	Empreza Lusitana...........	26 13	20	5.th each mo.	E. George, 4, rua do Ferregial de Cima.
	Royal Mail Steam Packet C.º	27	20	13.th and 29.th each mo.	R. Knowles & C.º, 31, rua dos Capellistas.
	Pacific Steam Navigation C.º	27	20	Fortnightly..	E. Pinto Basto & C.º, 64, caes do Sodré.
	Messageries maritimes.....	30	20	Monthly	Torlades & C.º, 1, travessa do Sequeiro das Chagas.
	Chargeurs réunis............	25	20 10	6.th and 20.th each mo.	Pereiras & La Rocque, 120, rua dos Capellistas.
Rio de Janeiro	Hamburg line.................	22	—	12.th and 26.th each mo.	E. George, 4, rua do Ferregial de Cima.
	Liverpool and River Plate ..	20	—	Fortnightly .	Garland, Laidley & C.º, 10, rua do Alecrim.
	Ryde line...................	27	—	20.th each mo.	Piomlino & Filhos, 7, beco dos Apostolos.
	Clyde line...................	20	16	Monthly	Joseph Medlicott, 23, travessa dos Romulares.
Rotterdam.....	Companhia Neerlandeza.....	8	—	Fortnightly..	E. George, 4, rua do Ferregial de Cima.
Santaren......	Liverpool and Amazon Steam line.	26 10	—	Every 2 mo.	José J. das Neves & Filhos, 4, praça de D. Luiz.
Santos..........	Chargeurs réunis............	25	20 10	6.th and 20.th each mo.	Pereiras & La Rocque, 120, rua dos Capellistas.

Destination.	Line of steamer.	Fare. 1st class. £ s.	Fare. 2nd class. £ s.	Date of sailing.	Lisbon agent's name and address.
Santos (con.)	Liverpool and River Plate	20	—	17.th each mo.	Garland, Laidley & C.o 10, rua do Alecrim.
	Hamburg line	22	—	13.th and 26.th each mo.	E. George, 4, rua do Ferregial de Cima.
S. Jorge	Empreza Insulana	7 2	5 7	15.th each mo.	G. S. Arnaud, 84, caes do Sodré.
S. Miguel	Empreza Insulana	6 13	4 18	15.th each mo.	G. S. Arnaud, 84, caes do Sodré.
S. Thiago	Empreza Lusitana	16	12	15.th each mo.	E. George, 4, rua do Ferregial de Cima.
S. Thomé	Empreza Lusitana	26 13	20	5.th each mo.	E. George, 4, rua do Ferregial de Cima.
S. Vicente	Empreza Lusitana	16	12	5.th each mo.	E. George, 4, rua do Ferregial de Cima.
	Royal Mail Steam Packet C.o	13	10	13.th and 29.th each mo.	R. Knowles & C.o 31. rua dos Capellistas.
Serpa	Liverpool and Amazon River Steam line.	30	—	Every 2 mos.	José J. das Neves & Filhos, 4, praça de D. Luiz.
Southampton	Royal Mail Steam Packet C.o	8	5	Fortnightly	R. Knowles & C.o, 31, rua dos Capellistas.
	Ryde line	8	4	Monthly	Piombino & Filhos, 7, beco dos Apostolos.
Terceira	Empreza Insulana	7 2	5 7	15.th each mo.	G. S. Arnaud, 84, caes do Sodré.
Valparaiso	Pacific Steam Navigation C.o	67	42	Fortnightly	E. Pinto Basto & C.o 64. caes do Sodré.
	Ryde line	67	—	20.th each mo.	Piombino & Filhos, 7. beco dos Apostolos.
Vigo	Spanish line	2 10	—	Irregular	J. M. Alcobia, 7, calçada do Ferregial.

6. MONEY, WEIGHTS AND MEASURES.

MONEY. (DINHEIRO.)

The coins current in Portugal are the:

GOLD.

	Value		
Moeda de cinco mil réis, marked 5000. réis 5$000 =	1l.	2s.	3d.
Libra or Soberano (English sov.)..... » 4$500 =	1	0	0
Meia libra or meio soberano (½ sov.) » 2$250 =		10	0
Moeda de dois mil réis marked 2000.. » 2$000 =		8	11

SILVER.

Meia Corôa, marked 500............ réis 500 =	0l.	2s.	3d.
Cruzado novo, marked 400........... » 480 =	0	2	2
Doze vintens, old, unmarked.......... » 240 =	0	1	1
Dois tostões, marked 200............ » 200 =	0	0	11
Seis vintens, old, unmarked.......... » 120 =	0	0	6
Tostão, marked 100................ » 100 =	0	0	5
Tostão, marked LXXX.............. » 100 =	0	0	5
Tres vintens, old, unmarked.......... » 60 =	0	0	3
Meio tostão, marked 50............. » 50 =	0	0	2½
Meio tostão, old, unmarked.......... » 50 =	0	0	2½

COPPER.

Pataco, marked 40................. réis 40 =	0l.	0s.	2d.
Vintem, marked XX .... » 20 =	0	0	1
Dez réis, marked X................ » 10 =	0	0	0½
Cinco réis, marked V............... » 5 =	0	0	0¼

Besides the above there are other coins, now no longer in circulation, such as the:

Dobrão....................... réis 30$000 =	6l.	13s.	4d.
Dobra........................ » 16$000 =	3	11	0
Peça......................... » 8$000 =	1	15	7

Accounts are kept in mil réis and réis; the sign $, called a *cifrão*, is used to denote mil réis; thus 14$000, or 14$ signifies fourteen mil réis. In speaking of amounts of money the following expressions are used in familiar discourse

Um conto for	a million réis
Uma moeda	4$800 »
Um quartinho.............................	1$200 »
Um pinto................................	$480 »
Um cruzado	$400 »

The English sovereign and half-sovereign have been adopted by the Portuguese government and made legal tender for 4$500 and 2$250. As the British government charges no seigniorage on the coinage of gold, the Portuguese, instead of going to the expense of coining gold, find it more economical to send it over to England and get it done *gratis*.

In changing circular notes etc., it is necessary to bear in mind that the sovereign represents in Portugal 4$500 réis and not a pound sterling. The amount to be received will of course vary according to the exchange, which fluctuates between 52^d and 54^d per milree. For instance a bill for £81 drawn on Lisbon at the exchange of 54^d would be paid by 80 sovereigns, for £81 @ 54^d = 360$000 réis or 80 times 4$500 réis. As to the origin of the Portuguese *real* see page 180.

The following tables may be found useful in reducing English to Portuguese money and vice-versa.

EXAMPLE — How much is 289$560 réis in English money?

Referring to the first part of table I.
we find 560 réis .... = 2s. 5 d.½
and in the other columns 289$000 réis ...... = 64l. 4 5

Ans. 64l. 6s. 10 d.½

AGAIN — How much is 196l. 11s. 6d. in Portuguese money?

In the pounds columns of table II. we find 196l. =. 882$000
and in the first column 11 s.= .... 2$475
and 7 d.= $131

Ans. Rs. 884$606

TABLE 1.

Portuguese to English money at the exchange of $53^{1}/_{3}$ per 1$000 réis, or 4$500 = £ 1.

Réis	£	s	D	Réis	£	s	D	Réis	£	s	D
10	0	0	$0^{1}/_{2}$	450	0	2	0	890	0	3	11
20	0	0	1	460	0	2	$0^{1}/_{2}$	900	0	4	0
30	0	0	$1^{1}/_{2}$	470	0	2	1	910	0	4	$0^{1}/_{2}$
40	0	0	2	480	0	2	$1^{1}/_{2}$	920	0	4	1
50	0	0	$2^{1}/_{2}$	490	0	2	2	930	0	4	$1^{1}/_{2}$
60	0	0	3	500	0	2	$2^{1}/_{2}$	940	0	4	2
70	0	0	$3^{1}/_{2}$	510	0	2	3	950	0	4	$2^{1}/_{2}$
80	0	0	4	520	0	2	$3^{1}/_{2}$	960	0	4	3
90	0	0	$4^{1}/_{2}$	530	0	2	4	970	0	4	$3^{1}/_{2}$
100	0	0	5	540	0	2	$4^{1}/_{2}$	980	0	4	4
110	0	0	$5^{1}/_{2}$	550	0	2	5	990	0	4	$4^{1}/_{2}$
120	0	0	6	560	0	2	$5^{1}/_{2}$				
130	0	0	$6^{1}/_{2}$	570	0	2	6	1$000	0	4	5
140	0	0	7	580	0	2	$6^{1}/_{2}$	2$000	0	8	11
150	0	0	8	590	0	2	7	3$000	0	13	4
160	0	0	$8^{1}/_{2}$	600	0	2	8	4$000	0	17	9
170	0	0	9	610	0	2	$8^{1}/_{2}$	5$000	1	2	3
180	0	0	$9^{1}/_{2}$	620	0	2	9	6$000	1	6	8
190	0	0	10	630	0	2	$9^{1}/_{2}$	7$000	1	11	1
200	0	0	$10^{1}/_{2}$	640	0	2	10	8$000	1	15	7
210	0	0	11	650	0	2	$10^{1}/_{2}$	9$000	2	0	0
220	0	0	$11^{1}/_{2}$	660	0	2	11	10$000	2	4	5
230	0	1	0	670	0	2	$11^{1}/_{2}$	11$000	2	8	11
240	0	1	$0^{1}/_{2}$	680	0	3	0	12$000	2	13	4
250	0	1	1	690	0	3	$0^{1}/_{2}$	13$000	2	17	9
260	0	1	$1^{1}/_{2}$	700	0	3	1	14$000	3	2	3
270	0	1	2	710	5	3	$1^{1}/_{2}$	15$000	3	6	8
280	0	1	$2^{1}/_{2}$	720	0	3	2	16$000	3	11	1
290	0	1	3	730	0	3	$2^{1}/_{2}$	17$000	3	15	7
300	0	1	4	740	0	3	3	18$000	4	0	0
310	0	1	$4^{1}/_{2}$	750	0	3	4	19$000	4	4	5
320	0	1	5	760	0	3	$4^{1}/_{2}$	20$000	4	8	11
330	0	1	$5^{1}/_{2}$	770	0	3	5	21$000	4	13	4
340	0	1	6	780	0	3	$5^{1}/_{2}$	22$000	4	17	9
350	0	1	$6^{1}/_{2}$	790	0	3	6	23$000	5	2	3
360	0	1	7	800	0	3	$6^{1}/_{2}$	24$000	5	6	8
370	0	1	$7^{1}/_{2}$	810	0	3	7	25$000	5	11	1
380	0	1	8	820	0	3	$7^{1}/_{2}$	26$000	5	15	7
390	0	1	$8^{1}/_{2}$	830	0	3	8	27$000	6	0	0
400	0	1	9	840	0	3	$8^{1}/_{2}$	28$000	6	4	5
410	0	1	$9^{1}/_{2}$	850	0	3	9	29$000	6	8	11
420	0	1	10	860	0	3	$9^{1}/_{2}$	30$000	6	13	4
430	0	1	$10^{1}/_{2}$	870	0	3	10	31$000	6	17	9
440	0	1	11	880	0	3	$10^{1}/_{2}$	32$000	7	2	3

Réis	£	s	D	Réis	£	s	D	Réis	£	s	D
33$000	7	6	8	82$000	18	4	5	131$000	29	2	3
34$000	7	11	1	83$000	18	8	11	132$000	29	6	8
35$000	7	15	7	84$000	18	13	4	133$000	29	11	1
36$000	8	0	0	85$000	18	17	9	134$000	29	15	7
37$000	8	4	5	86$000	19	2	3	135$000	30	0	0
38$000	8	8	11	87$000	19	6	8	136$000	30	4	5
39$000	8	13	4	88$000	19	11	1	137$000	30	8	11
40$000	8	17	9	89$000	19	15	7	138$000	30	13	4
41$000	9	2	3	90$000	20	0	0	139$000	30	17	9
42$000	9	6	8	91$000	20	4	5	140$000	31	2	3
43$000	9	11	1	92$000	20	8	11	141$000	31	6	8
44$000	9	15	7	93$000	20	13	4	142$000	31	11	1
45$000	10	0	0	94$000	20	17	9	143$000	31	15	7
46$000	10	4	5	95$000	21	2	3	144$000	32	0	0
47$000	10	8	11	96$000	21	6	8	145$000	32	4	5
48$000	10	13	4	97$000	21	11	1	146$000	32	8	11
49$000	10	17	9	98$000	21	15	7	147$000	32	13	4
50$000	11	2	3	99$000	22	0	0	148$000	32	17	9
51$000	11	6	8	100$000	22	4	5	149$000	33	2	3
52$000	11	11	1	101$000	22	8	11	150$000	33	6	8
53$000	11	15	7	102$000	22	13	4	151$000	33	11	1
54$000	12	0	0	103$000	22	17	9	152$000	33	15	7
55$000	12	4	5	104$000	23	2	3	153$000	34	0	0
56$000	12	8	11	105$000	23	6	8	154$000	34	4	5
57$000	12	13	4	106$000	23	11	1	155$000	34	8	11
58$000	12	17	9	107$000	23	15	7	156$000	34	13	4
59$000	13	2	3	108$000	24	0	0	157$000	34	17	9
60$000	13	6	8	109$000	24	4	5	158$000	35	2	3
61$000	13	11	1	110$000	24	8	11	159$000	35	6	8
62$000	13	15	7	111$000	24	13	4	160$000	35	11	1
63$000	14	0	0	112$000	24	17	9	161$000	35	15	7
64$000	14	4	5	113$000	25	2	3	162$000	36	0	0
65$000	14	8	11	114$000	25	6	8	163$000	36	4	5
66$000	14	13	4	115$000	25	11	1	164$000	36	8	11
67$000	14	17	9	116$000	25	15	7	165$000	36	13	4
68$000	15	2	3	117$000	26	0	0	166$000	36	17	9
69$000	15	6	8	118$000	26	4	5	167$000	37	2	3
70$000	15	11	1	119$000	26	8	11	168$000	37	6	8
71$000	15	15	5	120$000	26	13	4	169$000	37	11	1
72$000	16	0	0	121$000	26	17	9	170$000	37	15	7
73$000	16	4	5	122$000	27	2	3	171$000	38	0	0
74$000	16	8	11	123$000	27	6	8	172$000	38	4	5
75$000	16	13	4	124$000	27	11	1	173$000	38	8	11
76$000	16	17	9	125$000	27	15	7	174$000	38	13	4
77$000	17	2	3	126$000	28	0	0	175$000	38	17	9
78$000	17	6	8	127$000	28	4	5	176$000	39	2	3
79$000	17	11	1	128$000	28	8	11	177$000	39	6	8
80$000	17	15	7	129$000	28	13	4	178$000	39	11	1
81$000	18	0	0	130$000	28	17	9	179$000	39	15	7

MONEY.

Réis	£	s	D	Réis	£	s	D	Réis	£	s	D
180$000	40	0	0	229$000	50	17	9	278$000	61	15	7
181$000	40	4	5	230$000	51	2	3	279$000	62	0	0
182$000	40	8	11	231$000	51	6	8	280$000	62	4	5
183$000	40	13	4	232$000	51	11	1	281$000	62	8	11
184$000	40	17	9	233$000	51	15	7	282$000	62	13	4
185$000	41	2	3	234$000	52	0	0	283$000	62	17	9
186$000	41	6	8	235$000	52	4	5	284$000	63	2	3
187$000	41	11	1	236$000	52	8	11	285$000	63	6	8
188$000	41	15	7	237$000	52	13	4	286$000	63	11	1
189$000	42	0	0	238$000	52	17	9	287$000	63	15	7
190$000	42	4	5	239$000	53	2	3	288$000	64	0	0
191$000	42	8	11	240$000	53	6	8	289$000	64	4	5
192$000	42	13	4	241$000	53	11	1	290$000	64	8	11
193$000	42	17	9	242$000	53	15	7	291$000	64	13	4
194$000	43	2	3	243$000	54	0	0	292$000	64	17	9
195$000	43	6	8	244$000	54	4	5	293$000	65	2	3
196$000	43	11	1	245$000	54	8	11	294$000	65	6	8
197$000	43	15	7	246$000	54	13	4	295$000	65	11	1
198$000	44	0	0	247$000	54	17	9	296$000	65	15	7
199$000	44	4	5	248$000	55	2	3	297$000	66	0	0
200$000	44	8	11	249$000	55	6	8	298$000	66	4	5
201$000	44	13	4	250$000	55	11	1	299$000	66	8	11
202$000	44	17	9	251$000	55	15	7	300$000	66	13	4
203$000	45	2	3	252$000	56	0	0	301$000	66	17	9
204$000	45	6	8	253$000	56	4	5	302$000	67	2	3
205$000	45	11	1	254$000	56	8	11	303$000	67	6	8
206$000	45	15	7	255$000	56	13	4	304$000	67	11	1
207$000	46	0	0	256$000	56	17	9	305$000	67	15	7
208$000	46	4	5	257$000	57	2	3	306$000	68	0	0
209$000	46	8	11	258$000	57	6	8	307$000	68	4	5
210$000	46	13	4	259$000	57	11	1	308$000	68	8	11
211$000	46	17	9	260$000	57	15	7	309$000	68	13	4
212$000	47	2	3	261$000	58	0	0	310$000	68	17	9
213$000	47	6	8	262$000	58	4	5	311$000	69	2	3
214$000	47	11	1	263$000	58	8	11	312$000	69	6	8
215$000	47	15	7	264$000	58	13	4	313$000	69	11	1
216$000	48	0	0	265$000	58	17	9	314$000	69	15	7
217$000	48	4	5	266$000	59	2	3	315$000	70	0	0
218$000	48	8	11	267$000	59	6	8	316$000	70	4	5
219$000	48	13	4	268$000	59	11	1	317$000	70	8	11
220$000	48	17	9	269$000	59	15	7	318$000	70	13	4
221$000	49	2	3	270$000	60	0	0	319$000	70	17	9
222$000	49	6	8	271$000	60	4	5	320$000	71	2	3
223$000	49	11	1	272$000	60	8	11	321$000	71	6	8
224$000	49	15	7	273$000	60	13	4	322$000	71	11	1
225$000	50	0	0	274$000	60	17	9	323$000	71	15	7
226$000	50	4	5	275$000	61	2	3	324$000	72	0	0
227$000	50	8	11	276$000	61	6	8	325$000	72	4	5
228$000	50	13	4	277$000	61	11	1	326$000	72	8	11

MONEY, WEIGTHS AND MEASURES.

Réis	£	s	D	Réis	£	s	D	Réis	£	s	D
327$000	72	13	4	376$000	83	11	1	425$000	94	8	11
328$000	72	17	9	377$000	83	15	7	426$000	94	13	4
329$000	73	2	3	378$000	84	0	0	427$000	94	17	9
330$000	73	6	8	379$000	84	4	5	428$000	95	2	3
331$000	73	11	1	380$000	84	8	11	429$000	95	6	8
332$000	73	15	7	381$000	84	13	4	430$000	95	11	1
333$000	74	0	0	382$000	84	17	9	431$000	95	15	7
334$000	74	4	5	383$000	85	2	3	432$000	96	0	0
335$000	74	8	11	384$000	85	6	8	433$000	96	4	5
336$000	74	13	4	385$000	85	11	1	434$000	96	8	11
337$000	74	17	9	386$000	85	15	7	435$000	96	13	4
338$000	75	2	3	387$000	86	0	0	436$000	96	17	9
339$000	75	6	8	388$000	86	4	5	437$000	97	2	3
340$000	75	11	1	389$000	86	8	11	438$000	97	6	8
341$000	75	15	7	390$000	86	13	4	439$000	97	11	1
342$000	76	0	0	391$000	86	17	9	440$000	97	15	7
343$000	76	4	5	392$000	87	2	3	441$000	98	0	0
344$000	76	8	11	393$000	87	6	8	442$000	98	4	5
345$000	76	13	4	394$000	87	11	1	443$000	98	8	11
346$000	76	17	9	395$000	87	15	7	444$000	98	13	4
347$000	77	2	3	396$000	88	0	0	445$000	98	17	9
348$000	77	6	8	397$000	88	4	5	446$000	99	2	3
349$000	77	11	1	398$000	88	8	11	447$000	99	6	8
350$000	77	15	7	399$000	88	13	4	448$000	99	11	1
351$000	78	0	0	400$000	88	17	9	449$000	99	15	7
352$000	78	4	5	401$000	89	2	3	450$000	100	0	0
353$000	78	8	11	402$000	89	6	8	451$000	100	4	5
354$000	78	13	4	403$000	89	11	1	452$000	100	8	11
355$000	78	17	9	404$000	89	15	7	453$000	100	13	4
356$000	79	2	3	405$000	90	0	0	454$000	100	17	9
357$000	79	6	8	406$000	90	4	5	455$000	101	2	3
358$000	79	11	1	407$000	90	8	11	456$000	101	6	8
359$000	79	15	7	408$000	90	13	4	457$000	101	11	1
360$000	80	0	0	409$000	90	17	9	458$000	101	15	7
361$000	80	4	5	410$000	91	2	3	459$000	102	0	0
362$000	80	8	11	411$000	91	6	8	460$000	102	4	5
363$000	80	13	4	412$000	91	11	1	461$000	102	8	11
364$000	80	17	9	413$000	91	15	7	462$000	102	13	4
365$000	81	2	3	414$000	92	0	0	463$000	102	17	9
366$000	81	6	8	415$000	92	4	5	464$000	103	2	3
367$000	81	11	1	416$000	92	8	11	465$000	103	6	8
368$000	81	15	7	417$000	92	13	4	466$000	103	11	1
369$000	82	0	0	418$000	92	17	9	467$000	103	15	7
370$000	82	4	5	419$000	93	2	3	468$000	104	0	0
371$000	82	8	11	420$000	93	6	8	469$000	104	4	5
372$000	82	13	4	421$000	93	11	1	470$000	104	8	11
373$000	82	17	9	422$000	93	15	7	471$000	104	13	4
374$000	83	2	3	423$000	94	0	0	472$000	104	17	9
375$000	83	6	8	424$000	94	4	5	473$000	105	2	3

TABLE II.

English to Portuguese money at the exchange of 53$^{1}/_{3}$ per 1$000 réis, or 4$500 = £ 1.

S	D	Réis	£	Réis	£	Réis
0	1	19	12	54$000	56	252$000
0	2	38	13	58$500	57	256$500
0	3	56	14	63$000	58	261$000
0	4	75	15	67$500	59	265$500
0	5	94	16	72$000	60	270$000
0	6	113	17	76$500	61	274$500
0	7	131	18	81$000	62	279$000
0	8	150	19	85$500	63	283$500
0	9	169	20	90$000	64	288$000
0	10	188	21	94$500	65	292$500
0	11	206	22	99$000	66	297$000
1	0	225	23	103$500	67	301$500
2	0	450	24	108$000	68	306$000
3	0	675	25	112$500	69	310$500
4	0	900	26	117$000	70	315$000
5	0	1$125	27	121$500	71	319$500
6	0	1$350	28	126$000	72	324$000
7	0	1$575	29	130$500	73	328$500
8	0	1$800	30	135$000	74	333$000
9	0	2$025	31	139$500	75	337$500
10	0	2$250	32	144$000	76	342$000
11	0	2$475	33	148$500	77	346$500
12	0	2$700	34	153$000	78	351$000
13	0	2$925	35	157$500	79	355$500
14	0	3$150	36	162$000	80	360$000
15	0	3$375	37	166$500	81	364$500
16	0	3$600	38	171$000	82	369$000
17	0	3$825	39	175$500	83	373$500
18	0	4$050	40	180$000	84	378$000
19	0	4$275	41	184$500	85	382$500
			42	189$000	86	387$000
£		Réis	43	193$500	87	391$500
			44	198$000	88	396$000
1		4$500	45	202$500	89	400$500
2		9$000	46	207$000	90	405$000
3		13$500	47	211$500	91	409$500
4		18$000	48	216$000	92	414$000
5		22$500	49	220$500	93	418$500
6		27$000	50	225$000	94	423$000
7		31$500	51	229$500	95	427$500
8		36$000	52	234$000	96	432$000
9		40$500	53	238$500	97	436$500
10		45$000	54	243$000	98	441$000
11		49$500	55	247$500	99	445$500

£	Réis	£	Réis	£	Réis
100	450$000	149	670$500	198	891$000
101	454$500	150	675$000	199	895$500
102	459$000	151	679$500	200	900$000
103	463$500	152	684$000	201	904$500
104	468$000	153	688$500	202	909$000
105	472$500	154	693$000	203	913$500
106	477$000	155	697$500	204	918$000
107	481$500	156	702$000	205	922$500
108	486$000	157	706$500	206	927$000
109	490$500	158	711$000	207	931$500
110	495$000	159	715$500	208	936$000
111	499$500	160	720$000	209	940$500
112	504$000	161	724$500	210	945$000
113	508$500	162	729$000	211	949$500
114	513$000	163	733$500	212	954$000
115	517$500	164	738$000	213	958$500
116	522$000	165	742$500	214	963$000
117	526$500	166	747$000	215	967$500
118	531$000	167	751$500	216	972$000
119	535$500	168	756$000	217	976$500
120	540$000	169	760$500	218	981$000
121	544$500	170	765$000	219	985$500
122	549$000	171	769$500	220	990$000
123	553$500	172	774$000	221	994$500
124	558$000	173	778$500	222	999$000
125	562$500	174	783$000	223	1:003$500
126	567$000	175	787$500	224	1:008$000
127	571$500	176	792$000	225	1:012$500
128	576$000	177	796$500	226	1:017$000
129	580$500	178	801$000	227	1:021$500
130	585$000	179	805$500	228	1:026$000
131	589$500	180	810$000	229	1:030$500
132	594$000	181	814$500	230	1:035$000
133	598$500	182	819$000	231	1:039$500
134	603$000	183	823$500	232	1:044$000
135	607$500	184	828$000	233	1:048$500
136	612$000	185	832$500	234	1:053$000
137	616$500	186	837$000	235	1:057$500
138	621$000	187	841$500	236	1:062$000
139	625$500	188	846$000	237	1:066$500
140	630$000	189	850$500	238	1:071$000
141	634$500	190	855$000	239	1:075$500
142	639$000	191	859$500	240	1:080$000
143	643$500	192	864$000	241	1:084$500
144	648$000	193	868$500	242	1:089$000
145	652$500	194	873$000	243	1:093$500
146	657$000	195	877$500	244	1:098$000
147	661$500	196	882$000	245	1:102$500
148	666$000	197	886$500	246	1:107$000

WEIGHTS.

After a probation of 20 years the Portuguese adopted the French metrical system, and in 1868 its use was made obligatory in all official documents and public or private transactions.

The following are the metrical weights compared with the English:

Milligramma, or thousandth of a gramma	0.015	grains Troy
Centigramma, or hundredth of a gramma	0.154	" "
Decigramma, or tenth of a gramma	1.543	" "
Gramma	0.035	ounce avoir
Decagramma, or ten grammas	0.352	" "
Hectogramma, or hundred grammas	3.527	" "
Kilogramma, or thousand grammas	2.201	lbs. avoir
Myriagramma, or ten thousand grammas	22.046	" "
Quintal metrico, or hundred thousand gr.	220.460	" "
Mil kilos, or million of grammas	2,204.600	" "

The term *kilogramma* is popularly abbreviated into *kilo*. The *gramma* and *kilogramma* are the only terms in general use, the others being ignored, thus 24,655 would be read 24 kilos and 655 grammas, and not 2 myriagrammas, 4 kilogrammas, 6 hectogrammas, 5 decagrammas, and 5 grammas.

In Lisbon these new weights are well understood and universally adopted in the shops, but in the provinces many people still cling to old Portuguese weights which are as follows:

Old Portuguese weights compared with the new metrical and with English weights.

Grão (grain) .... grammas	0.049	0.77	grain troy
Escropulo (scruple) = 24 grãos	1.195	18.4	"
Oitava = 3 escrupulos	3.585	55.3	"
Onça (ounce) = 8 oitavas	28.683	1.0116	oz. avoirdupois
Marco (mark) = 8 onças	229.434	8.093	"
Libra (apothecary's pound) = 1½ marcos	344.136	12.140	"
Arratel (pound) = 2 marcos	459.000	1.0116 lb.	"
Arroba = 32 arrateis	14:685.000	32.374	"
Quintal (hundred weight) = 4 arrobas	58:742.000	129.498	"
Tonelada (ton.) = 13½ quintaes	793:028.000 = 1748.225		"

Table for the reduction of Portuguese to English weight.

Numerals	Grammas	10	100	Kilos	Pounds avoirdupois			
					10	100	1000	10000
1	0	0	0	2	2	0	4	6
2	0	0	0	4	4	0	9	2
3	0	0	0	6	6	1	3	8
4	0	0	0	8	8	1	8	4
5	0	0	1	1	0	2	3	0
6	0	0	1	3	2	2	7	6
7	0	0	1	5	4	3	2	2
8	0	0	1	7	6	3	6	8
9	0	0	1	9	8	4	1	4

The above table gives the equivalents in pounds or decimals of a pound of any number up to 9, of kilos or its multiples or submultiples. Care must be taken to put the decimal point in its right place according to the directions at the top of the perpendicular lines. For instance 2 kilos = 4.4092 lbs, 200 kilos = 440.92 lbs or 20 grammas = .044092 lbs. Having clearly understood how to place the decimal point, the reader will find no further difficulty in applying this useful little table:

EXAMPLES — How much is 258 kilos in English weight?

$$
\begin{aligned}
200 \text{ kilos} &= 440.92 \\
50 \text{ kilos} &= 110.230 \\
8 \text{ kilos} &= 17.6368 \\
\hline
\text{Ans. } 568.7868 \text{ lbs.}
\end{aligned}
$$

How much is 33 kilos 675 grammas in English weight?

$$
\begin{aligned}
30 \text{ kilos} &= 66.138 \\
3 \text{ kilos} &= 6.6138 \\
600 \text{ grammas} &= 1.32276 \\
70 \text{ grammas} &= 0.154322 \\
5 \text{ grammas} &= 0.011023 \\
\hline
33{,}675 \quad \text{Ans. } 74.239905 \text{ lbs.}
\end{aligned}
$$

Of course minute decimals may be omitted to shorten the operation.

Table for the reduction of English into Portuguese metrical weights.

Lbs.	Kilos.	Cwt.	Kilos.	Tons.	Kilos.
1	0,454	1	50,802	1	1:016,048
2	0,907	2	101,604	2	2:032,096
3	1,361	3	152,406	3	3:048,144
4	1,814	4	203,208	4	4:064,192
5	2,268	5	254,010	5	5:080,240
6	2,722	6	304,812	6	6:096,288
7	3,175	7	355,614	7	7:112,336
8	3,629	8	406,416	8	8:128,384
9	4,082	9	457,218	9	9:144,432
10	4,536	10	508,020	10	10:160,480
11	4,989	11	558,822	11	11:176,528
12	5,443	12	609,624	12	12:192,576
13	5,897	13	660,426	13	13:208,624
14	6,350	14	711,228	14	14:224,672
15	6,804	15	762,030	15	15:240,720
16	7,257	16	812,832	16	16:256,768
17	7,711	17	863,634	17	17:272,816
18	8,165	18	914,436	18	18:288,864
19	8,618	19	965,238	19	19:304,912
20	9,072			20	20:320,960
21	9,525				
22	9,979				
23	10,433				
24	10,886				
25	11,340				
26	11,793				
27	12,247				

Qrs.	Kilos.
1	12,700
2	25,401
3	38,101

EXAMPLES—How much is 25 lbs. in Portuguese weight? Ans. 11.340 kilos. How much is 2 tons, 15 cwt., 3 qrs., 21 lbs.?

```
2 tons.  =   2:032,096
15 cwt.  =     762,030
3 qrs.   =      38,101
21 lbs.  =       9.525
       Ans.  2:841,752 kilos.
```

MEASURES.

Like the weights, the measures at present officially recognized, are copied from the French metrical system with slight modifications of the names.

Long measure.

Millimetro, or thousandth of a metro. =	0.03937 inches			
Centimetro, or hundredth of a metro . =	0.3937	"		
Decimetro, or tenth of a metro...... =	3.937	" or	0.032809	feet.
Metro............................ =	39.37	" "	3.2809	"
Decametro, or ten metros........... =	32.809	feet "	10.936	yards.
Hectometro, or hundred metros..... "	328.09	" "	109.36	"
Kilometro, or thousand metros...... =	3280.9	" "	1,093.63	"
5 kilometros (the modern league)..... =	5468.16	yds. "	3.1019	miles.

Old Portuguese long measure compared with the metrical and with English.

Ponto (point)...............	0,0002	metro or	0.0075	inches.
Linha (line) = 12 pontos.... =	0,0023	"	0.0902	"
Pollegada (inch) = 12 linhas =	0,0275	"	1.0827	"
Palmo (palm) = 8 pollegadas =	0,22	"	8.6614	"
Covado = 3 palmos......... =	0,66	"	25.9842	"
Pé (foot) = 12 pollegadas ... =	0,33	"	12.9921	" = 1.0826 feet.
Vara = 3 ⅓ pés or 5 palmos =	1.1	"	43.307	" = 3.609 "
Braça = 2 varas............ =	2.2	"	86.614	" = 7.218 "
Milha (mile)...............	1851,8	"	2,025.22	yds = 1.1507 mile.
Legua (league) = 3 milhas.. =	5555,5	"	6,075.67	" = 3.4521 "

Tables for the reduction of the metrical long measure to English inches, feet or yards.

(For explanation see preceding table for kilogrammas, page 310.)

Numerals	Inches.						Numerals	Feet.					
	Millimetros	Centimetros	Decimetros	Metro	10 metros	100 metros	Kilometros	Centimetros	Decimetros	Metro	10 metros	100 metros	Kilometros
1	0	3	9	3	7	0	1	0	3	2	8	0	9
2	0	7	8	7	4	0	2	0	6	5	6	1	8
3	1	1	8	1	1	0	3	0	9	8	4	2	7
4	1	5	7	4	8	0	4	1	3	1	2	3	6
5	1	9	6	8	5	0	5	1	6	4	0	4	5
6	2	3	6	2	2	0	6	1	9	6	8	5	4
7	2	7	5	5	9	0	7	2	2	9	6	6	3
8	3	1	4	9	6	0	8	2	6	2	4	7	2
9	3	5	4	3	3	0	9	2	9	5	2	8	1

EXAMPLES—How much is 5 metros in English inches? Ans. 196,85.
How much is 5 metros in English feet? Ans. 16,4045.
How much is 5 metros in English yards? Ans. 5,468165.
How much is 23.460 metros in English inches?

MEASURES.

```
20 metros        =  787.4
 3 metros        =  118.11
 0,4 decimetros  =   15.748
 0,06 centimetros=    2.3622
                    ─────────
23,46 Ans.       =  923.6202
```

Numerals	Yards							
	Millimetros.	Centimetros.	Decimetros.	Metros.	10 metros.	100 metros.	Kilometros.	10 kilometros.	100 kilometros.	1,000 kilometros.

Numerals	Millimetros.	Centimetros.	Decimetros.	Metros.	10 metros.	100 metros.	Kilometros.	10 kilometros.	100 kilometros.	1,000 kilometros.
1	0	0	1	0	9	3	6	3	3	
2	0	0	2	1	8	7	2	6	6	
3	0	0	3	2	8	0	8	9	9	
4	0	0	4	3	7	4	5	3	2	
5	0	0	5	4	6	8	1	6	5	
6	0	0	6	5	6	1	7	9	8	
7	0	0	7	6	5	5	4	3	1	
8	0	0	8	7	4	9	0	6	4	
9	0	0	9	8	4	2	6	9	7	

Table for reducing English inches, feet and yards to metros.

Numerals	Metros.				
	Yards.	10 yards.	100 yards.	1,000 yards.	10,000 yards.
1	0	9	1	4	4
2	1	8	2	8	8
3	2	7	4	3	2
4	3	6	5	7	6
5	4	5	7	2	0
6	5	4	8	6	4
7	6	4	0	0	8
8	7	3	1	5	2
9	8	2	2	9	6

Numerals	Metros.				
	Feet.	10 feet.	100 feet.	1,000 feet.	10,000 feet.
1	0	3	0	4	8
2	0	6	0	9	6
3	0	9	1	4	4
4	1	2	1	9	2
5	1	5	2	4	0
6	1	8	2	8	8
7	2	1	3	3	6
8	2	4	3	8	4
9	2	7	4	3	2

Inches.	Metros.
1	.025
2	.051
3	.076
4	.102
5	.127
6	.152
7	.178
8	.203
9	.229
10	.254
11	.279

Examples — How much is 8 yards in Portuguese metros?
Ans. 7,3152.

How much is 80 yards in Portuguese measure? Ans. 73,152.

How much is 239 yards in metrical measure?

```
200 yards  =  182.88
 30   "    =   27.432
  9   "    =    8.2296
___                _____
239   Answer   218.5416 metros
```

How many metros is 69 feet, 5 inches?

```
60    feet    =  18.288
 9    "       =   2.7432
 5    inches  =    .127
___                 _____
69-5  Answer   21.1582 metros
```

Square measure.

Milliare, or a tenth of a square metro =   1.076 square feet.
Centiare, or a square metro.......... = 10.764   "
Deciare, or ten square metros .... = 11.96 square yds.
Are, or hundred square metros ...... = 119.6   "
Decare, or thousand square metros... = 1196.0   "
Hectare, or ten thousand square metros = 2.4711 acres.

Dry and liquid measure.

Millilitro or thousandth of a litro =   .061 cubic inch.
Centilitro or hundredth of a litro =   .61   "
Decilitro or tenth of a litro... =   6.1
Litro...................... = 61.028   = .22 gall.
Decalitro or ten litros .... =   2.2   "
Hectolitro or hundred litros .... = 22.0   "
Kilolitro or thousand litros (cubic metro)..... = 220.0   "

Old Portuguese liquid measure.

Quartilho................ =   .3531 litros =   .0779 gall.
Canada = 4 quartilhos..... =   1.4125   "   =   .3107   "
Pote = 6 canadas........... =   8.475   "   = 1.8645   "
Almude, Lisbon = 12 canadas = 16.95   "   = 3.729   "
Almude, Oporto............ = 25.45   "   = 5.6   "
Pipa = 25 almudes........ = 423.75   "   = 93.225   "
Tonel = 2 pipas........... = 847.50   "   = 186.45   "

MEASURE OF TEMPERATURE.

Centigrade thermometer compared with Fahrenheit.

Degrees.		Degrees.		Degrees.	
Cent.	Fahr.	Cent.	Fahr.	Cent.	Fahr.
0	32 freezing.	34	93.2	68	154.4
1	33.8	35	95.0	69	156.2
2	35.6	36	96.8	70	158.0
3	37.4	37	98.6	71	159.8
4	39.2	38	100.4	72	161.6
5	41.0	39	102.2	73	163.4
6	42.8	40	104.0	74	165.2
7	44.6	41	105.8	75	167.0
8	46.4	42	107.6	76	168.8
9	48.2	43	109.4	77	170.6
10	50.0	44	111.2	78	172.4
11	51.8	45	113.0	79	174.2
12	53.6	46	114.8	80	176.0
13	55.4	47	116.6	81	177.8
14	57.2	48	118.4	82	179.6
15	59.0	49	120.2	83	181.4
16	60.8	50	122.0	84	183.2
17	62.6	51	123.8	85	185.0
18	64.4	52	125.6	86	186.8
19	66.2	53	127.4	87	188.6
20	68.0	54	129.2	88	190.4
21	69.8	55	131.0	89	192.2
22	71.6	56	132.8	90	194.0
23	73.4	57	134.6	91	195.8
24	75.2	58	136.4	92	197.6
25	77.0	59	138.2	93	199.4
26	78.8	60	140.0	94	201.2
27	80.6	61	141.8	95	203.0
28	82.4	62	143.6	96	204.8
29	84.2	63	145.4	97	206.6
30	86.0	64	147.2	98	208.4
31	87.8	65	149.0	99	210.2
32	89.6	66	150.8	100	212 boiling.
33	91.4	67	152.6		

END.

INDEX.

	Page.
Academy of Fine arts	204
„ Sciences	144
Affonso Henriques	32
Agricultural institute	231
Agua vae	87
Ajuda, palace	167
Alani, the	31
Alcaçarias, baths of	6
Alcaçar-Quibir, battle of	48
Alfandega grande	241
Aljubarrota, battle of	46
Aljube, prison	227
Anglican church	233
Anthony, St. (Life of)	147
Antiquities, Roman	212
Aqueduct, great	215
Arch of Rua Augusta	99
„ Doric, of Aqueduct	216
„ of D. Diniz	155
Architecture of dwellings	85
Archives, national	138
Arsenal, military	225
Arsenal, naval	224
Association, commercial	8
Baixa, the	83
Banks and Bankers	2
Barracks	233
Baths, public	5
Battle of Alcaçar-Quibir	48
„ Aljubarrota	46
„ Ourique	33
Beco	83
Belem tower	239
Bilhete de residencia	1
Birds, singing	255
Black-Horse-Square	96
Boa Hora	223
Boats	291
Bolsa, or Praça	96

Botanical garden	230
British legation and foreign consulates	1
Bull-fight	189
Burning of Lisbon by D. Henrique	41
Caes das Columnas	96
Cafés	5
Calçada	83
Camara dos deputados	137
Camara dos pares	136
Camara municipal	278
Camões (Luiz de), life of	107
Campo de Sant'Anna	112
Capote e lenço	91
Carriage Company	288
Carthaginians, the	29
Cart drawn by oxen	89
Casa dos bicos	249
Casa pia	124
Castle of St. George	237
Cemetery of Ajuda	236
» English	236
» French	236
» German	236
» Jewish	236
» Prazeres	235
» Alto de S. João	235
» Valle Escuro	236
Centigrade thermometer compared with Fahrenheit	315
Chronographic map of Portuguese, Italian, Spanish, French and English classic writers	27
Chronological résumé of the history of Portugal	10
Church, Ajuda	166
» Anjos	166
» Carmo	144
» Cathedral	113
» Chagas	164
» Collegio Inglez	129
» Conceição Nova	166
» Conceição Velha	159
» Coração de Jesus (parish)	166
» Coração de Jesus (Estrella)	139
» Corpo Santo	130
» Encarnação	150
» Estrella	139
» Graça	140
» Jeronymite	117
» Jesus	143
» Lapa	166
» Loretto	152
» Martyres	150
» Memoria	159
» do Monte	156

Church, Pena 166
» Penha de França 148
» Sacramento 166
» Santa Cruz 166
» Santa Engracia 161
» Santa Izabel 166
» Santa Luzia 166
» Santa Magdalena 163
» Santa Maria de Belem (Jeronymos) 117
» Santa Maria Maior (Cathedral) 113
» Santo Antonio 146
» Santo Estevão 166
» Santos, o Velho 157
» S. Christovão 166
» S. Domingos 153
» S. Francisco de Paula 164
» S. João da Praça 166
» S. Jorge 166
» S. José 154
» S. Julião 162
» S. Lourenço 166
» S. Luiz 166
» S. Miguel 166
» S. Nicolau 163
» S. Paulo 163
» S. Pedro d'Alcantara 166
» S. Roque 125
» S. Sebastião 166
» S. Thiago 166
» S. Thomé 166
» S. Vicente 134
» Sé (Cathedral) 113
» Soccorro 165
Cintra 256
    Castello dos Mouros 262
    Collares 263
    Cork convent 262
    Monserrate 264
    Palacio da Pena 260
    Palacio real 258
    Pedra de Alvidrar 264
    Penha Verde 265
    Quinta do Marquez de Vianna 258
    Quintas, various 266
    Ramalhão 257
    Setiaes 266
Civility and civilization 253
Climate 92
Clubs 7
Coach-House, Royal 236
Coches reaes 236
Collegio dos aprendizes 233

Collegio inglez	129
Conservatory	232
Constitutional charter	70
Consulates	1
Convent of Albertas	167
» Bom Successo	164
» Chellas	167
» Desaggravo	165
» Encarnação	166
» Esperança	167
» Francezinhas	166
» Madre de Deus	165
» Odivellas	155
» SS. Sacramento	166
» Salessias	167
» Sant'Anna	166
» Santa Brigida	131
» Santa Martha	166
» Santa Monica	166
» Santos o Novo	156
» S. Bento	136
» S. Domingos	164
» S. Patricio	165
» S. Pedro d'Alcantara	167
» Trinas	167
Convention of Cintra 69	266
Cordoaria	241
Corn-market	247
Court-house	223
Courts of justice	224
Crusaders, the	34
Currency, Portuguese	301
Currency, Roman	178
Curso superior de letras	232
Custom-house	241
Custom-house, municipal	248
Deputies, Chamber of	137
Dias Santos	113
Directions to travelers arriving at Lisbon	1
Dom, title of	277
Dominicans, Irish	130
Earthquake, great	52
Eating-houses	4
Environs of Lisbon	250
Estrella, passeio da	230
Exports to Great-Britain	245
Expulsion of the Spaniards in 1640	49
Feira da ladra	229
Fernando and D. Leonor Telles	41
Fire-signal	279
Fires	87
Flight of the court to Brazil	67

INDEX.

Fountains	218
French invasions	68
Gallegos	88
Gama, D. Vasco da (life of)	102
General view of Lisbon	80
Geographical position	80
Goths, the	30
Gremio litterario	7
Hackney carriages	288
Historical sketch of Lisbon	28
Holidays, official	118
Horses, Lusitanian	254
Hospital, British naval	222
» do Desterro	223
» da Estrellinha	223
» da Marinha	223
» de S. José	222
» de S. Lazaro	223
Hotels	3
Illustrious men born at Lisbon	72
Imports from Great-Britain	244
Imprensa nacional	249
Industrial institute	232
Inglezinhos	129
Investiture of Portugal	82
Italian memorial	109
Jardim botanico	230
Jews, massacre of the	48
Lancaster, Duke of	276, 43
Language and literature, Portuguese	20
Largo das Amoreiras	111
» do Barão de Quintella	112
» de Belem	110
» do Carmo	112
» do Pelourinho	110
» do Rato	111
» de S. Paulo	111
» de S. Roque	109
Latin, great similarity of Portuguese and	22
Laus perennis	92
Lazaretto	241
Legation, British	1
Letting, system of	86
Library of academy of sciences	144
» at Ajuda	184
» of the Convent of Jesus	143
» national	200
Limoeiro, prison of	226
Literature, Portuguese	20
Lotteries	90
Lyceum	233
MAFRA	266

Mae d'agua	217
Manners, Portuguese	251
Market, feira da ladra	229
» fish	228
» Praça da Figueira	227
» Ribeira Velha	229
Marquis of Pombal (life of)	101
Massacre of the Jews	48
Matadouro	248
Measures, Portuguese	312
Mestre d'Avis	42
Miguelite war	71
Mint, the	246
Moeda, casa da	246
Money, Portuguese	301
Moorish invasion	31
Mules	254
Municipal custom-house	248
» revenue and expenditure	278
Municipality, the	278
Museum, Archaeological	146
» Colonial	225
» Industrial	232
» National	210
Newsrooms	7
Nobility, titles of	275
Numismatic cabinet (Ajuda)	177
Nuno Alvares Pereira (life of)	101
Observatory, astronomical	220
» meteorological (de D. Luiz)	221
Octroi duties	279
Omnibuses	291
Origin of Lisbon	28
Ourique, battle of	33
Palace, Ajuda	167
» Belem	186
» Bemposta	187
» Caxias	189
» Necessidades	185
» Queluz	188
Parochial divisions	112
Passeio, da Estrella	230
» publico	229
» de S. Pedro d'Alcantara	230
Pedro V., D	72
Peers, Chamber of	136
Pereira, Nuno Alvares (life of)	101
Picture Gallery, Ajuda	172
» » National	204
Pish-sh	90
Police force	87
Politeness, Portuguese	252

INDEX.

Pombal, Marquis of (life of)	101
Population of Lisbon	80
Ports with which there is regular steam communication, alphabetical list of	294
Portuguese language and literature	20
Post-office and postages	281
Praça da Alegria	112
» do Commercio	96
» da Figueira 111.	227
» das Flores	112
» de Luiz de Camões	105
» de D. Pedro IV	104
» do Principe Real	111
» dos Romulares	111
Praça dos Touros	189
Press, the	8
Printing-office, the national	249
Prison, Aljube	227
» Castello de S. Jorge	227
» S. Julião da Barra	227
» Limoeiro	226
» Torre de Belem	227
Processions, religious	91
Public amusements	189
Railways, Portuguese	283
Railway fares to the principal cities of Europe	287
Rainfall	95
Real, the Portuguese	180
Rebuilding of the city	66
Ribeira nova	228
Ribeira velha	229
Roads, Portuguese	89
Roman antiquities	212
Roman conquest	29
Rope-walk	241
Royal family, the	273
Rua	83
Saloios	90
S. Pedro de Alcantara, Passeio de	230
School, commercial	232
» medical	231
» military	232
» naval	232
» pharmaceutical	231
» polytecnic	231
Sebastião's (D.) departure to Africa	48
Ships, number of, entering Lisbon	242
Siege of Lisbon by Affonso Henriques	34
Siege of Lisbon by D. Juan of Castile	43
Siligni, the	31
Site of the duke of Aveiro's palace	111
Slaughter-house	248

Squares	96
Statistics, exports and imports	243
» shipping	242
» weather	94
Statue of Camões	105
» equestrian of D. José I	96
» of D. Pedro IV	101
» of St. John Nepomucene	247
Steamers, to foreign ports	291
Steamers, river	290
Streets of Lisbon, the	83
Streets, double nomenclature of	81
Streets, generic names of	83
Suevi, the	31
Table by which to ascertain the name of the principal buildings	73
Telegraph	280
Temperature, diurnal variation of	94
Temperature, mean, maximum, and minimum	94
Terreiro do Paço	96
Terreiro do trigo	247
Theater, S. Carlos	196
» Gymnasio	199
» D. Maria II	198
» Principe Real	199
» rua dos Condes	199
» Trindade	198
» Variedades	200
the Portuguese	194
Thermometer, centigrade	315
Titles of nobility	275
Tobacco, introduction of	247
Torre do Tombo	138
Tower of Belem	239
Trade with foreign nations	243
Tramway	291
Tramway, steam	292
Travessa	83
Tribunal of commerce	224
» ecclesiastical	224
» of 2.nd instance	224
» supreme military	224
» supreme, of Justice	224
Tribunals of 1.st instance	224
Vandals, the	31
Vasco da Gama (life of) 16,	102
Viriatus, (life of)	103
Visigothic invasion	30
Weather statistics	94
Weights, Portuguese	309
Wind, prevailing direction of	95
Xabregas	246

5	Rua de S. Paulo..........................	P
1	» de S. Pedro de Alcantara...............	Q
7	» de S. Sebastião da Pedreira	Q
6	» de S. Thomé	T
3	» de S. Vicente........................	T
	» dos Sapateiros.......................	R
9	» da Saudade..........................	S
7	» da Senhora da Graça	U
2	» do Sol do Rato......................	O
5	» do Tethal...........................	R
4	» do Terreiro do Trigo.................	T
4	» dos Terremotos......................	L
4	» da Torre da Polvora..................	L
1	» da Trinas do Mocambo................	N
4	» do Valle de Pereiro..................	Q
5	» do Valle de Santo Antonio............	V
9	» de Vasco (D.).......................	F
4	Travessa do Pintor.........................	S
6	» do Pombal.........................	P
3	» de Santo Amaro	H
1	» da Veronica........................	U
4		

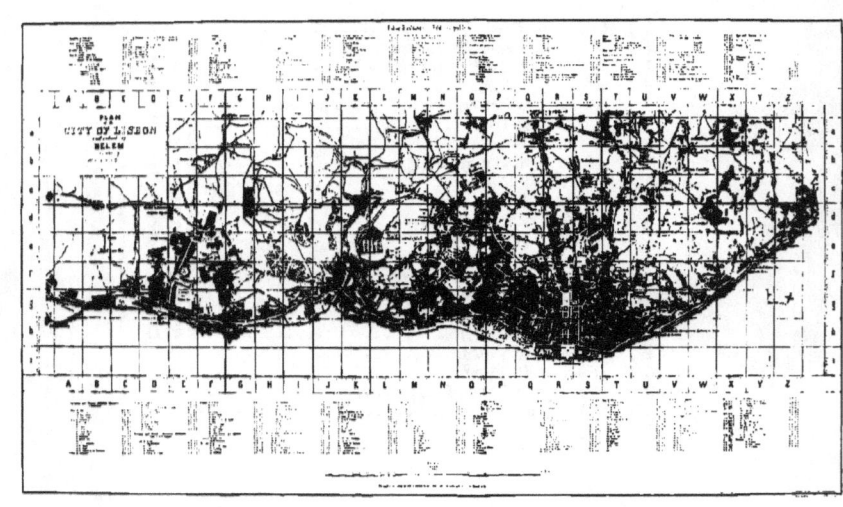

www.ingramcontent.com/pod-product-compliance
Lightning Source LLC
Chambersburg PA
CBHW021149230426
43667CB00006B/321